day trips® series

day trips® from
philadelphia

first edition

 **getaway ideas for the local traveler**

renee pires

travel

Guilford, Connecticut

All the information in this guidebook is subject to change. We recommend that you call ahead to obtain current information before traveling.

To buy books in quantity for corporate use or incentives, call **(800) 962-0973** or e-mail **premiums@GlobePequot.com**.

Editor: Kevin Sirois
Project Editor: Lynn Zelem
Layout: Joanna Beyer
Text Design: Linda R. Loiewski
Maps: Daniel Lloyd © Morris Book Publishing, LLC.
Spot photography throughout © Paul S. Wolf/licensed by Shutterstock.com

ISBN 978-0-7627-7935-2

Printed in the United States of America
10 9 8 7 6 5 4 3 2

contents

about the author

Renee Pires was born in Philadelphia and has lived there most of her adult life, exploring its many outlying areas on weekend jaunts. A freelance writer, she has covered dining, travel, and local arts and entertainment for a number of publications.

acknowledgments

Many thanks to the visitor centers, chambers of commerce, and tourism bureaus that have helped with the compilation of information and guided me through the many trips that make up this book. Thanks especially to the Greater Philadelphia Tourism and Marketing Corporation for its vast and accessible resources.

>> introduction

When touting the merits of our great city, we native Philadelphians love to think of it as the center of everywhere. As a starting point for day trips, it doesn't get much better. Sandwiched between New York City and Washington D.C., Philadelphia is an easy drive from both the nation's capital and its largest metropolis. One need not drive far to observe a dramatic change of landscape. To the east is the Jersey shoreline and its string of distinct and storied beach towns. To the northwest are the Pocono Mountains, with their myriad ski resorts and outdoor adventures. And the ring of land hugging the city offers an incredible range of vistas, from the rolling farmland of Lancaster County to the charming little towns of Phoenixville and New Hope and the postindustrial cities of Allentown and Bethlehem.

But the diversity here is not just visual—it's cultural as well. As some of the original colonies of the US, Pennsylvania, New Jersey, Maryland, and Delaware are rich with early American history. In Valley Forge and the Brandywine Valley visitors can explore Revolutionary War battlefields; in Bucks County is the site of Washington's Crossing, where he led the Continental army into New Jersey. A walk through the brick-laid streets of New Castle, Delaware, with their brick Dutch and colonial homes is the best glimpse into 17th-century American life north of Williamsburg, Virginia. Civil War history buffs will find plenty to study in the Underground Railroad sites in Kennett Square, the ships in Baltimore's harbor, and the amazing store of artifacts collected in Harrisburg's Civil War Museum.

While the Industrial Revolution and urbanization forged its way through this region, the 19th century left an enduring mark in the covered bridges of Bucks County, the living history museums at Holcombe farm and Batsto Village, and the Victorian architecture of Cape May and Spring Lake.

Some of the region's small towns seem almost untouched by modern life—this is especially true of Bird-in-Hand and many other Amish villages in Lancaster County where cars share the road with horse-drawn buggies and a good deal of the population wears handmade clothing. With more tourists than residents, the sleepy villages of Stockton and Skippack feel blissfully removed from the city.

Agrarian life is still alive and well here, and the local-food movement thrives around Philadelphia, the numerous farms and wineries in easy reach attracting gourmands and agri-tourists to Chester County, Bucks County, Montgomery County, and farther west.

In the postindustrial age, many of the Mid-Atlantic's larger cities and towns—Allentown, Bethlehem, and Red Bank, to name a few—fell on harder times. In recent decades they've rebounded with creative reuse of factories and warehouses. Their newly animated economies rely on the service industries, and these boroughs have emerged as fun and interesting places to visit.

There are plenty of urbane pleasures here, too. As a major metropolitan area, this region has a wealth of sophisticated shopping (one of the world's largest malls is in King of Prussia) and high-end restaurants from celebrity chefs. Arts and entertainment are vital to this region. Visitors might be surprised to find world-class museums, galleries, and theater so far away from the city, but they're there for the exploring in Princeton, Doylestown, Reading, and Red Bank.

And then there's just plain fun for all ages. A ride on a historic steam engine (Flemington), a ghost tour (Ocean City), a giant castle playground (Doylestown), a thrilling spin on a roller coaster, or a glimpse of a chocolate factory (Hershey). To steal a phrase from Walt Whitman, a onetime resident of New Jersey, this region contains multitudes. And from the jingling, flashing Atlantic City Boardwalk to the snow-covered mountaintops of Big Boulder, the day trips that follow offer a universe of possibilities.

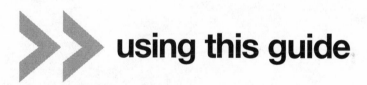

using this guide

This guide is organized starting with destinations north of Philadelphia and working clockwise around the compass. Each day trip is designed to bring out the best attractions, and some include more than an average person might see in a single day. Some day trips can be strung together for a weekend trip—in particular New Hope and Lambertville with Stockton, Frenchtown, and Flemington; or the Brandywine Valley with Kennett Square and Wilmington. Some trips, such as Stone Harbor, Avalon, and Wildwood, can easily be whittled down to a single destination.

Activities, shops, and restaurants have been chosen with a wide range of travelers in mind—from couples looking for a romantic getaway, to friends on an adventure, to families with young children. In general, this guide emphasizes small, independent businesses over large national chains to support local economies and provide local flavor.

Listings under Where to Go, Where to Eat, Where to Shop, and Where to Stay are organized in alphabetical order, except for in the Where to Go category, when some first-stop attractions, such as visitor centers, are listed first.

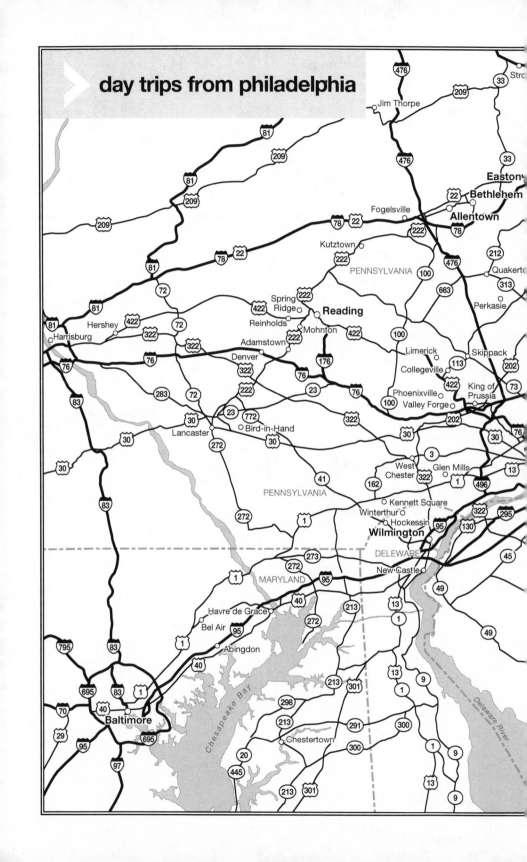

day trips from philadelphia

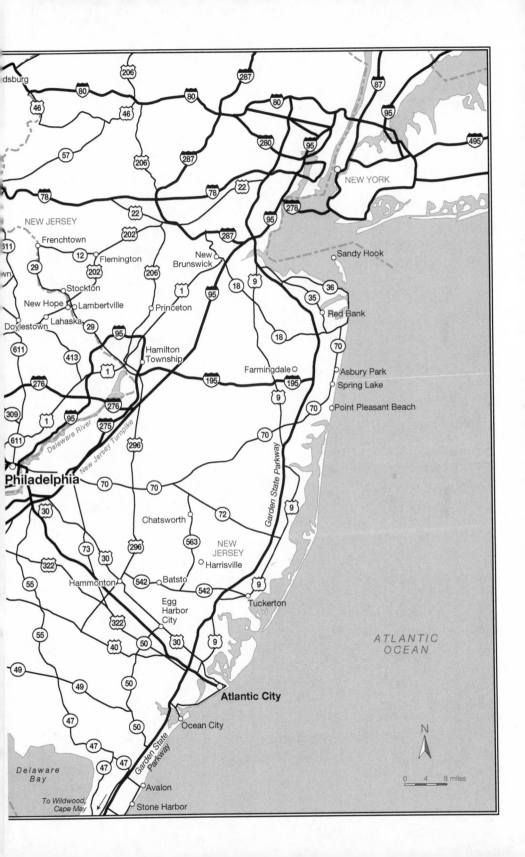

hours & prices

In the interest of accuracy and because they are subject to change, hours of operation and attraction prices are given in general terms. Always remember to call ahead. If you have questions, contact the establishments for specifics.

pricing key

The price codes for accommodations and restaurants are represented as a scale of one to three dollar signs ($). You can assume all establishments listed accept major credit cards unless otherwise noted. For details, contact the locations directly.

accommodations

The price code reflects the average cost of a double-occupancy room during the peak price period (not including tax or extras). Always ask if any special discounts are available.

$ less than $150
$$ $150 to $200
$$$ more than $200

restaurants

The price code reflects the average price of dinner entrees for two (excluding cocktails, wine, appetizers, desserts, tax, and tip). You can usually expect to pay less for lunch and/or breakfast, when applicable.

$ less than $10
$$ $10 to $25
$$$ more than $25

driving tips

Leaving Philadelphia during rush hour on one of the major highways—I-95 or I-76—is not advised, as traffic gets very heavy during these times. The maximum speed limit in Pennsylvania is 65 mph on many highways and 55 mph on most. In Pennsylvania you may turn right on red lights, and all passengers must wear seat belts.

Bucks County, Lancaster County, and Hunterdon County have plenty of back roads for meandering drives. When driving around in Lancaster County, be aware of Amish horse-drawn buggies, which share the road with cars.

New Jersey's traffic laws can confuse visitors, particularly on roads where left-hand turns are prohibited—in many cases there are rotaries or jug handles on the right-hand side for left turns. Right turns on red lights are not permitted in New Jersey.

One last note: The Philadelphia region is prone to harsh winters. Use caution when driving on snowy, icy roads.

highway designations

- *Interstates* are prefaced by "I" (for example, I-270) and are generally multilane divided highways.

- *US highways* are two- and three-lane undivided roads and prefaced by "US" (for instance, US 68).

- *State highways* are paved and divided and prefaced by "PA" (for example, PA 3).

travel tips

Area Codes: Some of the area codes you'll encounter on these day trips include:

- **215 and 267:** southeastern Pennsylvania, including northern and eastern suburbs of Philadelphia

- **610 and 484:** eastern and southeastern Pennsylvania, including Allentown, Bethlehem, Reading, and much of the Delaware Valley

- **609:** southeastern and central New Jersey, including Princeton, Atlantic City, and much of the Jersey shore

- **732:** Jersey shore

- **908:** northern New Jersey, including Hunterdon County

- **302:** Delaware

- **410 and 443:** eastern Maryland

- **717:** south central Pennsylvania, including Harrisburg and Lancaster

- **570:** northeast Pennsylvania, including the Poconos

Sales Tax: Pennsylvania's sales tax rate is 6 percent, and food is usually exempted. New Jersey's sales and use tax rate is 7 percent (not applied to unprepared food or clothing), and additional local sales taxes are imposed on certain items sold in Atlantic City and Cape May County. There is no sales tax in Delaware. Maryland's sales tax is 6 percent; 9 percent for alcohol.

Seasonal Issues: The Mid-Atlantic is truly a four-season region, with spring and fall the most mild and temperate times of year. Day-trippers can get the most out of visits to the shoreline during the summer—or early September to beat the crowds. Hurricane season—generally felt more strongly on the coastline—is officially from early June to November, with the majority of activity in August and September. Leaf-peeping in the rural areas, such as Hunterdon, Lancaster, and Bucks and Berks Counties, hits its peak in mid to late October. Snow and winter sporting may take place anytime between November and March.

for more information

Within each chapter we provide contact information for chambers of commerce and/or convention and visitor bureaus. Here are some additional general resources:

Delaware Tourism Office
www.visitdelaware.com

Greater Philadelphia Tourism Marketing Corporation
www.visitphilly.com

Maryland Bed and Breakfast Association
www.marylandbb.com

Maryland Office of Tourism
401 E. Pratt St., 14th Floor
Baltimore, MD 21202
(866) 639-3526
www.visitmaryland.org

National Register of Historic Places
http://nrhp.focus.nps.gov

New Jersey Division of Travel and Tourism
www.visitnj.org

Pennsylvania Tourism Office
400 North St., 4th floor
Harrisburg, PA 17120-0225
www.visitpa.com

Preferred Inns of New Jersey Bed & Breakfast Association
(866) 449-3535
www.njinns.com

north

day trip 01

north

artist's retreat:
doylestown, pa

doylestown, pa

Twenty-seven miles almost directly north of Philadelphia is the picturesque borough of Doylestown, where mild-mannered small-town life is enlivened by bright bursts of arts and culture. The seat of Bucks County, Doylestown is strategically located between Norristown and New Hope and connected to Philadelphia by PA 611. First settled in 1745, Doylestown became known as the home of Henry Chapman Mercer, who left his mark with a trio of buildings—the Mercer Museum, the Fonthill museum, and the Moravian Pottery and Tile Works. Today it's a low-key tourist destination peppered with historic landmarks, fun and funky shops, global dining options, and a reputation as a refuge for creative Manhattanites and Philadelphians. Diminutive though it may be, Doylestown is rich enough to merit a day trip all its own.

getting there

From Philadelphia, take Broad Street to PA 611, heading north for 10.7 miles. Continue north on US 202, which zags to the east, and follow to E. State Street. Turn left to drive into the center of town. Total travel time is about 54 minutes, not accounting for heavy traffic.

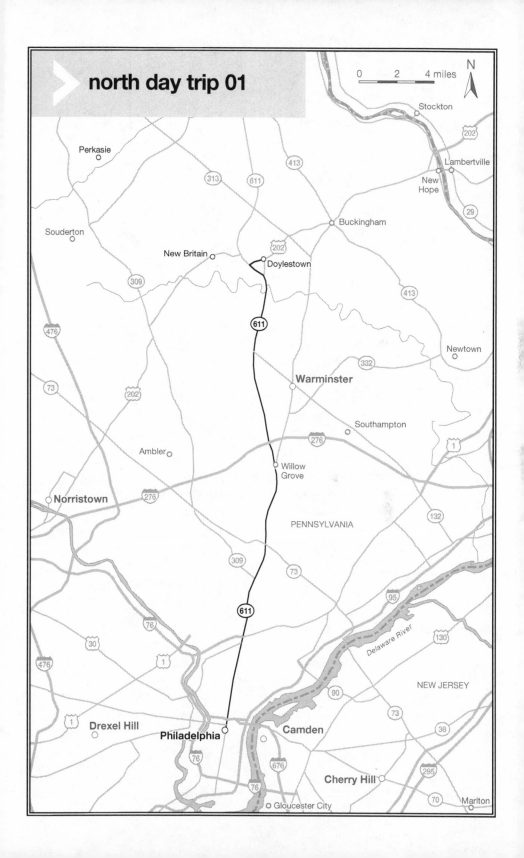

where to go

County Theater. 20 E. State St.; (215) 345-6789; www.countytheater.org. First opened in 1938, the Art Deco County Theater was for many years a major center of Doylestown life—that is, until the multiplex came into fashion. In the early 1990s the theater was saved from destruction by the nonprofit community group Closely Watched Films. Restored and reopened in 1997, the building was given another chance, with fresh seating and a new projection booth, and the marquee's neon tower was refurbished the following year. Most recently the landmark theater has been brought up to date with digital media equipment. Film buffs will appreciate the selection of art, independent, and foreign screenings, and families are drawn to the Saturday matinees for kids. Local filmmakers, discussion groups, and lectures round out the programming. Open daily.

Fonthill Castle. E. Court St. and PA 313; (215) 348-9461; www.mercermuseum.org. Henry Mercer's brilliant eccentricities are manifest in his 1912 reinforced poured-concrete home embedded with handmade tiles. This timeless manse showcases not only his love of ceramics but also his passion for books, antiques, and prints. Mercer designed the interior first and then completed the exterior to accommodate his singular vision. Visits through the 44 rooms are by guided tour only. (A Mercer Experience Ticket covers both the Mercer and Fonthill museums.) The surrounding park is a good place for hiking or a picnic. Open daily, and tour reservations are strongly advised.

James A. Michener Art Museum. 138 S. Pine St.; (215) 340-9800; www.michener museum.org. The best place to view art inspired by and made in Bucks County, this museum is named for the famed novelist, Pulitzer Prize winner, and Doylestown native James A. Michener. Founded in 1988, the Michener was built on the site of the 19th-century Bucks County jail, with modern annexes expanding the space. Today the museum houses a substantial number of Pennsylvania Impressionist paintings. Changing contemporary exhibits and a stunning installation of works by furniture maker George Nakashima are additional draws for visitors, as is an outdoor sculpture garden and terrace built into the original prison yard. Closed Mon.

Kids Castle. 425 Wells Rd.; (215) 348-9915. Visiting families will not want to miss this spectacular 35-foot-high, 8-story playground structure in Central Park with its myriad compartments for hiding and seeking, slides, swings, ropes, and bridges. Beyond the castle's drawbridge is a very friendly dragon, a tree house, a barnyard, and a climbable rocket ship for imaginative and active play. A smaller promenade keeps toddlers busy and the community-built complex is surrounded by sand for lower-level amusement. Central Park also features tennis and basketball courts, soccer fields, a picnic pavilion, walking and jogging trails, an amphitheater, and restrooms. Open year-round.

Mercer Museum. 84 S. Pine St.; (215) 345-0210; www.mercermuseum.org. Fearing the obliterating sweep of the Industrial Revolution, historian and archaeologist Henry Mercer

(1856–1930) collected nearly 30,000 functional items used in American life, then designed and built a museum to house them in 1916. The 6-story concrete castle is an eye-popping walk through the history of everyday objects, including cobblers' tools, candle molds, bloodletting razors, log sleds, threshing machines, tin-smithing paraphernalia, a Conestoga wagon, and a whaling boat. A collection of giant cigar-store figures and a vampire-killing kit add a creepier dimension to the displays. Stations throughout allow kid visitors to try on colonial clothes, create tile rubbings, and participate in other hands-on activities. (A Mercer Experience Ticket covers both the Mercer and Fonthill museums.) Open daily.

Moravian Pottery and Tile Works. 130 E. Swamp Rd.; (215) 348-6098; www.bucks county.org/government/departments/tileworks/visitus.aspx. The third destination of the Mercer trifecta in Doylestown is this working history museum in which reproductions of Mercer's Arts and Crafts–style tiles depicting Pennsylvania flora and fauna are produced. Like the Mercer and Fonthill museums, the Tile Works is listed on the National Register of Historic Places and is built out of Mercer's favorite material, poured concrete. The low-lying U-shaped structure has a wraparound colonnade and a grass courtyard in the style of California mission architecture. Mercer's decorative tiles are set in both the exterior and interior walls. The current building is technically the second Tile Works; the first was destroyed by fire. A self-guided tour showcases the production methods and original tile installations. Open daily.

Pine Valley Covered Bridge. Old Iron Hill Rd., New Britain, PA. The first known covered bridge in the US was built in Philadelphia in 1805, and at one time the state had about 1,500 covered bridges. One of the few remaining, the red-painted covered bridge on Old Iron Hill Road offers a glimpse of bucolic days past. The 1842 landmark is 82 feet long, built from native hemlock and pine, and spans the Pine Run stream, named for the native trees that

> ## mercer & his tiles
>
> *Fearing the dehumanizing touch of industrialization, renaissance man Henry Chapman Mercer set out to revive traditional pottery in Bucks County, and when that failed, he set his sights on tile-making, founding the Moravian Pottery and Tile Works in 1912. In keeping with the Arts and Crafts movement, Mercer's tiles were carved into clay, cast into plaster, then pressed into more clay to imprint the design. They were then dipped into glaze for a rustic look. Reproductions of the original designs using Mercer's techniques are still being made at the Tile Works, with new reissues introduced constantly. The tiles can be found in hundreds of private homes, churches, and other buildings around the country.*

were abundant near the water. Because the bridge still gets quite a bit of car traffic, it's best viewed from outside. Pull over at the park at the foot of the bridge to get a look.

where to shop

Booktenders' Secret Garden Bookstore. 20B Donaldson St.; (215) 348-7160; www .booktenderssecretgarden.com. The oldest children's-only bookstore in the tristate area is a frequent best-of award winner for its dedication to quality products and the personal service from its owner, a former schoolteacher. Set back behind the shopping thoroughfare of State Street, Booktenders' is a hidden enclave for children's lit both new and used, plus games, puzzles, greeting cards, activity kits, audio books, and gifts. Regularly hosted events include appearances by authors and illustrators. The store also maintains an art gallery specializing in original prints and illustrations, with a Wall of Fame signed by visiting artists. Open daily.

Chris' Cottage. 38 W. Oakland Ave; (215) 345-1550; www.chriscottage.com. The shabby-chic look is alive and well at this homey, charming shop just off the main drag of Doylestown. Marrying the rural heritage of Bucks County with a sophisticated flair for interior design, the Cottage offers a mix of new and refurbished vintage furnishings, plus home accessories (glassware, china, candles, linens, pillows, vases), lighting, artwork, and gifts (picture frames, tea towels, handmade soaps). American-made Lee upholstered furniture can be customized with a variety of fabrics and frames. Closed Sun.

Cowgirl Chile Co. Jewelry. 52 E. State St.; (215) 348-4646; www.cowgirlchile.com. You don't have to ride a horse or even don a hat to appreciate the yee-haw spirit of Cowgirl Chile jewelry. This relative newcomer to the State Street shopping scene trades in handmade jewelry featuring sculpted metalwork and both precious and semiprecious stones—all crafted with a western aesthetic. On display are dangling gemstone earrings, chunky beaded wrap bracelets, layered pearl and silver charm necklaces, cocktail rings, hammered silver pendants on handmade chains, and dramatic statement pieces. Custom designs are also available. Open Tues through Sun.

Shop Sixty-Five. 53 W. State St.; (215) 348-8250; www.shopsixtyfive.com. A Czech fashion editor and former New York stylist has brought downtown to Doylestown with this chic unisex boutique in an airy LEED-certified showroom. Both couture and independent labels are represented, including Nanette Lepore, Rebecca Taylor, and Ella Moss for women, and Diesel for men. Many of the lines are made with organic fabrics. The entire second floor is devoted to denim, with a brand, fit, and cut to flatter every body. Sixty-Five also stocks dresses for all occasions, plus designer handbags, trendy jewelry, and other accessories. Open daily.

Siren Records. 25 E. State St.; (215) 348-2323; www.sirenrecords.com. In the age of the dwindling music store, Siren Records is a reliable standby. Vinyl collectors, music geeks, and movie fans of the digital and analog variety alike endorse this independent with a wide selection and attentive customer service. More than 200,000 new and used records and DVDs fill the shelves with punk, hardcore, psychedelia, soul, reggae, hip-hop, and indie selections, and the staff encourages customer selling and trading. The store also supports local and emerging acts with live in-store shows and appearances. Open daily.

where to eat

Cross Culture. 62–64 W. State St.; (215) 489-9101; www.crosscultureindiancuisine.net. Doylestown is full of small cultural surprises, like this Indian eatery housed in a federal-style building in the town's "restaurant row" on State Street. Authentic cuisine (curries, kormas, masalas) is served in a stylish dining room with exposed brick walls. There's also a veranda for al fresco eating. Home-baked breads from the tandoor are superior, and meatless options like *paneer tikka* will please vegetarian diners. While the a la carte prices are a bit steep, *thali* specials make for an excellent lunchtime value. BYOB. $$.

Crossroads Bake Shop. 812 N. Easton Rd.; (215) 348-0828; www.crossroadsbakeshop .com. Everything is made from scratch with natural, high-quality ingredients at this sunny bakery and cafe. Traditional breads from French *epis* to cinnamon raisin and "beneficial" breads, such as six-grain and German rye, are the mainstay here, but the full menu of flaky morning pastries, cookies, cakes, and tarts makes Crossroads an ideal stop for a coffee break. The featured beans are from Princeton-based Small World; Rishi teas, chai, and green tea lattes are also available. Take along a bag of molasses nut granola or a dozen olive rolls for freezer stocking. $.

Domani Star. 57 W. State St.; (215) 230-9100; www.domanistar.com. At this small family-owned and -operated restaurant, the daily specials reflect the season, and local produce shines. The Italian-inflected cooking marries red-sauce favorites with lighter specialties and house-made pastas. Enjoy a grilled pork, mozzarella, and red onion panini for lunch, or lump crab cakes with basil-pesto aioli for dinner in the casual, parlor-like dining room. Open for lunch and dinner on weekdays, dinner Saturday, and Sunday brunch. There's a 3-course prix fixe on Sunday nights. Bring your own bottle with no corkage fee. $$.

Honey. 42 Shewell Ave.; (215) 489-4200; www.honeyrestaurant.com. The borough's edgiest restaurant is a sleek and sexy hideaway serving small and large plates. Honey's trendy dining room is warmly lit with candles and decorated, appropriately enough, in golden hues. A seasonally changing menu wows patrons with surprising fare like veal cheek *carnitas* and tea-glazed spareribs with ginger ice cream. Wines are available by the glass and there's a wide selection of Pennsylvania craft beers. Honey is also Doylestown's best spot for serious cocktails, such as locally distilled Bluecoat gin with muddled blackberry and red shiso. Dinner only, 7 nights a week. $$.

Jules Thin Crust. 78 S. Main St.; (215) 345-8565; www.julesthincrust.com. The crust is indeed very thin at this local mini-chain of restaurants, founded by a health-conscious father, with a slice of cheese pizza adding up to no more than 190 calories. But it's the toppings on the 28 different varieties (think fig jam, gorgonzola and prosciutto, or roasted potato, mozzarella, and rosemary) that make the mod pizzeria a standout. Quality is evident in the hormone-free meats, organic flour, and local ingredients. Ultra-fresh salads, dairy-free cheese by request, and a full slate of gluten-free options means there's something for every eater. $.

Lilly's Gourmet. 1 W. Court St.; (215) 230-7883; www.lillysgourmet.com. Situated at a five-point intersection in the heart of town, Lilly's Gourmet is a local pillar of noshing. This casual cafe offers generous portions of straightforward breakfast and lunch fare. Baked goods and prepared foods (salads, vegetables, lasagna) are excellent for picnics in nearby parks. The menu of sandwiches named for artists (Claude Monet = ham, turkey, and brie on sourdough) hews to the town's creative spirit. While the desserts are killer, there are also multiple healthy and vegetarian options. Sidewalk tables provide outdoor seating. Open Mon through Sat. $.

where to stay

1818 Stone Ridge Farm Country Inn. 956 Bypass Rd., Perkasie, PA; (877) 855-2276; www.stoneridge-farm.com. This 10-acre farm, which once belonged to author Pearl Buck, was converted into a bed-and-breakfast in 1999. Set outside Doylestown in nearby Perkasie, Stone Ridge is about a 15-minute drive from the town's center. Old hewn barn beams, plank floors, stone walls, antique decor, and handmade quilts add to its rustic appeal, but the rooms are outfitted with A/C and cable TV, and suites have whirlpool baths and private entrances. The sitting room in the original barn is warmed by a wood-burning stove and there's a swimming pool on the premises for use in warmer months. Horses are welcome, too. $$.

Hargrave House. 50 S. Main St.; (215) 348-3334; www.hargravehouse.net. Situated in the center of Doylestown's historic district, this bed-and-breakfast is a historic landmark in its own right, built by marble masons in 1815. The 7 bright but simply decorated rooms feature en suite bathrooms, king- or queen-size feather beds, flat-screen TVs, and Internet access, and many have fireplaces and 2-person hot tubs. Keurig coffeemakers and a basket of snacks are provided for in-room refreshment. Breakfast is cooked to order and served in a cozy communal dining room. There's free on-site parking in a private lot. $$.

Highland Farm Bed & Breakfast. 70 East Rd.; (215) 345-6767; www.highlandfarmbb .com. Broadway aficionados will be interested to know that the wraparound porch at this newly renovated B&B was the site where Oscar Hammerstein wrote the lyrics for *Oklahoma!* As such, the rooms are named for his most famous plays: *South Pacific, King & I, Carousel,* and, of course, there's an *Oklahoma!* suite. The nicer ones are outfitted with wood-burning fireplaces and marble baths but all feature Egyptian cotton sheets, free wireless Internet access, and handmade mattresses and box springs. A wine and cheese reception greets guests in the evenings and a hot breakfast is served in the dining room. $$–$$$.

worth more time

Peace Valley Park. 230 Creek Rd., New Britain, PA; (215) 922-8608. North of Doylestown is Lake Galena, around which lie some 1,500 acres of woods and meadowlands worth at least half a day's exploration. At the east end is the Peace Valley Nature Center, housed in a barn. From the center, choose a map and set out among the 14 miles of trails. There are blinds for watching some of the 250 species of birds that touch down here. Osprey, kingfishers, egrets, turtles, and other wildlife can be viewed from the Chapman Road Bridge. The park also offers boat launching facilities and rentals in the spring and summer, blacktop trails for biking and walking, and plenty of picnicking space. Guided family nature walks are scheduled on Sunday afternoons and summer evenings. Open 8 a.m. to sunset.

day trip 02

north

eat, bike, shop:
stockton, nj; frenchtown, nj;
flemington, nj

A slow crawl up NJ 29, winding along the Delaware and Raritan (D&R) Canal, reveals a peek into western New Jersey's preindustrial past and its present-day beauty. While it's most spectacular during leaf-peeping season, there are reasons to visit this region year-round. This day trip explores the blink-and-you-may-miss-it town of Stockton, a popular stopover for bikers, hikers, and inngoers. Continue north into the more heavily touristed hamlet of Frenchtown, whose stroll-worthy streets are now dotted with boutiques and antiques stores, then take a turn east for the decidedly 20th-century town of Flemington, which is best known for its outlet mall but is also the site of quirkier attractions.

stockton, nj

A tiny jewel on the eastern banks of the D&R, Stockton looks much like it did in the 18th century. The picturesque mill town was named for Senator Robert Field Stockton, a major player in creating the canal. While its .6 square mileage requires no more than an hour or two to explore, Stockton is a worthwhile stop-off for its well-preserved historic flavor, along with a few choice eateries.

getting there

From Philadelphia, take I-95 North for about 30 miles and exit at NJ 29, heading north. Continue to follow NJ 29 for about 13 miles, then make a slight right onto Stockton

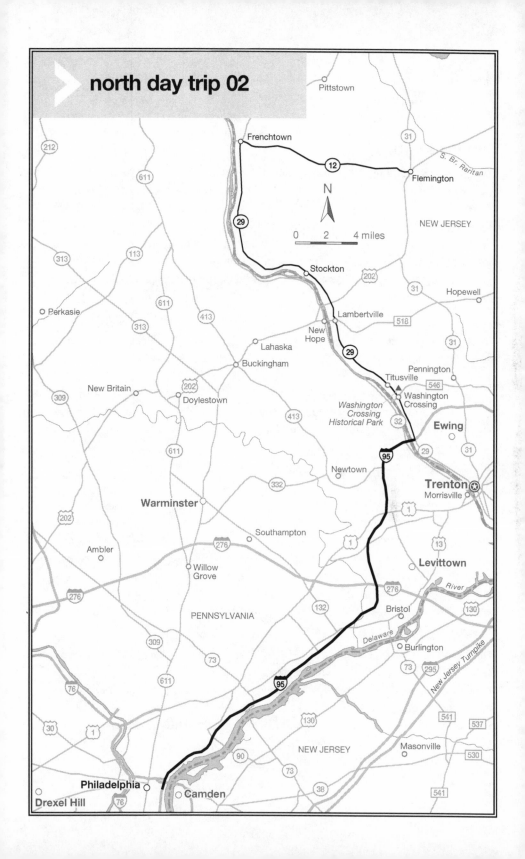

Sergeantsville Road and the first right onto Broad Street to enter Stockton. Travel time is 56 minutes.

where to go

Delaware and Raritan Canal Biking and Hiking Trail. Along the D&R Canal; www .dandrcanal.com. Once upon a time, mule barges and steam tugboats carried coal and other freight down the D&R waterway. These days it's used less for transport and more for recreation. This 77-mile towpath trail runs through Frenchtown, Byram, Lambertville, Washington's Crossing, and Trenton. The trail also goes through Bull's Island, a small forested area for camping north of Stockton, which makes a great launching point for fishing, canoeing, and kayaking. There are designated parking lots at Prallsville Mills and Bull's Island recreation area.

Prallsville Mills. NJ 29 and Risler St. The literal heart of Stockton when it was first built in the 1790s by American Revolution veteran and quarry owner John Prall, Prallsville was an industrial complex that included a linseed oil mill, gristmill, sawmill, grain silo, railroad trestle, and several outbuildings.

Most of the buildings, which ceased operations in the 1950s, have been preserved and restored, listed on the National Register of Historic Places, and protected by the surrounding state parkland. Today the Mills hosts private events, art exhibitions, and antiques shows, and houses a year-round crafts gallery.

where to shop

Phillips' Fine Wines. 17 Bridge St.; (609) 397-0587; www.phillipsfinewines.com. The well-curated array of wines, beers, and spirits at this deceptively small-looking, family-run shop are sold with personal recommendations. A recent renovation expanded the beer selection with a special "Beer Emporium" room stocked with over 100 artisanal and craft brews from around the world and highlighting a different microbrewery every month. In-store tastings and other events with vintners, brewers, and cheesemakers make it a destination for regional oenophiles. The owners also maintain a list of local BYOB restaurant recommendations.

Riverbank Arts. 19 Bridge St.; (609) 397-9330; www.riverbankarts.com. Fine art lines the walls and floor of this store and exhibition space, representing over 300 artists with a large array of works by Pennsylvania Academy of Fine Arts alumni. Reflecting the academy's artistic tradition, the emphasis is on representational contemporary painting, prints, and sculpture with some abstract expressionism thrown in for good measure. The contemporary crafts selection includes wood furniture, jewelry, pottery, and more. Pet and human portraits are available by commission. Open daily.

Sunflower Glass Studio. 877 Sergeantsville Rd.; (609) 397-1535; www.sunflowerglass studio.com. Glass—stained, beveled, fused, and art—is the primary product at this artisan studio and gallery space just north of Stockton. The aesthetic is varied, ranging from botanical renderings, to Arts and Crafts designs, to modern abstract fused-glass platters. In keeping with the area's historic heritage and American stained-glass techniques, the works are handmade. From boxes and frames to custom crafted windows and "miniature buildings," Sunflower's selection is extensive. Open daily.

where to eat

Meil's. Bridge and Main Streets; (609) 397-8033; www.meilsrestaurant.com. Stockton's best bet for a comfort-food fix has character to spare. Set in an old gas station tricked out with vintage magazine covers and handmade quilts, this local institution has a quaint, homey feel. The hearty, rib-sticking eats, such as potato pancakes, meatloaf, crab cake sandwiches, and chicken pot pie with noodles, are served in hefty portions. Fresh-baked muffins and pastries will sate lighter appetites. Open daily for breakfast, lunch, and dinner, except on Thanksgiving and Christmas Day. $–$$.

Via Ponte Pizzeria Trattoria. 13 Bridge St.; (609) 397-9397; www.viapontestockton.com. In such a small town it may be surprising to encounter a memorable pizzeria, let alone an authentic one, but Via Ponte rates among its big-city brethren. Sicilian expatriate Giuseppe Finazzo has made it his life's work to share true Italian cuisine with American patrons, and his homey eatery delivers, with fresh-cut pasta in slow-cooked ragout and scallops tossed with sun-dried tomato and basil. The tiled brick oven produces superb thin crust pizza topped with anchovy, mozzarella, and breadcrumbs. Bring your own wine or beer. $–$$.

where to stay

Stockton Inn. 1 S. Main St.; (609) 397-1250; www.stocktoninn.com. Built in 1710, this landmark hotel—one of Stockton's main attractions—was memorialized in the Rodgers and Hart song "There's a Small Hotel." The current ownership has renovated the property and hosts annual blues and music festivals as well as live arts entertainment around the year. Eleven guest suites, studios, and bedrooms—some of which are located in the separate Carriage House, Wagon House, and Federal House buildings—are cleanly decorated with a nod to the past; most feature fireplaces. A tavern, a fine dining restaurant with fire-lit mural rooms, and a garden bar are also on the premises. $–$$.

Woolverton Inn. 6 Woolverton Rd.; (888) 264-6648; www.woolvertoninn.com. Cushily appointed rooms in a bucolic setting make the Woolverton Inn the area's most sumptuous lodging option. The 1792 stone manor house is located on the hillsides of Stockton, surrounded by 300 acres of preserved farmland dotted with grazing sheep. Themed suites with 19th-century-inspired decor feature showers for two, sunken tubs, and fireplaces for added romance. Smaller rooms and individual cottages with private entrances are also available. Three-course local and seasonal breakfasts (served in bed or in the dining room, porch, or patio), complimentary beverages, and fresh flowers gild the lily of luxury. $$$.

frenchtown, nj

With its backdrop of rolling green hills, this Victorian village on the banks of the Delaware is a day-tripper's jackpot. Planned by Scotsmen who immigrated to America in the 18th century, Frenchtown's orderly streets are lined with colorfully painted clapboard houses, art galleries, and boutiques.

getting there

From Stockton, head left on Stockton Sergeantsville Road and turn right on NJ 29 North/ Risler Street for about 12 miles, then turn left on Harrison Street. From Philadelphia, take I-95 North to NJ 29 North to Frenchtown. Total travel time from Stockton is 18 minutes.

where to go

Delaware River Tubing. 2998 NJ 29; (908) 996-5386; www.delawarerivertubing.com. Outdoor types will want to take advantage of the relaxing, slow-crawling pace of the Delaware River by setting out on a waterborne excursion. Self-guided tubing, rafting, canoeing, and kayaking trips are available here. Rental periods include an optional stop at the Famous River Hot Dog Man's semi-submerged island eatery for a barbecue lunch or dinner. On-site facilities at the former Frenchtown roller rink include restrooms, changing rooms, showers, and a snack bar. Shuttle bus rides to and from the river are included.

Old Stone Church. CR 519 and Oak Summit Rd. Now the home of the First Unitarian First Universal Fellowship, this church is one of the oldest buildings in Frenchtown. The original 1754 stone meeting house, which stood across the street by the Oak Summit Cemetery, was an important part of Revolutionary history: For 10 days during December 1778, members of the Continental army camped there while transporting British and Hessian prisoners to Virginia. In the years following the Revolution, the building's condition deteriorated and its Presbyterian congregation built the present structure in 1837, using some of the old church's stones.

where to shop

Alchemy. 17 Bridge St.; (908) 996-9000; www.alchemyclothing.com. This fresh and offbeat clothing store stocks more than 50 organic lines and small labels for the cutting-edge shopper, all with an emphasis on sustainable fabrics, handcrafted details, and arty textures. The apparel runs the gamut from casual to formal, including black-tie gowns and

Nataya bridal fashions. There's also a wide selection of artisan beaded jewelry and dyed silk scarves, bags, hats, GoodyGoody slippers, and home accessories. Open daily.

Book Garden. 28 Bridge St.; (908) 996-2022; www.bookgarden.biz. Set in an 1860s Victorian home with gingerbread trim, this independent bookstore is bursting with local interest titles, puzzles, games, and books of all kinds. A collection of museum goods includes fine-art cards, art books, reproduction jewelry, and imported gifts from Germany, Egypt, Russia, and Japan. In the children's room is a selection of eco-friendly building blocks, cars, trucks, model kits, music boxes, and dolls. Open Thurs through Sun.

Designs for Tranquility Gallery. 41 Bridge St.; (908) 996-9990; www.designsfor tranquility.com. Because nobody's modern life is free of stress, peace is both the theme and the product at this gallery and store. The art (paintings, glass, sculpture) and crafts (jewelry, handbags, lamps, and Judaica) are hand selected to soothe and promote serenity with natural themes and meditative imagery. Limited-edition giclées, handmade water fountains, leather accessories, and other gifts round out the calming offerings. Changing exhibits showcase a wide variety of artists. Most of the wares are made in the US. Open Wed through Sun.

Two Buttons. 62A Trenton Ave.; www.twobuttons.com. Author Elizabeth Gilbert (*Eat, Pray, Love*) and her husband, Jose Nunes—yes, the one from the book—have filled their 2,200-square-foot warehouse with art objects, furniture, ceremonial pieces, jewelry, textiles, and antiques from their extensive travels around the world. Wander the aisles and don't be surprised to see a 6,000-pound white marble Buddha, a 3-tiered parasol, a set of Thai "greeting ladies," or Gilbert herself, who's been known to serve as a sales clerk. Open Wed through Sun.

where to eat

Bridge Cafe. 8 Bridge St.; (908) 996-6040; www.bridgecafe.net. Frenchtown's original train depot is now the site for this easygoing eatery, and diners can sit outside on the waiting platform and overlook the Delaware River and Frenchtown-Uhlerstown Bridge. The eclectic fare changes by the day but might include veggie spinach and feta cakes, burgers, and fish and chips. Homemade baked goods (muffins, doughnuts, cake) are a standout, as is the coffee, which is from Small World in Princeton. BYOB. Hours change seasonally. $–$$.

Cocina del Sol. 10 Bridge St.; (908) 996-0900; www.cocinadelsolnj.com. Mexican fare with a Tex twist (think fajitas, burritos, and tacos) gives Frenchtown a little south-of-the-border flavor. This casual, low-key gathering place across the street from the former railroad station is family friendly and decorated with bright Mexican art and artifacts. Cocina del Sol has a BYO policy, so diners must supply their own Coronas and Negro Modelas—the kitchen will provide the limes. Open for lunch and dinner. Closed Mon. $$.

Frenchtown Inn. 7 Bridge St.; (908) 996-3300; www.frenchtowninn.com. A 19th-century inn with a formal, tablecloth-and-chandelier vibe, the Frenchtown serves hearty if slightly dated haute cuisine with Francophile leanings: duck breast over whipped horseradish potatoes, rare yellowfin tuna over jasmine rice, and pork tenderloin over bacon risotto. For consistent, upscale eating and service it's the preeminent choice in town. At the informal grill room, the food is more casual (burgers, warm goat cheese salad, and crab cakes) and so are the prices. $$–$$$.

Lovin' Oven. 62 Trenton Ave.; (908) 996-7714; www.lovinovenfrenchtown.com. While this bright and funky bistro is open all day Wed through Sat, the meal of choice is breakfast/ brunch, with creative bites like a southwestern tofu and tortilla scramble, challah French toast with cream cheese drizzle, and eggs and crispy potatoes served over a sweet potato biscuit with kale and sausage gravy. Comfort food with a healthy twist is the emphasis, and gluten-free and vegan options are cheerfully provided for diners with special needs. $–$$.

where to stay

National Hotel. 31 Race St.; (908) 996-3200; www.thenationalhotelnj.com. Established in 1850, the National Hotel stands proudly at Frenchtown's entrance point. Its vibrant past includes stops from Buffalo Bill Cody and Annie Oakley. The current management took over in 2009 and rehabbed the entire property. The centrally located lodge offers quiet rooms, many with whirlpool tubs and some with private porches. All feature free Wi-Fi, cable TV, and complimentary continental breakfast. The on-site restaurant and bar area is a popular local hangout, as is the speakeasy basement bar the Rathskeller. $–$$.

Widow McCrea House. 53 Kingwood Ave.; (908) 996-4999; www.widowmccrea.com. An Italianate Victorian B&B named for its original owner, the Widow is located just off the main strip of Frenchtown. Lodging ranges from a private cottage to 2 luxury suites and 3 individual guest rooms, all decorated with period antiques and feather beds. The romance is in the details: Complimentary wine en suite, afternoon tea, and candlelit multicourse breakfast are included, and in-room spa services are available for guests who need a little extra pampering. $$–$$$.

flemington, nj

Acquired by William Penn from the Lenni Lenape Indians, Flemington was settled in the 18th century. For many visitors, the main attraction is the local outlet mall, but Flemington has more to offer, namely some historic sites, independent businesses, and one of the quirkiest railroad attractions in the country. The stately Main Street is still lined with Victorian homes, shops, and restaurants, and during the holiday season, the town takes on a nostalgic glow.

getting there

From Frenchtown, travel west over NJ 12 and turn left onto Main Street to enter Flemington. Total travel time from Frenchtown is 18 minutes.

where to go

Black River and Western Railroad. Stangl Rd. and NJ 12; (908) 782-9600; www.brwrr .com. The antique locomotive engines (either steam or diesel) on the Black River and Western short line transport riders from Flemington to Ringoes in their restored 19th-century coaches, parlor cars, and cabooses. This purely pleasure ride, established in 1970, offers scenic pastoral views and a fun experience for kids. While the 1-hour round-trip trains operate regularly in summer, seasonal excursions (to a corn maze in autumn, a ride with Santa during the winter holidays) are available in the off months.

Historic Hunterdon County Courthouse. 75 Main St.; (908) 284-4814; www.co.hunt erdon.nj.us/facts/chpics.htm. This temple of justice was built in Greek revival style in 1828, but it's best known for hosting the "Trial of the Century," aka the 1935 proceedings for the Lindbergh baby kidnapping. Today the local court proceedings have moved to the more modern Justice Complex but would-be detectives and historians, and those convinced of the accused Bruno Richard Hauptmann's innocence continue to flock here on a regular basis to see the famous setting. Visitor tours wend through the courtroom, deliberation rooms, and cell block. On display are original furniture and memorabilia from the trial.

Northlandz. 495 US 202; (908) 782-4022; www.northlandz.com. It's every little boy's dream come true: 16 acres of space with 8 miles of track and 100 trains that add up to the world's largest model railroad setup. Opened in 1996, this quirky roadside attraction was 25 years in the making and the brainchild of one passionate man, Bruce Williams Zaccagnino. If his grandiose vision doesn't sell you, the museum with more than 200 collectible dolls, the 94-room dollhouse with indoor swimming pool, and the expansive art gallery just might. Closed Tues.

where to shop

Comic Fusion. 42 Main St.; (908) 788-0599; www.comicfusion.com. Comics, graphic novels, trading cards, games, statues and models, and other collectibles abound at this Main Street staple. Product themes range from horror and sci-fi to anime and cartoons, TV shows, and superheroes. Publishers carried here include Dark Horse, Marvel, DC, First Issues, Image, Crossgen, and plenty of independents. The friendly and approachable staff assists the most seasoned collectors and novices alike, and visiting artists regularly stop in to sign work. Bring along old comics to trade. Open daily.

Dutch County Farmers' Market. 19 Commerce St.; (908) 806-8476; www.dutchfarmers market.com. This covered market boasts an authentic Pennsylvania Dutch experience out-side of Pennsylvania. Stock up on apple fritters, shoofly pie, or whoopee pies at the bakery, country-style crafts, the pickled vegetable condiment known as chow-chow, apple butter, and hand-rolled Amish-style soft pretzels. Vendors carry an array of fresh produce, cheeses, and more. Visitors with a little more time can stop into the Lancaster County Home Style Cooking restaurant for some old-fashioned eggs and scrapple. Open Thurs through Sat.

Liberty Village Premium Outlets. 1 Church St.; (908) 782-9550; www.premiumoutlets .com/libertyvillage. This outdoor discount mall—the nation's first outlet village—has driven tourism to Flemington for decades since its founding in 1981, and there are still plenty of great bargains to be had here. The 40 stores in the colonial-style complex include many of the usual suspects and popular brands—among them J. Crew, Ann Taylor, Brooks Broth-ers, Nautica, Ralph Lauren, Nike, Le Creuset, and Coach. Open daily. Additional discounts are usually available online.

where to eat

Blue Fish Grill. 9 Central Ave.; (908) 237-4528; www.thebluefishgrill.com. Bring your own bottle of wine (white, of course) to this casual seafood shack on the mainland that offers both generous portions and affordable prices. Tacos and sandwiches are filled with all man-ner of fish, while fillets are cooked over the wood-fired grill for simple, satisfying entrees. A kids' menu is available and the no-frills atmosphere with plastic tableware and paper towel napkins makes it an appealing place to bring little ones. Be prepared for a wait on weekend nights. $.

Matt's Red Rooster Grill. 22 Bloomfield Ave.; (908) 788-7050; www.mattsredroostergrill .com. Flemington's answer to upmarket cuisine is this contemporary American BYO set in an old Victorian house with a covered porch. The Red Rooster serves up familiar yet well-crafted bistro cooking: grilled romaine salad, blackened day-boat scallops with can-died onion marmalade, and vegetarian stuffed eggplant with herbed orzo. Finish it all off with sticky-sweet *tres leches* bread pudding. Sit by the open kitchen to watch Chef Matt McPherson at work or find a table by the wood-burning stove on a chillier night. Closed Mon. $$–$$$.

Shaker Cafe. 31 Main St.; (908) 782-6610; www.shakercafe.com. Named for the original owners' vast collection of salt and pepper shakers, this unassuming eatery with funky decor changed hands in 2010. The comfort-food menu now features local farm ingredients. On the regular list are basic omelets, sandwiches, and salads, along with inventive creations like the Fruity French Pig (a ham, brie, and raspberry jam omelet). Daily changing specials also expand the offerings, and Friday nights are always devoted to Mexican food. Open daily for breakfast, lunch, and dinner. $$.

where to stay

Main Street Manor Bed and Breakfast. 194 Main St.; (908) 782-4928; www.mainstreet manor.com. Flemington's only inn is prominently located on Main Street, and the well-maintained property is a classic Victorian B&B down to the lace doilies, iron beds, and floral wallpaper. Main Street Manor ups the fancy quotient further with fresh flowers, afternoon tea, feather beds, 24-hour snacks and coffee, and candlelight breakfasts in the Arts and Crafts paneled dining room. There are 5 guest rooms and a porch for people-watching. Holiday time brings a host of special events and a showy display of vintage decorations. $$–$$$.

day trip 03

north

a bridge over the delaware:
new hope, pa; lambertville, nj

The twin towns of New Hope, PA, and Lambertville, NJ, offer at least a day's worth of exploration—this trip could easily fill a weekend—and an essential Philadelphia getaway. Rolling hills, preserved forest, working farmland, and the wending Delaware River provide a scenic backdrop for these two vibrant centers of modern life. With only a short walk over the steel-truss bridge separating the two, New Hope and Lambertville are forever entwined, though they each offer distinct pleasures to the day-tripping visitor. Our trip starts at the funkier and more bustling New Hope, then ambles across the water to the more reserved streets of Lambertville.

new hope, pa

The town once known as Coryell's Ferry—an important site in the American Revolution and the halfway point between New York City and Philadelphia—is home to few but, with a well-established tourist trade, visited by many. Still, the constant influx of sightseers has done little to erode its charisma. When most of the town's mills were destroyed by fire, the "new hope" was rebuilt and renamed in 1790, and became a major destination for artists, gay travelers, and motorcyclists in the 20th century. More recently its inns have provided a weekend respite for urbanites looking for antiques, regional art, and strolls along the canal.

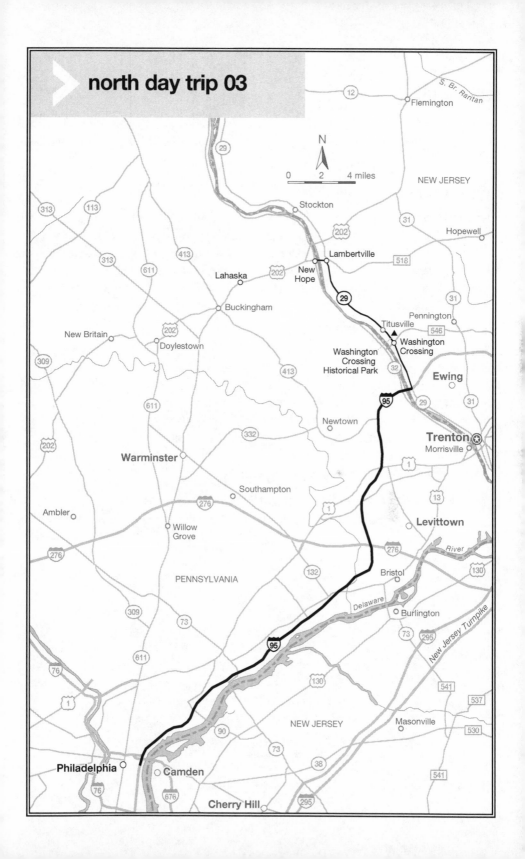

getting there

Take I-95 North from Philadelphia and follow exit 1 to NJ 29/River Road, following the water for about 10 miles. Make a slight right onto NJ 165 and then a left onto Bridge Street. Total travel time, without traffic, is 50 minutes.

where to go

New Hope Visitor's Center. 1 W. Mechanic St.; (215) 862-5030; www.newhopevisitor center.org. Set in New Hope's first town hall, school, and jail—a single all-purpose building constructed in 1839—the local visitor center has a notable architectural feature: the square glass in the large arch window facing Main Street. Inside staff offer detailed information on lodging, dining, and attractions as well as listings and maps. The store is stocked with all manner of New Hope memorabilia, from snow globes and paperweights to thimbles and hat tacks. Open daily but hours are seasonal.

Bowman's Hill Wildflower Preserve. 1635 River Rd.; (215) 862-2924; www.bhwp.org. Binoculars are a must-have here. Featuring 134 acres of native Pennsylvania plants in a natural setting, Bowman's Hill is a nonprofit park open to the public. There are 2.5 miles of trails through woodlands and meadows, plus a pond and creek banks for visitors to explore, either on self-guided walks or official tours. The free seasonal bloom guide can help identify flowering plants like redbud, mistflower, and American basswood. The preserve also hosts native plant sales in fall and spring. Open daily. There's a picnic pavilion and restrooms on the grounds.

George Nakashima. 1847 Aquetong Rd.; (215) 862-2272; www.nakashimawoodworker .com. You don't need to be a furniture expert to recognize the artistry of Nakashima, a

arts colony

Founded by William Langson Lathrop in 1898, the arts colony of New Hope quickly drew fellow artists with its scenic vistas and rural pace of life. Spanning Impressionism to modernism, the colony evolved over the decades and developed important affiliations with other groups of artists in the region. Among some of its most famous residents are painters Edward Redfield (1869–1965), Daniel Garber (1880–1958), and George Sotter (1879–1953). The artists held exhibitions in the Phillips Mill building north of New Hope. Eventually the group splintered off into smaller subgroups, but the colony cemented New Hope's reputation as a center of creativity.

masterful midcentury woodworker. This complex, operated today by Nakashima's daughter Mira, showcases his singular creative vision. Eight of the 14 Nakashima-designed and landscaped buildings on the property, including the house, working studio, and showrooms, are open for visitors. Architectural highlights include the conoid shell roof of the studio, made from reinforced concrete, and the plywood parabolic shell roof of the Minguren Museum. Open Sat from 1 to 4:30 p.m. Tours for 15 or more people can also be arranged.

New Hope & Ivy Land Railroad. 32 W. Bridge St.; (215) 862-2332; www.newhoperail road.com. Hop aboard a 1920s passenger coach and ride a short-line locomotive train from New Hope to Lahaska, or vice versa. The 1-hour ride rolls through the backwoods of Bucks County and an open car provides better viewing. A section of the 9-mile route was used in the 1914 film series *Perils of Pauline* and is still called Pauline's Trestle. There's a picnic grove at the Lahaska Station and a gift shop at New Hope. Special events include brunch and dinner rides catered by area restaurants, murder mystery events, and wine and beer tastings. Open daily.

Parry Mansion. 45 S. Main St.; (215) 862-5652; www.newhopehs.org. Built in 1784, this Georgian-style home was commissioned by the "father of New Hope," Benjamin Parry, and housed the ensuing generations of the Parry family until 1966. Visitors can tour the 11 rooms that they occupied and take a walk through decorative history. Designed by noted historian and interior designer Charles Lamar, they span 125 years of interior trends, from Chippendale furniture and candlesnuffers to William Morris wallpaper and whale oil lighting. Tours are available on weekends from May to Oct. The Historical Society, which is located in the mansion, also offers walking tours with various themes.

Washington Crossing Historical Park. 1112 River Rd., Washington Crossing, PA; (215) 493-4076; www.ushistory.org/washingtoncrossing. Revolutionary War history comes alive at this site where General George Washington and the Continental army and militia crossed the Delaware River on Christmas 1776—a critical moment in their ultimate victory. Founded in 1911, the current park has grown to 841 acres of historic sites and recreational areas. The visitor center is the best place to start an excursion and orient to the park. From there, circle around to view Durham boat replicas; the 18th-century McConkey's Ferry Inn, where soldiers stood guard; the Bowman's Hill Tower, built in 1931 to commemorate the Revolution; soldiers' graves; and more. The natural area in the northwest quadrant of the park contains 140 acres of mixed forest and fields with a nature center for environmental education activities. Guided tours are available Thurs through Sun seasonally.

where to shop

A Mano Galleries. 128 S. Main St.; (215) 862-5122; www.amanogalleries.com. Contemporary crafts fill this colorful gallery on Main Street—there's a sibling store across the river in Lambertville and both represent artisans from the region and beyond. Hand-painted Sticks furniture, brass and glass kaleidoscopes, Judaica from both America and Israel, and parchment and ceramic lamps are among the many one-of-a-kind wares for sale. A Mano also carries beaded silk jewelry, tabletop fountains, quirky office accessories, and eco-friendly items like bags and artwork made from recycled materials.

Farley's Bookshop. 44 S. Main St.; (215) 862-2452; www.farleysbookshop.com. This tightly quartered independent packs books into every narrow aisle, nook, and cranny. The specialties are local authors, musical scores, literature, and children's selections, though there's a little something for everyone. A longtime supporter of poetry, Farley's also sells limited-edition broadsides it produces in conjunction with Moontree Letterpress and collaborates with other indie presses to make available a wider array of reading material. Moving with the times, the store has also recently begun to sell ebooks.

Love Saves the Day. 1 S. Main St.; (215) 862-1399. Its moniker (and the associated acronym) reveals this vintage store's hippie roots, but the glittery costumes, jewelry, movie memorabilia, and toys display a high camp sensibility. Browsing the hectic clutter of objects can feel more like visiting an attraction than shopping, and some of the items have museum-quality prices. Yet amid the racks of vintage clothes, shoes, and purses are stylish designer finds and wares that go back to the Victorian era. Even if a KISS lunchbox or Pee-Wee Herman doll isn't on the shopping list, it's a fun diversion.

Peddler's Village. US 202 and PA 263, Lahaska, PA; (215) 794-4000; www.peddlersvillage .com. Arranged like an 18th-century town center, Peddler's Village is a quaint if slightly hackneyed tourist stop. Wander along the well-manicured walkways to explore the 70 shops, which range from a boutique coffee roaster to PJ and Jammies, devoted entirely to sleepwear. Six on-site restaurants include a murder-mystery dinner theater and the Cock n' Bull restaurant, which offers colonial-style dinners with live music. Immensely popular seasonal festivals draw nostalgic crowds and the Giggleberry Fair attraction for children is the ideal place to let the little ones blow off some steam.

Rice's Country Market. 6326 Greenhill Rd.; (215) 297-5993; www.rices.com. Bucks County's largest and oldest open-air market is for some visitors reason enough to make a pilgrimage to the region. Over 500 vendors convene to sell antiques, art, clothing, jewelry, produce, and Amish baked goods. But it's not all vintage finds—a large section is devoted to inexpensive, mass-manufactured new items, like eyeglasses, handbags, and socks. Arrive early for the best selection. Expect to pay for parking. Open Tues year-round, and Sat, Mar through Dec, 7 a.m. to 1 p.m.

where to eat

C'est La Vie. 20 S. Main St.; (215) 862-1956. A petite French bakery and cafe off the beaten path, C'est La Vie has a low-key charm. Its location on a hidden alleyway makes it the ideal place to duck out of the New Hope crowds for a light breakfast of authentically flaky savory and sweet croissants, or a lunch of quiche or sandwiches on crusty bread. Tea-timers will be rewarded with meringues, turnovers, and other treats. There are a few small tables inside and some additional seating is available outside. $.

Marsha Brown. 15 S. Main St.; (215) 862-7044; www.marshabrownrestaurant.com. The old church building, with its stained-glass windows, high ceilings, and pews, makes for a dramatic setting, but Marsha Brown's Creole cooking has got plenty of verve on its own. N'awlins classics like jambalaya and étouffée are the mainstay, along with straight-ahead steaks and chops and a raw bar. There are also some more creative inventions, like a divinely rich lump crab and smoked gouda cheesecake. A small but selective wine list and full bar complement the hearty eats. Open daily. $$$.

Sprig & Vine. 450 Union Square Dr.; (215) 693-1427; www.sprigandvine.com. Vegans rejoice at this chic modern bistro and meatless mecca near the New Hope and Ivyland Railroad. While the tagline is "pure vegetarian," there's no cheese, eggs, or milk to be found here and the produce is local and sustainable to boot. Brunch features peach French toast with vanilla cashew cream and candied pecans and tempeh sausage; lunchtime brings edamame falafel wraps and grilled eggplant *banh mi*; dinner might be a platter of fennel seed–crusted tofu over creamy saffron polenta. BYO. $$.

Tastebuds. 49 W. Ferry St.; (215) 862-9722; www.tastebuds-newhope.com. A minimal Danish modern interior accented with orange is the setting for brightly flavored food at this memorable BYO. The limited menu of local, sustainably minded cuisine changes seasonally but might include a baby spinach salad with bing cherries, feta, and a maple-cream dress-ing; beef tenderloin rubbed with ancho chile and served with a Cuban espresso sauce over whipped potatoes; or Arctic char with crushed cherry tomatoes, red couscous, and basil. Cash only. Closed Mon and Tues. $$–$$$.

where to stay

Inn at Bowman's Hill. 518 Lurgan Rd.; (215) 862-8090; www.theinnatbowmanshill.com. An upscale, luxury inn with 4 guest rooms and 2 suites, Bowman's Hill is situated on a meticulously maintained 5-acre estate, surrounded by woodlands. The grounds enchant with their weeping willows, fountain pond, and free-roaming chickens. All of the country-romantic rooms include full breakfast (the house specialty is the full English), 1-person tubs, fireplaces, and king-size beds. Spa services are available, and a heated pool and hot tub are on the property. $$$.

Pineapple Hill B&B Inn. 1324 River Rd.; (888) 866-8404; www.pineapplehill.com. This colonial manor set between central New Hope and Washington Crossing Park is a well-situated jumping-off point for visitors—especially those interested in area history. The atten-tive innkeepers value personal attention: They offer complimentary beverages and snacks on arrival as well as plenty of suggestions about area attractions. The 5 rooms and 4 suites could use a bit of updating but they're clean and affordable, and many feature fireplaces. A full breakfast is served every morning and there's an outdoor pool, charmingly situated near the ruins of an old barn, open for swimming in warmer months. $$–$$$.

lambertville, nj

In perfect symmetry to New Hope is the city of Lambertville. Incorporated in 1849, the one-time factory town used to produce underwear, rubber bands, and other basic but necessary goods. With the advent of the automobile and the decline of canal commerce, Lambertville went through a period of neglect and became something of a redheaded stepchild to bustling New Hope in the early to mid-20th century. The 1970s marked its revival as a tourist destination, giving new life to its Victorian and federal buildings. With its current batch of shops, galleries, restaurants, and inns, not to mention a reputation as the "Antiques Capital of New Jersey," Lambertville has gone decidedly upscale.

getting there

From New Hope, head east on Bridge Street one-half mile.

where to go

Lambertville Historical Society/Marshall House. 60 Bridge St.; (609) 397-0770; www .lambertvillehistoricalsociety.org. The Marshall House Museum narrates the story of Lambertville and one of its most famous sons. James Wilson Marshall left his hometown in the mid-1800s for California, where he was the very first person to find gold in Coloma, thus setting off the Great Gold Rush. Marshall's New Jersey home was nearly destroyed in the 1960s, before it was saved by the state. A walk through period rooms reveals an extensive collection of objects and documents and noteworthy period details, like chimney cupboards in the parlor and an Adams-style decorative frieze over the doorway. Guided walking tours are available. Open weekend afternoons from Apr to Oct.

Museum at Holcombe. NJ 29; (609) 397-2752; www.holcombe-jimison.org. This 19th-century farmstead is situated on 10 acres of land and operated by a nonprofit educational organization. Holcombe showcases old farming equipment, a country kitchen, a print shop, a post office, a blacksmith shop, a doctor's office, and the oldest surviving stone house in Hunterdon County. With the museum barn's displays of early homemaking and farming tools, Holcombe gives visitors a taste of agricultural life from 1700 to 1900. Open to the public Sun and Wed from May to Oct, and by appointment during the rest of the year.

River Horse Brewing Company. 80 Lambert Ln.; (609) 397-7776; www.riverhorse.com. With a hippo as mascot and a changing lineup of creative beers, River Horse epitomizes the laid-back sensibility of the American microbrewery scene. This craft brewery, best known for its Belgian-style ale and Oatmeal Milk Stout, is a beer snob must-see, but because it's tucked away in a retrofitted snack factory on a dead-end street in Lambertville, it can be easy to miss. The brewery opens its doors for free self-guided (or occasionally guided) tours of the brewing and bottling process and tastings of the finished product with dangerously inexpensive ($1 for 4) pours on weekends.

where to shop

Golden Nugget. 1850 NJ 29; (609) 397-0811; www.gnmarket.com. This indoor-outdoor flea market is one of the largest of its kind on the East Coast, with over 60 indoor shops and 200 outside dealers. Emphasizing antique and vintage goods, dealers encourage bartering, though the indoor "stores" typically feature higher-price items. From spring through fall, the Green Market showcases regionally grown produce and plants and locally made food and crafts. Open year-round Wed, Sat, and Sun, 6 a.m. to 4 p.m.

Pure Energy Cycling and Java House. 99 S. Main St.; (609) 397-7008; www.pureenergy cycling.com. Custom cycling meets cappuccino in this unique full-service bike shop that emphasizes personal attention and the perfect fit. Catering to cycling nerds and leisure cruisers alike, Pure Energy is a favorite stop-off for canal-path riders planning routes, getting tune-ups, or relaxing with a hot cup of Small World Coffee, and a plate of locally made baked goods. The cement floors are cleat-friendly and mounted TVs show cycling races for spectator types.

Rago Arts and Auction Center. 333 N. Main St.; (609) 397-9374; www.ragoarts.com. The owners of this major auction house for 20th-century design appear regularly on *The Antiques Roadshow* and they've served thousands of buyers since opening their business in 1995. Specialties include fine art, decorative arts, currency, furnishings, jewelry, and artifacts, and while 20th-century work is the focus, there are items from across the ages. Free valuations of personal property are offered for walk-in visitors on Monday. Auctions are held throughout the year with items on exhibit in Rago's galleries.

where to eat

Hamilton's Grill Room. 8 Coryell St.; (609) 397-4343; www.hamiltonsgrillroom.com. This canal-side bistro with al fresco courtyard seating is open for brunch and dinner. Set in an alley off the main streets of Lambertville, Hamilton's has a romantic, hideaway feel with a European flair. The menu emphasizes simple, clean cooking with Mediterranean flavors: grilled turbot with celery salad, grilled shrimp with anchovy butter, and rack of spring lamb. Reservations are recommended on weekends. The policy is bring your own bottle, so consider getting a pre- or postmeal drink at the nearby Boat House. Open daily. $$$.

Marhaba. 77 S. Union St.; (609) 397-7777; www.marhabalambertville.com. With Lambertville's star on the rise, it can be challenging to find a great budget-conscious meal. Enter

Marhaba. Fresh, casual, Middle Eastern eats (kebabs, falafel, *pitza*) make this little cafe a favorite for a quick lunch or inexpensive dinner. Portions are generous and all of the platters are served with basmati rice and a cucumber salad. Try the hibiscus tea, anything to dip with the homemade pita bread, chicken *shawarma*, and baklava. Food is halal. BYO. $–$$.

where to stay

Inn at Lambertville Station. 11 Bridge St.; (609) 397-8300; www.lambertvillestation .com. A centrally located hotel with river-view rooms, the Inn at Lambertville Station is more contemporary than quaint. Its proximity to New Hope makes it a good choice for visitors exploring either town. And while visitors would be advised to skip the touristy in-house train station restaurant, the overnight accommodations are spacious and well appointed. Suites have fireplaces, and all rooms include flat-screen TVs, wireless Internet access, continental breakfast, and a complimentary newspaper. $$–$$$.

Lambertville House Hotel. 32 Bridge St.; (888) 867-8859; www.lambertvillehouse.com. This nationally registered landmark building once provided lodging to Andrew Johnson and Ulysses S. Grant. Today the Lambertville House is a decidedly boutique affair with 26 guest rooms that feature amenities like marble baths with jetted tubs, plush bathrobes, and private balconies. An expanded continental breakfast is included and there are Keurig machines on every floor. The quieter rooms face the courtyard. The hotel bar, Left Bank Libations, serves up a menu of signature cocktails. $$$.

day trip 04

north

mountain destination:
stroudsburg, pa

stroudsburg, pa

Directly north of Philadelphia is the Pocono Mountain range and the borough of Strouds-burg. Founded by Colonel Jacob Stroud in the mid-18th century, Stroudsburg has served as a commercial hub for the Pocono region since its founding. More recently it's become a tourist destination, with many ski resorts nearby. Main Street is still the town's biggest thoroughfare, anchored on one end by the Stroud Mansion and on the other by the Holland Thread Mill, which has been revamped to enclose shops, loft apartments, and offices. In between are Victorian buildings now occupied by a lively mix of galleries, boutiques, and restaurants.

getting there

From Philadelphia, travel north on I-476, then merge onto US 22 for 16.4 miles. Then follow PA 33 north toward Stroudsburg. Turn right on US 209 and travel for 3 miles, turning left on Main Street (PA 611) to enter town. Total driving time, without traffic, is just under 2 hours.

where to go

Bell School. Cherry Valley Rd., Stormville, PA; (570) 421-7703; www.monroehistorical .org. This 1-room schoolhouse is located just southwest of Stroudsburg and gives visitors a fascinating glimpse into 19th-century education in general and that of Monroe County in particular. As a matter of fact, the small brick Bell School hosted students until 1953. Named for the bell on its cupola, the building now houses a display of books, photographs, and other artifacts. Open Sun in July and Aug, and by appointment other times of the year.

Cherry Valley Vineyards. 5100 Lower Cherry Valley Rd., Saylorsburg, PA; (570) 992-2255; www.cherryvalleyvineyards.com. The creation of an Italian immigrant, Cherry Valley brings southern Italian viticulture to the Pocono region. The grapes are French hybrids, typical in Pennsylvania but not elsewhere in the States: Marechal Foch, Baco Noir, Leon Millot, and Chambourcin. The winery also produces Merlot, Cabernet, and Pinot Grigio wines, as well as sparkling and fruit wines. Visitors can tour the facility and learn about the winemaking process and sample vintages. Surrounding the vineyard is a park and wildlife refuge. Open daily from 10 a.m. to 6 p.m.

Pocono Indian Museum. US 209, Bushkill, PA; (570) 588-9338; www.poconoindian museum.com. The only cultural institution dedicated to the Delaware tribe of Native Americans, this museum traces their history back thousands of years. The colonial-style manor in which it's housed was used as a safe house for slaves on the Underground Railroad, then as a speakeasy during Prohibition before it was purchased and established as the Pocono Indian Museum in 1976. Exhibits showcase artifacts, weapons, and tools, while telling the story of the tribe's tragic losses at the hands of the conquering white settlers. Hours change seasonally.

Stroud Mansion Museum. 900 Main St.; (570) 421-7703; www.monroehistorical.org. When it was built in 1795, founding father Jacob Stroud's mansion was the finest example of Georgian architecture for miles. The Revolutionary War hero intended the 12-room building as a home for his son, and it remained in the family until 1893. Now listed in the National Register of Historic Places, the mansion is filled with 4 floors of galleries about the history of Monroe County, including permanent and changing exhibits. Visitors can explore the colonial-era cellar kitchen, Victorian parlor, and other rooms. Open Tues through Fri, and the first and third Sat of the month from 10 a.m. to 4 p.m.

where to shop

Dawn of New York. 542 Main St.; (570) 421-5560; www.dawnofnewyork.com. A onetime photo stylist has put down roots in Stroudsburg with this trendy fashion emporium, replete with luxe furniture and crystal chandeliers. Owner Dawn Notaro still splits her time between here and New York City, scouting out the latest affordable pieces for her store. The result is a mix of labels and styles with clothing for a range of occasions, from casual daywear to evening gowns, all with a fresh, creative sensibility. Open daily.

Josephine's Fleur-de-Lis. 601 Main St.; (570) 476-7909; www.josephinesonmain .com. Two New Yorkers opened this female-centric, multipurpose lifestyle boutique in

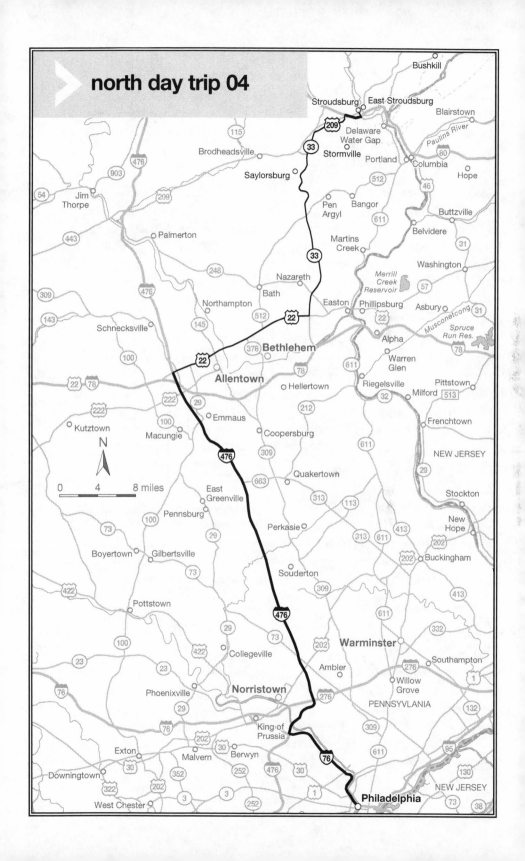

north day trip 04

Stroudsburg to bring high style to Main Street. Their product lines include such luxuries as Vietri tableware and home accents, Lundburg art glass, Italian leather handbags, Cleo & Patek evening bags and briefcases, and Caswell-Massey spa and bath products. Rounding out the selection are candles, baby gifts, and paper products. The in-store Creative Center encourages customers to build their own jewelry.

Main Street Jukebox. 606 Main St.; (570) 424-2246. Since 1994 this colorful, independently owned music store has provided a steady supply of tunes to Stroudsburg residents. Carrying both new and used records and CDs, the Jukebox specializes in rare and limited-edition titles. Also on the shelves are DVDs—for the especially nostalgic shopper, VHS and audio cassettes—plus music and pop culture books, collectibles, toys, art, and turntables. Prices are affordable and there's a listening area in-store. Open daily.

where to eat

Stone Bar Inn. US 209; (570) 992-6634; www.stonebar.com. This roadside restaurant, first opened in 1936, is a local favorite for dining experiences ranging from happy hour snacks to an elegant meal in the wine cellar or on the veranda, weather permitting. The menu offers some expected selections—homemade applewood-smoked trout with dill cream and crab-stuffed mushrooms—and some not-so-expected, such as the Spanish paella and the steaks topped with foie gras. For its part, the namesake stone bar is stocked with a decent wine and beer selection and intriguing cocktails, like the Butterpecantini. Closed Mon. $$$.

Stroudsmoor Inn. RD #4 Stroudsmoor Rd.; (570) 421-6431; www.stroudsmoor.com. One of the area's oldest inns also features an affordable Italian-American restaurant. Lunch is a selection of sandwiches, salads, and soups, plus pasta specialties and entrees that include the soup and salad bar. Midweek dinner features tomato zucchini bisque, veal scaloppini with Marsala demi-glace, and "light and healthy" options such as whole wheat penne with broccoli. Weekends bring buffets—Festa di Mare seafood buffet on Friday, the Grand Buffet on Saturday with live piano music, and the Brunch and American Harvest Dinner Buffet on Sunday. Open daily. $–$$.

where to stay

Cranberry Manor B&B. 114 Cherry Lane Rd., East Stroudsburg, PA; (570) 620-2246; www.cranberrymanor.com. This former summer boarding home circa 1880 is situated on a 14-acre lot at the edge of the Tannersville Cranberry Bog—thus, the name. The 5 guest rooms are feminine but not overly frilly and feature large private baths with separate soaking tubs and showers, plus gas fireplaces, air-conditioning, and DirecTV. Also available to guests: a pool table, library, and butler's pantry stocked with complimentary snacks and beverages. Candlelight breakfast is served in the formal dining room or on the porch. $$.

northeast

day trip 01

northeast

brain trust:
princeton, nj

princeton, nj

While it's known to many as a college town—home to the eponymous Ivy League university—Princeton has much to offer visitors who are not necessarily interested in applying early decision. The town was first settled by Europeans in the 17th century, then later witnessed the Battle of Princeton during the Revolutionary War and served as the hometown to two signers of the Declaration of Independence, Richard Stockton and John Witherspoon. In recent decades Princeton's already elite intellectual heritage has been enhanced by the arrival of corporations such as ETS, Bristol-Myers Squibb, and Dow Jones & Company, all of which are headquartered here. Throughout its history the Princeton community has provided a high quality of life for its residents with its mix of colonial and Victorian architecture, a lively arts and culture scene, boutique shopping, and myriad restaurants.

getting there

From Philadelphia, take I-95 North for 36 miles to exit at US 206 North. Follow for 6 miles, then turn right into Princeton. Travel time is about 50 minutes.

where to go

Grounds for Sculpture. 18 Fairgrounds Rd., Hamilton, NJ; (609) 586-0616; www.grounds forsculpture.org. Founded in 1992 by J. Seward Johnson, sculptor and heir to the Johnson

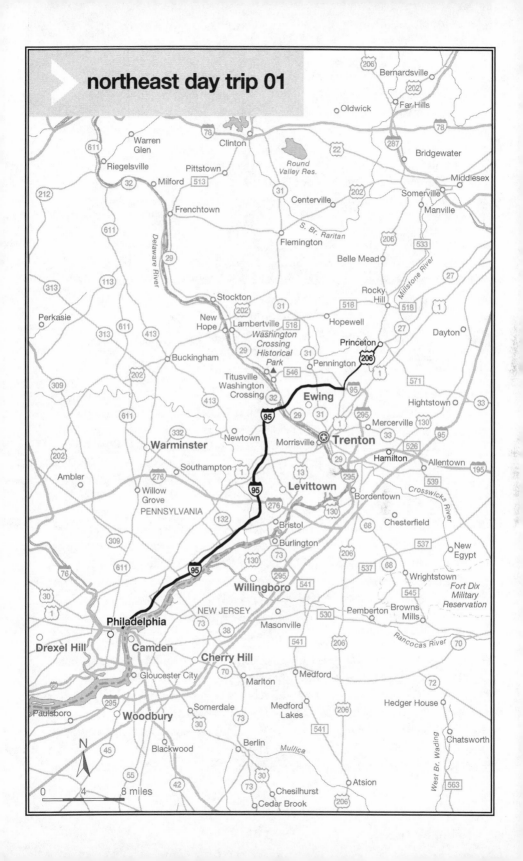

& Johnson fortune, Grounds for Sculpture is a 42-acre art park on the site of the former New Jersey State Fairgrounds. A permanent collection of outdoor sculpture is embellished with stunning gardens, ponds, and bamboo forests, and excavated waterways add striking contours to the surroundings. Among the artists represented here are Kiki Smith, Magdalena Abakanowicz, Red Grooms, and Johnson himself. Indoor galleries host changing exhibitions of mostly contemporary works. On-site are a casual cafe, bookstore, and a more formal restaurant called Rat's. Guided and self-guided tours are available. Open Tues through Sun 10 a.m. to 6 p.m.

Historic Society of Princeton. 158 Nassau St.; (609) 921-6748; www.princetonhistory .org. The headquarters for the Historical Society are contained in the mid-period Georgian-style Bainbridge House, built by a cousin of Richard Stockton, and include exhibition space and a small museum shop. Changing exhibits focus on the lives of famous Princetonians and draw from the extensive collections of furniture, paintings, household items, and clothing from the 18th and 19th centuries. The Society is open Tues through Sun and holds guided two-hour walking tours on Sunday mornings, as well as other special events. There's also a research library on the premises.

McCarter Theatre Center. 91 University Place; (609) 258-2787; www.mccarter.org. This world-class cultural center is the only organization in the US that's both a professional producing theater and a major presenter of the performing arts. Opened in 1930, the theater gained popularity as an early showcase for Broadway previews but has since branched out considerably. McCarter hosts a core theater series, focusing on both new works and classic plays, as well as music, dance, and children's events in a wide variety of genres. Touring theater productions are also hosted here.

Morven Museum and Gardens. 55 Stockton St.; (609) 924-8144; www.historicmorven .org. This onetime home to Richard Stockton now serves as a museum of fine and decorative arts with changing exhibitions that illustrate the history and culture of New Jersey. The Boudinot Collection, on loan from the Princeton University Art Museum, contains furniture, porcelain, portraits, and silver that descended through the Boudinot family, which was interwoven with the Stocktons. The pristine grounds encompass a formal lawn with heirloom 18th- and 19th-century annuals and a colonial revival–style garden. Open Wed through Sun.

Princeton Cemetery. 29 Greenview Ave.; (609) 924-1369; www.princetonol.com/groups/ cemetery. The American version of Père Lachaise, this 18th-century cemetery owned by the Nassau Presbyterian Church is the final resting place for such notable people as Grover Cleveland, George Gallup, Kurt Gödel, John O'Hara, and Richard Stockton. While there are many old stones to view, the oldest monument on-site is for Aaron Burr Jr., vice president of the US from 1801 to 1805 (best known as the man who killed Alexander Hamilton in a duel). Maps are available online for self-guided tours.

Princeton Tour Company. 100 Nassau St.; (609) 902-3637; www.princetontourcompany .com. Explore the area by bus, by foot, or by bike on one of these tours, and get an earful of townie folklore and plenty of gossip about Princeton's most famous residents from Revolutionary times to the present day. Itineraries typically include stops at the university campus through to the town's side streets lined with stately homes, covering both town and gown. Themed tours of ghosts, Einstein, architecture, and literary greats are also available. The Genius Vision tour uses iPads to enhance the experience.

Princeton University. (609) 258-3000; www.princeton.edu. The idyllic campus of the fourth-oldest college in the US is an architectural cornucopia. Highlights include the gothic University Chapel, the iron FitzRandolph Gateway, the sleekly modern Woodrow Wilson School building, and the storied Nassau Hall, which was occupied during the Revolution. The library has its own galleries showcasing art and special collections as well as the excellent Cotsen children's area with a storybook reading room and interactive exhibits. Information for self-guided tours is on the university's website.

Princeton University Art Museum. McCormick Hall; (609) 258-3788; http://artmuseum .princeton.edu. The collections of Princeton's museum include some 72,000 works of art, spanning ancient to contemporary, concentrating on the Mediterranean, Western Europe, Asia, and the Americas. Greek and Roman antiquities include mosaics, ceramics, marble, and bronzes, while the medieval Europe collection features sculpture, metalwork, and stained glass. Chinese tomb figures, painting, and calligraphy are among the most notable holdings. Works by Frederick Remington, Pablo Picasso, Henri Matisse, Hieronymus Bosch, and Augustus Saint-Gaudens are displayed. Self-guided tours are the norm, but small groups (6 or more) can arrange a docent-led tour for a small fee. Closed Mon.

where to shop

Landau's. 102 Nassau St.; (800) 257-9445; www.landauprinceton.com. Open for nearly a century, Landau's is a third-generation family-run specialty store focused on globally made woolens. Iceland's president nicknamed the Landaus "The Wool Family" in 1982, and the epithet stuck. Their tiny outlet is crammed with textile products, from throws and shawls to Loden coats, fisherman sweaters, scarves, socks and slippers. And inside is the Einstein Museum, a display of Albert Einstein memorabilia donated from community residents including those that knew him personally.

Palmer Square. 40 Nassau St.; (609) 921-2333; www.palmersquare.com. A courtyard mall in the center of Princeton, Palmer Square was originally built by Edgar Palmer, the heir to the New Jersey Zinc Company fortune and designed by Thomas Stapleton in the colonial revival style during the 1930s. Today the square houses a mix of reliable chain stores (J. Crew, Ann Taylor, Banana Republic) and boutique-y independents (Corkscrew Wine Shop, Jazams toys, Spruce floral design, Zoë fashion). Tucked in between are gourmet eats, upscale cosmetics, artisan jewelry, and a full-service salon. The plaza in front is the town's major bus stop and features a sculpture by Seward Johnson.

Princeton Record Exchange. 20 S. Tulane St.; (609) 921-0881; www.prex.com. The Record Exchange is a landmark for college DJs and music lovers of all stripes. Prex, as it's affectionately called, buys estate collections, private collections, radio station surplus, and retail inventory, and the result is a massive stock of new and rare finds. The proceedings are overseen by a friendly, knowledgeable staff that's as passionate about their wares as their customers are. With over 50,000 CDs, DVDs, and LPs under $5 and 140,000 total music and movies on sale, a short pop-in can quickly escalate into an hour or two of shopping.

where to eat

Bent Spoon. 35 Palmer Sq. West; (609) 924-2368; www.thebentspoon.net. Princeton has become something of a mecca for cold-confection seekers, and it's all because of this new-style ice cream parlor, which is regularly featured in national media. The artisan ice creams and sorbets with fresh, local ingredients in flavors like peach mascarpone, ricotta pistachio, pluot, and more daringly, tomato basil, are the main draw here, but excellent cookies and cupcakes, and killer hot chocolate are a few other reasons to stop in. The inside seating is limited but there are plenty of benches in the surrounding Palmer Square. $.

Elements. 163 Bayard Ln.; (609) 924-0078; www.elementsprinceton.com. Its sleek dining room with rustic overtones is as soothing as a spa, and this locavore bistro delivers equally fresh and wholesome cuisine, such as Griggstown chicken with corn and black trumpet mole, and an eggplant soup spiked with chile, coconut, and tapioca. Specialty cocktails like the Green Plum (damson plum gin, elderflower cordial, green tomato and plum juice), an excellent selection of whiskeys, and a nice sampling of wines by the glass round out the offerings. Open for brunch, lunch, and dinner. A chef's table can be reserved for special-occasion dining. Valet parking is available. Reservations recommended. $$–$$$.

Hoagie Haven. 242 Nassau St.; (609) 921-7723; www.hoagiehaven.com. Outside of Phila-delphia proper, this local institution circa 1970 is one of the better places to nab an authen-tic hoagie — the famed Italian sandwich of cold cuts and cheese on a long roll. Generously portioned sandwiches are extremely inexpensive, and the atmosphere is strictly no-frills. The student-friendly hangout also gives a nod to the nearby New Brunswick grease-truck scene with its subs filled with mozzarella sticks, french fries, and chicken tenders. $.

Rat's. Fairgrounds Rd., Hamilton, NJ; (609) 584-7800; www.groundsforsculpture.org. Named for a *Wind in the Willows* character, the resident fine-dining restaurant at Grounds for Sculpture is designed to look like a Claude Monet painting come to life. The French-inspired fare includes steak tartare with quail egg and chive, halibut over *brandade* cannel-loni, and short-rib bourguignon. An outdoor patio overlooks the lily-padded pond. To get the full experience, purchase admission to the grounds and stroll around before or after the meal. $$$.

Triumph Brewing Company. 138 Nassau St.; (609) 924-7855; www.triumphbrewing .com. One of 3 local locations of this locally based microbrewery, the Princeton outpost is a crowd-pleasing hangout for the casual diner. The menu is laden with beer-friendly grub like fried green tomatoes, roast pork sandwiches, and fish and chips. The Epic Burger, with a fried egg, pork belly, caramelized onion, truffle aioli, *and* Mornay sauce, may be Triumph's contribution to the local pharmaceutical companies but it's also a standout. The 6 taps rotate with house-brewed selections and the pub hosts live music on weekends. $$.

where to stay

Inn at Glencairn. 3301 Lawrenceville Rd.; (609) 497-1737; www.innatglencairn.com. Located about 5 minutes from the center of Princeton, the Inn at Glencairn is a fitting layover for the traveler seeking the region's historic sights. The 5 rooms of this newly renovated Georgian manor are decorated with 18th-century antiques and gussied up with Egyptian cotton linens, flat-screen TVs, and feather beds. The common areas and guest rooms are decorated with a revolving art collection and oriental carpets. The inn's green philosophy is showcased in its nontoxic cleaning products and the organic, local ingredients in the complimentary breakfast. $$–$$$.

Nassau Inn. 10 Palmer Sq.; (800) 862-7728; www.nassauinn.com. Located in the heart of Palmer Square, the Nassau looks charmingly small and quaint on the outside but is surprisingly expansive and modern on the inside. The elegant lobby serves complimentary cookies and maintains a bustling energy all day long. The 200 pet-friendly guest rooms don't offer many amenities, but the in-house restaurant and bar make the Nassau a mainstay for Princeton parents and a convenient launching pad for visitors. Bed-and-breakfast packages are available. $$$.

Peacock Inn. 20 Bayard Ln.; (609) 924-1707; www.peacockinn.com. A landmark 18th-century mansion is the setting for this boutique luxury hotel a block from Princeton's campus. The 16 minimalist chic guest rooms offer privacy and comfort and 7 of them feature fireplaces. Heated bathroom floors, flat-screen televisions, complimentary wireless Internet access, Hollandia mattresses, Ben Shahn artwork, and take-home slippers pamper guests, along with a light continental-style breakfast served every morning. Both valet parking and self-parking are available. $$$.

day trip 02

northeast

meeting of many cultures:
new brunswick, nj

new brunswick, nj

The hometown of Rutgers University was occupied by white settlers in 1681, and New Brunswick (named after the German city Braunschweig) became an important hub for colonial travelers and traders before it was occupied by the British during the Revolutionary War. In the early 20th century it drew a large population of Hungarian emigrés who found work at the city's Johnson & Johnson factories, and later, Hispanic and Indian immigrants employed by the electronic, biotech, and information industries. Though a period in the 1960s and 1970s brought white flight and urban decay, the city has since had a revival. Current-day New Brunswick is an expanded college town with the cultural life of a much bigger city.

getting there

From Philadelphia, take I-95 North for 38.3 miles, then pick up US 1 North for 16 miles. Exit onto Livingston Avenue to enter New Brunswick. Total travel time without traffic is 1 hour and 10 minutes.

where to go

Jane Voorhees Zimmerli Art Museum. 71 Hamilton St.; (732) 932-7237; www.zimmerli museum.rutgers.edu. A modern brick structure named for the mother of philanthropist Alan Voorhees, Rutgers's art museum is rich in Russian and Soviet art—the centerpiece of which

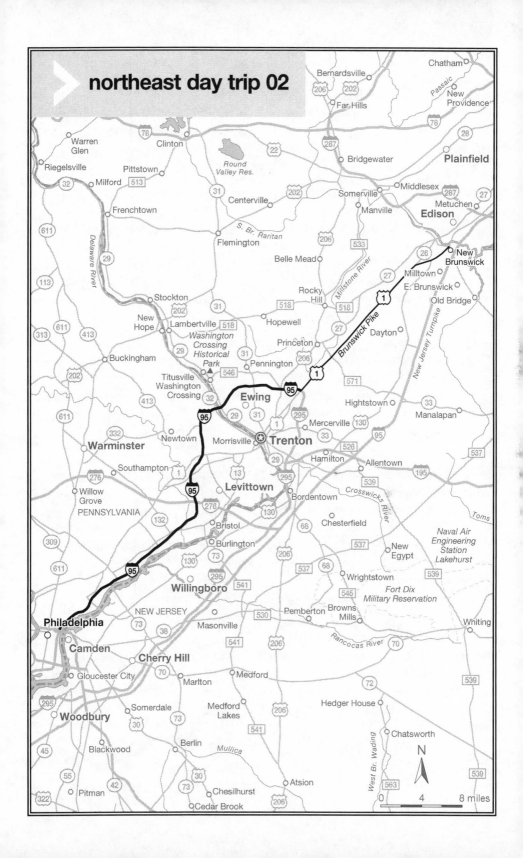

northeast day trip 02

is the Dodge Collection, the single largest collection of Soviet nonconformist works outside of Russia. In addition, there are extensive holdings in 19th-century French paintings and American art from the 18th century through the present with an emphasis on contemporary prints. The museum also mounts a diverse slate of changing exhibitions. With over 60,000 works in total, it's one of the largest university art museums in the country.

Museum of the American Hungarian Foundation. 300 Somerset St.; (732) 846-5777; http://hstrial-pfazekaz.homestead.com/museum.html. Reflecting New Brunswick's rich Hungarian culture, this museum, which opened in 1989, captures the Hungarian immigrant experience, focusing especially on fine art and folk art. The permanent and temporary exhibitions showcase Hungarian contributions to US life, particularly those artists born in Hungary who have made an impact on the American art world. The museum store proffers Hungarian embroidery, Zsolnay porcelain, books, music, and other items. There's a library, and archives housed here as well. Open Tues through Sun.

Rutgers Gardens. 112 Ryders Ln.; (732) 932-8451; www.rutgersgardens.rutgers.edu. The university's 50 acres of horticultural, display and botanical gardens are open to the public and beautiful in any season. Among the collections and exhibits are an evergreen garden, water conservation terrace area, shrub and shade-tree forest, rhododendron and azalea garden, bamboo forest, and more. There's no fee to tour them, and visitors can roam through a self-guided tour. Of special interest is the log cabin overlooking Westons Mill Pond, which was built by the Works Progress Administration in 1936. Free and open daily.

State Theatre. 15 Livingston Ave.; (732) 246-7469; www.statetheatrenj.org. The calendar of national and international performing arts events at this historic nonprofit venue is impressive for its range and scope, encompassing theater, blues, jazz, comedy, classical, dance, and more. Founded in 1921, the theater hosted vaudeville and played silent films, and eventually became part of the RKA chain. It served a brief stint as an adult movie theater in the 1970s before being purchased by the New Brunswick Development Corporation and has since been renovated twice over. The latest round has brought the theater back to its original appearance with plaster repair, lighting, and other decorative detail.

where to shop

Pop Trash Boutique. 29-A Easton Ave.; (732) 247-1190; www.frankenknuckle.com/web stage/pop/index.html. Punk flavor with a pop edge is the aesthetic at this hot pink shop that thinks outside of the mall box. The fun and funky selection of new and vintage women's apparel is mostly casual and aimed at twenty-somethings and teens, with a nice array of jeans, tops, dresses, and skirts. The youthful but feminine designers include BB Dakota, Lux De Ville, Sailor Jerry, and Soundgirl. Pop Trash also stocks jewelry, outerwear, cosmetics, belts and other accessories.

Thomas Sweet Next Door. 55 Easton Ave.; (732) 828-3855; www.thomassweet.com. The Thomas Sweet ice cream parlors are a local chain, notable for their enticing homemade flavors like French Kiss (chocolate raspberry mousse with chocolate chips), Grand Marnier, and Eastern Chai. This tempting gift shop is stocked with Sweet's hand-dipped chocolates, truffles, pralines, fresh fudge in an array of flavors (dulce de leche, peanut butter cup, and the intriguingly named Prozac), plus slightly less serious treats like chocolate-covered Oreos. There's also a selection of nonedible (and less caloric) gifts and cards.

where to eat

Due Mari. 78 Albany St.; (732) 296-1600; www.duemarinj.com. Traditional Italian fare is given an upmarket twist at Due Mari. Start the meal with *sfizi,* or pre-appetizers, and a signature cocktail like the house Negroni with Hendrick's gin. Then ease into menu highlights such as the Kobe beef carpaccio with truffle vinaigrette; Berkshire pork chop with cavatelli, fava beans, and shallot butter, and homemade pastas. There's live jazz at the bar and lounge area on Thursday and Friday nights, and the casual menu here includes lighter fare like sandwiches and pizza. Open for lunch and dinner. $$$.

The Frog and the Peach. 29 Dennis St.; (732) 846-3216; www.frogandpeach.com. The name may sound like a children's fable but this warmly lit fine-dining restaurant in a former warehouse serves up sophisticated, decidedly adult-friendly cookery. The farm-to-table prix-fixe dinners offer the best value but there are plenty of a la carte options. The chef favors contemporary American creations such as seared foie gras over grilled peach with bacon and port reduction, or local sea scallops with black sesame hummus, couscous, and carrot vinaigrette. The diverse, dynamic wine list includes selections from around the world. There's a small lot for free parking, and reservations are recommended. $$$.

Hansel & Griddle. 53 Mine St.; (732) 846-7090; www.hanselngriddle.com. Brunch and lunch are the meals of choice at this sandwichery, which is inexpensive enough to appeal to the college crowd, and fast enough to appeal to the workaday break crowd. Some of the most oft-ordered menu items include the Home Fry, egg 'n' cheese roll-up, the spicy oven-toasted Italian panini, and the char-grilled barbecue bacon chicken sandwich on a semolina roll. Outdoor seating spills out from the side alley to the sidewalk. $.

PJ's Grill and Pizza. 166 Easton Ave.; (732) 249-1800; www.pjsgrill.com. No visit to New Brunswick is complete without sampling the local "grease truck" cuisine—the cheap slices and sandwiches on which the student population subsists. At the top of the food chain is PJ's, whose pizza wins high accolades, and whose menu of fat sandwiches (a local delicacy that stuffs as many deep-fried items into a roll as possible) is extensive. Still, a hangover is not required to enjoy a Fat Moon (chicken fingers, bacon, egg, fries, lettuce, tomato, mayo, and ketchup). $.

where to stay

Heldrich Hotel. 10 Livingston Ave.; (866) 609-4700; www.theheldrich.com. Close to the performing arts centers and preferred dining establishments in downtown New Brunswick, this high-rise hotel is a favorite for theatergoers. In total, the Heldrich offers 235 guest rooms with 13 suites decorated with an urban boutique flair. While the provided amenities are not in the luxury realm, the decor is modern and minimal, and rooms are clean and quiet, most offering skyline views. Rooms feature wireless Internet access, and a restaurant and bar, fitness center with pool, and a full-service spa are on site. Valet parking is also available. $$–$$$.

east

day trip 01

east

gazebos & boardwalks:
spring lake, nj;
point pleasant beach, nj

Travel to the central Jersey shoreline directly east of Philadelphia and you'll discover two distinct kinds of resort towns. Both Spring Lake and Point Pleasant came of age in the late 1800s, but while Spring Lake has preserved that history and Victorian ambience, appealing to an older crowd, Point Pleasant Beach is known for its lively boardwalk and kid-friendly vibe. This day trip starts at Spring Lake and travels south to Point Pleasant Beach.

spring lake, nj

This sleepy borough, also known as the "Jewel of the Jersey Shore," first attracted barons of industry during the Gilded Age of the 1800s. Their grand Victorian homes still line its streets, though many of them are now inns. While Spring Lake never quite reached the status of Newport, Rhode Island, it remains a popular destination for summertime visitors, and the large local Irish-American population has landed it a prominent spot on the so-called Irish Riviera of New Jersey. (These days it's best known as a year-round residential community.) The freshwater spring-fed lake for which the town is named is stocked with trout for fishing and surrounded by weeping willows, shady nocks, and rock gardens. Unlike many Jersey towns' boardwalks, Spring Lake's is a quiet, unassuming stretch of promenade, with no carnival rides or amusements—simply an appealing view of the two miles of sandy ocean beaches and grassy windswept dunes.

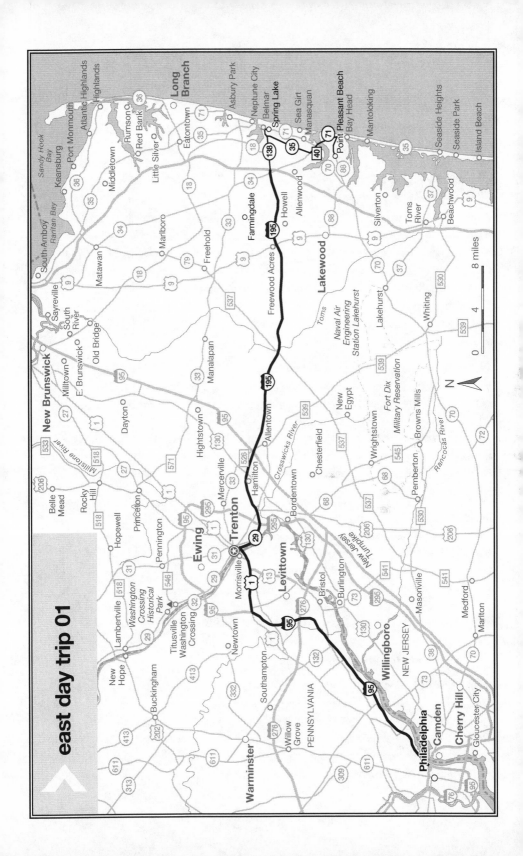

east day trip 01

getting there

From Philadelphia, head north on I-95 for about 24 miles, and continue east on I-195, then NJ 138 for 3 miles. From there pick up NJ 35 South to CR 40 and turn right onto NJ 71 South. Total travel time is about 1 hour and 23 minutes.

where to go

Beach and Boardwalk. Spring Lake's beach is among the purest in New Jersey and the town has managed to maintain its integrity over the years. Walk along the longest uninterrupted noncommercial boardwalk in New Jersey and enjoy its serene views of the Atlantic Ocean without the hectic badgering of food vendors, gift shops, or amusement parks. On either end of the planks are 2 large beach houses that shelter saltwater pools inside. Spring Lake Beach and the beach house pools are open to the general public with the purchase of daily admission badges during the summer months, and these are often provided gratis by inns.

Divine Park. Lake Ave. Emanating from underground streams, the freshwater Spring Lake is a center point of the eponymous town, attracting fishing enthusiasts with its regular stock of trout. On summer days ducks and Canada geese swim lazily over its crystalline surface. The surrounding Divine Park epitomizes Spring Lake's old-timey charms, with 2 romantic wooden footbridges that cross the lake and a large gazebo that houses live music and theater events at the northwest end. Weeping willows sway over shaded paths, and squirrels, chipmunks, and rabbits scamper across the walkways.

Historic Village of Allaire. 4263 Atlantic Ave., Farmingdale, NJ; (732) 449-0772; www .allairevillage.org. About 6 miles farther inland from Spring Lake is this living-history museum where visitors can experience life in an early 19th-century bog iron town. Nestled in Allaire State Park, the village was once called Williamsbridge Forge but was later renamed after New York brass founder James P. Allaire, who developed the area around his foundry. Among the restored buildings are trade shops where craftsmen in period dress practice their arts for visitors. At the manager's house, female workers demonstrate domestic skills, while the Howell Works Bakery produces fresh "flatcakes," and the general store showcases commerce of the 1800s. Tours are available and special events including craft markets are held throughout the year.

Spring Lake Historical Society. Warren and Fifth Avenues; (732) 974-1476; www.spring lake.org/historical. To best understand Spring Lake's illustrious past, this small museum is a good place to start. The 1897 Borough Hall building once housed the town's first public school. The top floor now contains its permanent collection, which spans Spring Lake's earliest days as an Indian settlement through to the Victorian era with photographs, artifacts, and other memorabilia, as well as scenes from famous movies that were filmed in town. The society also offers walking tours, house tours, and other special events. Free. Open Thurs from 10 a.m. to noon and Sun from 1:30 to 3:30 p.m.

where to shop

EurOrganics. 1219 Third Ave.; (732) 359-7880; www.eurorganicsbeauty.com. This little boutique with Scandinavian flair was started by two well-traveled women who found that most of their favorite beauty secrets were not available stateside. EurOrganics offers hundreds of natural and organic skincare, hair, and cosmetic lines from across Europe, hand selected for their therapeutic effects to offer visitors a "passport to beauty." Most of the 20 brands, which include Dermika, Ole Henriksen, Phyto, and Ainhoa, are free of chemicals like synthetic coloring, parabens, and mineral oils, and many are certified 100 percent organic. Both men's and women's products are available. Open daily

Irish Centre. 1120 Third Ave.; (732) 449-6650; www.irishcentre.net. Celebrating Spring Lake's rich Irish-American heritage, the Centre is a little bit of the Emerald Isle set on the Third Avenue drag. The largest importer of famed Belleek china, the store also carries a wide array of Waterford crystal, china, stemware, and flatware. Among the other products showcased here are gold and silver jewelry with ancient Irish and Celtic symbolism, Aran sweaters, tweed jackets, and capes for both men and women, as well as giftware with plenty of ideas for weddings, new babies, and other occasions. Open daily.

Juli Mei. 1303 Third Ave.; (732) 449-0021; www.julimei.com. Catering to the pampered crowd, Juli Mei is a chic boutique and facial spa embellished with crystal chandeliers, white orchids, and French furniture. Youthful fashion-forward apparel brands include designers like Flora Bella, Elan, Tart, and Krisa, while the jewelry collection proffers stunning pieces by Melissa Joy Manning and Alexis Bittar. The beauty treatments with Jurlique and Cosmedix products run the gamut from facials and corrective peels to brow styling and mineral-makeup application. Home accessories and gifts round out the offerings. Open daily.

where to eat

Bistro by the Beach. 7 Atlantic Ave.; (732) 449-8800; www.sandpiperinn.com. A relatively new player in the Spring Lake restaurant scene, Bistro by the Beach is an expansive restaurant opened by a New England Culinary Institute graduate on the ground floor of the Sandpiper Inn. Breakfast fare includes eggs and omelets as well as the chef's signature peanut butter and jelly French toast on brioche. Lunch and dinner tend toward more local, seasonally inspired eats, like a crab cake sandwich with pico de gallo and avocado, and pan-seared day-boat scallops over tricolor beet puree. Open daily. $$.

Breakers on the Ocean. 1507 Ocean Ave.; (732) 449-7700; www.breakershotel.com. Specializing in Northern Italian cookery, the restaurant at the Breakers hotel is an atmospheric spot for Spring Lake dining. Sit inside or on the wraparound porch for oceanfront views. White tablecloths set a stage for elegance but the food is homey, starting with baked artichoke hearts with mozzarella and prosciutto or tortellini *en brodo* and moving on to veal Milanese Breakers style with oreganato bread crumbs, to be topped off with classic tiramisu or a cannoli. A prix-fixe meal is available for early diners. Open daily for breakfast, lunch, and dinner. $$.

Hoffman's Ice Cream. 569 Church St.; (732) 974-2253; www.hoffmansicecream.net. A Jersey shore tradition since 1986, this sibling of a 3-store chain makes all of its flavors in-house. While the selection skews traditional, the rich buttery taste of pralines and cream or cake batter will convert skeptics—or perhaps the eager crowds (take a number before getting into line) and the gigantic portions will do the trick. Sherbets, sorbets, and frozen yogurts are some concessions to the health-conscious, as are take-home treats like bon-bons, ice cream pies, and Bobsicles (an ice cream sandwich on a stick that's dipped in chocolate and rice crunch) for the patient. Open daily. $.

Whispers Restaurant. 200 Monmouth Ave.; (732) 974-9755; www.whispersrestaurant .com. While hotel dining can be mediocre in many cities, the opposite is true of Spring Lake, and this creative, upscale BYO in the lakefront Hewitt-Wellington Hotel is a standout. Chef Scott Giordano's signature dishes draw from an array of culinary influences and include sautéed shrimp over a black bean cake with grilled pita bread and a honey red curry sauce, and broiled Chilean sea bass with baby bok choy over rock shrimp mashed potatoes. The relaxed atmosphere in the Victorian dining room is an inviting place to linger over a bottle of wine before an evening stroll through Divine Park. Open nightly. $$$.

where to stay

Breakers on the Ocean. 1507 Ocean Ave.; (732) 449-7700; www.breakershotel.com. The central draws of this classic waterfront hotel, first built in the late 1800s, are its terrifically unfettered ocean views and easy access to Spring Lake's beautiful beach. Guest rooms are slightly dated in their cabbage rose decor but they're large, clean, and comfortable. The luxury rooms are the most sizeable and include granite or marble gas fireplaces and whirlpool baths. Most rooms overlook the water, but be sure to ask when making a reservation. The hotel's wraparound porch, lined with wicker chairs, offers a pleasant spot for an afternoon cocktail. $–$$$.

Evergreen Inn. 206 NJ 71; (732) 449-9019; www.evergreeninn.net. The storied history of this Victorian B&B includes turns as the Villa Park General Store, a luncheonette, and a brothel. Its present-day incarnation as a friendly and somewhat quirky inn has netted owners multiple awards. The 9 guest suites have tree-related themes and are outfitted with colorful decor and designer linens, plus AC and cable TV. Several feature whirlpools and fireplaces. The innkeepers provide a gourmet breakfast and complimentary snacks as well as a cache of DVDs, beach towels, chairs, and bikes for guests to borrow as needed. $$$.

Sandpiper Inn. 7 Atlantic Ave.; (732) 449-6060; www.sandpiperinn.com. The onetime summer home to the Mexican ambassador to the US, the Sandpiper is an 1888 cottage that was purchased and renovated by its current owners in 2005. The 15 air-conditioned rooms feature private baths, refrigerators, corner views, and a country-eclectic decor. Note that all rooms are on the upper floors and there is no elevator. A heated indoor pool offers an alternative from the nearby beach. Cooked-to-order breakfast is served every morning and beach badges, towels, and chairs are available for guests. The Sandpiper is open only during the summer season. $$-$$$.

point pleasant beach, nj

Situated on the Barnegat Peninsula, a barrier island that divides the Barnegat Bay from the Atlantic Ocean, Point Pleasant Beach—often confused with the nearby town of Point Pleasant—was inhabited by Lenape Indians before Henry Hudson first spied the landmass on his way north to New York. The first European settlers here were fishermen, laying the foundation for Point Pleasant's reputation as the Jersey shore's destination for seafood. With the Victorian era came the development of a resort town, and most visitors today come for the bustling privately owned boardwalk—a favorite hangout for kids and teens—and the white, serene stretches of beach. Other notable attractions include antiques shopping and an aquarium.

getting there

From Spring Lake, take NJ 71 South for 3.6 miles, then continue on NJ 35 South for a little over a mile. Turn right onto Arnold Avenue and then take a slight right on Ocean Road to enter Point Pleasant Beach. Total travel time without traffic is 14 minutes.

where to go

Jenkinson's Aquarium. 300 Ocean Ave.; (732) 899-0600; www.jenkinsons.com. This small aquarium is owned by the same family that operates the boardwalk and is one of its most prominent attractions. The tanks exhibit Atlantic and Pacific sharks, coral reefs, alligators, penguins, and seals. Visitors can get a little bit closer to the sea creatures in the touch tank. The second floor houses a rainforest exhibit with pygmy marmosets, poison dart frogs, and macaws. Go early to avoid the crowds. Open year-round, daily until 5 p.m.

Jenkinson's Boardwalk. 300 Ocean Ave.; (732) 892-0600; www.jenkinsons.com. This 1.5-mile family-owned-and-maintained stretch of beachfront is the quick-beating heart of Point Pleasant Beach. At any rate, most visitors end up here at one time or another. The major bulk of the boardwalk's activity is in the center, a packed assortment of brightly colored snack shacks, pizza stands, arcades, minigolf courses, batting cages, and carnival games. The blinking lights of rides—Ferris wheel, swings, bumper cars, roller coasters, and

antiquing in point pleasant beach

One of Point Pleasant Beach's chief attractions is its antiques shopping, most of which is clustered around the commercial downtown area on Arnold Avenue, Bay Avenue, and NJ 35. The following are some of the highlights for collectors and bargain hunters:

- *Ambiance. 707 Arnold Ave., Point Pleasant Beach; (732) 295-9202. Shabby-chic decor, tin signs, vintage clothing, primitive and folk art.*

- *Antique Emporium. Bay and Trenton Avenues, Point Pleasant Beach; (732) 892-2222. Three floors of goods, including furniture, lighting, art, jewelry, dolls, and toys.*

- *Canvas House Antiques. 614 Trenton Ave., Point Pleasant Beach; (732) 701-0255; www.canvashouseantiques.blogspot.com. A 30-dealer mall showcasing quilts, furniture, shabby chic, pottery, jewelry, and collectibles.*

- *Fond Memories. 628 Bay Ave., Point Pleasant Beach; (732) 892-1917. Furniture, jewelry, dolls, and gifts.*

- *Point Pavilion Antique Center. 608 Arnold Ave., Point Pleasant Beach; (732) 899-6300; www.pointpavilionantiques.com. A former Woolworth building featuring 60 dealers selling textiles, furniture, silver, books, porcelain, architectural elements, art, and more.*

- *Thoughtful Treasures. 641 Arnold Ave., Point Pleasant Beach; (732) 899-1155; www.thoughtfultreasuresantiques.com. Tin signs, vintage clothes, quilts, primitives, toys, and collectibles.*

Fun House—beckon kids of all ages. For the twenty-something crowd, the Jenkinson's Entertainment Complex is a nightspot overlooking the water, featuring live music daily during the summer.

where to eat

Jack Baker's Lobster Shanty. Channel Dr.; (732) 899-6700; www.jackbakerslobster shanty.com. Point Pleasant Beach is known for its seafood, and this restaurant, situated among the commercial fishing boats, is a great place to sample it. The elegant dining room is appointed with stunning views of the river and inlet islands, and live piano music. The classic American cookery includes raw-bar selections, clams casino, and mussels marinara, followed by fried and broiled seafood platters laden with local flounder, day-boat scallops, and lobster. Friday nights bring a festive seafood buffet. Hours change seasonally. $$.

Voila. 816 Arnold Ave.; (732) 295-1005; www.voilaresto.com. A new addition to Point Pleasant Beach, Voila is a cozy BYO owned and operated by a French couple. Original artwork, soft music, and faithful renditions of French classics have transformed a downtown storefront into the area's most romantic destination. Atlantic bouillabaisse makes the most of local bounty, while the cassoulet and rack of lamb Dijonnaise are heartier entrees. Desserts are classic French confections like apple tarte tatin, profiteroles, and crème brûlée. Reservations suggested. Hours change seasonally. $$.

where to stay

Surfside Motel. 101 Broadway; (732) 899-1109; www.surfside-motel.com. In its peak season, Point Pleasant Beach can be a hectic place, and this family-owned motel offers a quiet respite. It's conveniently located 3 blocks from the beach, boardwalk, and the Manasquan Inlet, and offers free parking. Rooms, ranging from single queen beds to 2 bedrooms, are simple and not particularly stylish but they're very clean, and they're outfitted with refrigerators, air-conditioning, and cable TV. Guests have access to the heated swimming pool and beach badges. $-$$.

Tower Cottage. 203 Forman Ave.; (877) 766-2693; www.thetowercottage.com. First built in 1883, Tower Cottage was used as a private summer retreat, and it has recently been restored to its original grandeur replete with the tower that was once destroyed by a hurricane. There are 5 double-occupancy guest rooms, including 1 suite. Most overlook Little Silver Lake and all are decorated in period furniture with marble fireplaces, sweeping drapery, and crystal fixtures. The complimentary hot breakfast is served in the second-floor breakfast room. Guests can make use of the inn's beach badges and towels. $$$.

day trip 02

east

ghost towns & cranberry bogs:
the pine barrens, nj

the pine barrens, nj

The Pine Barrens (also known as the Pinelands) encompasses the forested stretch of southern New Jersey's coastal plain and was so named by European settlers for its acidic, difficult soil. During the colonial era, industries such as bog iron mining activated the area but as these activities dropped off in the mid-19th century, they left behind ghost towns and the persistent legend of the Jersey Devil—a mysterious flying creature—in their wake. The entire 1.1 million acres was named the country's first National Reserve in 1978. Even today much of this region between Philadelphia and the Jersey shore remains unpopulated but the Pine Barrens is a fascinating and often-overlooked region to visit. Ideally this day trip should begin at Hammonton and Historic Batsto Village and move north to Chatsworth.

getting there

From Philadelphia, head east on I-76 and continue east onto the Atlantic City Expressway for 16 miles. Take exit 28 toward Hammonton. Travel time is about 42 minutes.

where to go

Buzby's Chatsworth General Store. 3959 NJ 563, Chatsworth, NJ; (609) 894-4415. The country store is alive and well in Chatsworth, the unofficial capital of the Pinelands. This 1865 landmark was owned by the Buzby family until 1967—it changed hands several

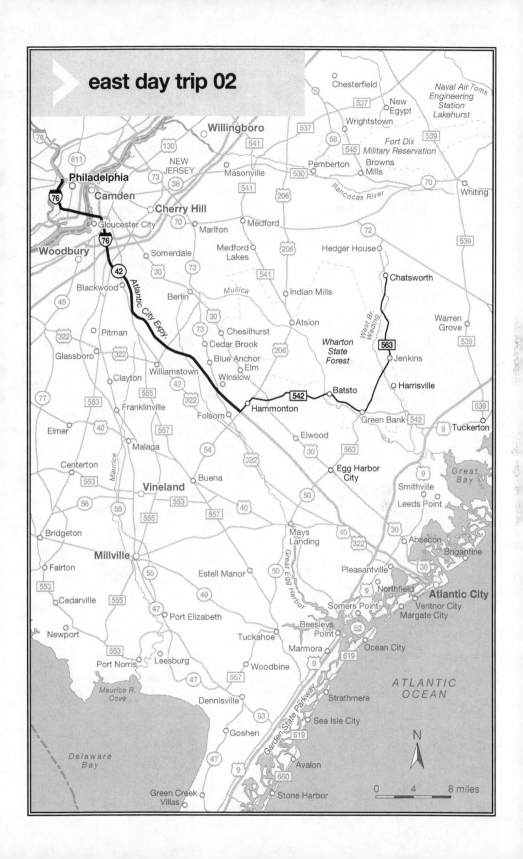

times until its current owners gave it an overhaul. Occupying the front is the Cheshire Cat Gift Shop, selling authentic "Piney" crafts by local artisans, books by authors who've written about the area (these include John McPhee and Henry Carlton Beck) and a small antiques area. In the back is the cafe that serves local specialties, like cranberry walnut pancakes and the Jersey Devil Monte Cristo. Call for hours.

Harrisville Village. CR 679 and Perimeter Rd., Harrisville, NJ; www.pinelandsalliance.org/ history/harrisvillepod. This ghost town exemplifies the importance of industry in American history and offers a cautionary tale about the dangers of the one-company town. Harrisville was abandoned in 1891 after its paper mill went out of business. The paper mill itself is still in ruins and is fenced off for safety but the remnants of a boardinghouse, workers' homes, the mill owner's mansion, store, and gristmill can be seen. The best way to tour this area is through a video podcast available on the Pinelands Alliance website.

Historic Batsto Village. 31 Batsto Rd., Hammonton, NJ; (609) 561-0024; www.batsto village.org. Deep within the Wharton State Forest is Batsto Village, a time capsule of colonial and 18th-century life in America. The village was first established in 1766, though some archaeological investigations have shown evidence of life in the region dating back several thousand years. The Batsto Iron Works, which mined bog ore from the nearby streams and rivers, manufactured supplies for the Continental army, and the village—mills, homes, a general store, post office, and craft shops—grew up around it. Start your exploration at the visitor center, which is open daily, and continue on through the museum, nature center, and other buildings. Self-guided tours can be conducted with a visitor center brochure, and there are regular guided tours of the Wharton Mansion. Open daily.

Tomasello Winery. 225 N. White Horse Pike, Hammonton, NJ; (800) 666-9463; www .tomasellowinery.com. This third-generation family vineyard and winery was established by a local fruit farmer in 1933, making it one of the region's oldest, well ahead of the current New Jersey winemaking boom. The grounds stretch across 70 acres with more than 30 varietals, including Native American, French, and classic wine grapes. In the tasting room visitors can sample some of the 30 still (Petit Verdot, Cabernet Sauvignon, Chardonnay, Pinot Grigio) and a number of sparkling wines. There are also some specialty wines made from local cranberries and blueberries. Open daily.

Wharton State Forest. 31 Batsto Rd., Hammonton, NJ; (609) 561-0024; www.nj.gov/ dep/parksandforests/parks/wharton.html. While Historic Batsto Village and Harrisville Vil- lage are major destinations for visitors to Wharton State Forest, the land's natural resources are an attraction all their own. The single largest park in the New Jersey state system encompasses hiking trails, rivers and streams for canoeing, unpaved roads for mountain biking and horseback riding, and a rich store of wildlife to observe. The Atsion Recreation Area, off US 206 in Shamong, offers a public beach, bathhouses, nature trails, and a picnic area as well as a view of the remains of another historic village.

where to eat

Casciano Coffee Bar and Sweetery. 212 Bellevue Ave., Hammonton, NJ; (609) 561-2600; www.cascianocoffee.com. This coffee bar on Hammonton's main drag was one of the first newer businesses to herald the town's revitalization, and it's a lively place for a quick, light meal. All the usual specialty coffee drinks, from mochas to lattes, are on the menu. Breakfast nibbles include yogurt parfaits and eggs frothed in the espresso machine, served on crusty bread or "no-carb" style in a cup. Grab-and-go sandwiches are available all day. "Junk in the trunk" cookies, monkey bread, and personal cheesecakes in flavors like cinnamon bun and s'more round out the sweet treats. Open daily. $.

Fiesta Mexicana. 327 12th St., Hammonton, NJ; (609) 704-1611; www.fiestamexicana-nj .com. It may look suspiciously like a Taco Bell from the outside but Fiesta Mexicana is an independent restaurant with Corona-hued walls and a clean, casual atmosphere. The authentic Mexican fare is there for the taking, in the form of Aztec tortilla soup, tamales, tacos, fried thin-pounded pork chops, and guacamole. There are also some Tex-Mex options, such as taco salad, fajitas, and (count 'em) four types of nachos. Beer and vegetarian options are available and the prices are affordable. Open daily for breakfast, lunch, and dinner. $–$$.

Illiano's. 705 12th St., Hammonton, NJ; (609) 561-3444; www.illianosrestaurant.com. Hearty Italian fare with a decidedly American twist is the kitchen's specialty here. Expect familiar dishes like fried calamari with marinara sauce, veal parmigiana subs, and pizza—nothing groundbreaking but all simple and satisfying. Pasta dinners of mix-and-match noodles and sauces are served family style and the veal, chicken, and seafood entrees, which include minestrone soup or salad and a side of pasta, are a good value. Open daily for lunch and dinner. There's a full bar with a small wine list. $$.

where to stay

Wharton State Forest campgrounds and cabins. www.nj.gov/dep/parksandforests/ parks/wharton.html. For those interested in exploring the Pinelands up close and personal, there are prodigious public campgrounds in Wharton State Forest. At Atsion there are 50 tent and trailer sites with fire rings, picnic tables, potable water, and flush toilets, open Apr through Dec. There's an additional campground at Godfrey Bridge that's open all year and primitive campsites around the forest at Bodine Field, Hawkins Bridge, Batona, Mullica River, and Goshen Pond. Alcohol is prohibited. $.

Tuscany House Hotel at the Renault Winery Resort. 72 N. Bremen Ave., Egg Harbor City, NJ; (609) 965-2111; www.renaultwinery.com. About 15 miles southeast of Hammonton is the Tuscan House Hotel, an old world–style inn across the street from the Renault Winery. From the outside the building, with its red tiled roof and white arches, approximates an Italian villa. While the 45 guest rooms don't look especially Mediterranean on the inside, the hotel's courtyard, verandas, golf course, and 2 outdoor pools contribute to the resort feel. Two restaurants on the premises, Joseph's and Renault's Gourmet, offer casual and upscale dining experiences, respectively. Tours and tastings at the winery can also be arranged. $$.

worth more time
tuckerton, nj

In the 18th century Tuckerton was known as the nation's "Third Point of Entry." Today this quaint little coastal town on the southern tip of Ocean County is often overlooked by the Jersey shore's summer vacationers, but it makes for an interesting detour. The Tuckerton Seaport, a working maritime village, is an engaging look at maritime life in New Jersey's history through exhibits, hands-on activities, and craftsmen demonstrating boatbuilding and other skills. Stop off for lunch at the Stewart's Root Beer drive-in for a 1950s-style lunch of burgers, onion rings, and fountain treats, served by carhops.

day trip 03

east

new jersey revival:
red bank, nj

red bank, nj

An hour south of Manhattan and an hour and a half northeast of Philadelphia, Red Bank is a hip (and growing hipper) town on the Navesink River, a few miles from the Atlantic coast. Red Bank's Victorian housing and river-town flavor belies its very modern and vibrant heart, and its growing population of fleeing urbanites. Once a major commercial center and port with steamboats carrying travelers up the river to Manhattan, Red Bank fell on harder times in the 1980s. The recently revitalized business districts along Broad Street and Monmouth Street are peppered with trendy restaurants and boutiques, and the arts, from film festivals to live performance, are fiercely supported here.

getting there

From Philadelphia, travel north on I-95 for 23 miles, then travel east on I-195 and NJ 138, and north again on the Garden State Parkway. Exit at CR 520 toward Red Bank. Travel time is an hour and a half.

where to go

Red Bank Visitors Center. 46 English Plaza; (888) HIP-TOWN; www.visit.redbank.com. Start your visit here at this organized and well-staffed visitor center and pick up transportation schedules, guides, and brochures for area activities and special events. The latest

jazz in new jersey

New Jersey was an important center for jazz's development in the early 20th century. Red Bank gave birth to bandleader Count Basie, and Englewood was home to Dizzy Gillespie. Nearby Newark was especially important, serving as the stomping ground for Sarah Vaughan, Willie "The Lion" Smith, Thomas "Fats" Waller, and Donald "The Lamb" Lambert, and a stop-off for many jazz musicians on their way to New York and global stardom. Later in the 20th century, Atlantic City and Camden, home of the Victor Talking Machine recording studio, developed equally jumpin' jazz scenes and would eventually rival Newark, attracting top performers and writing their own pages in New Jersey's musical history.

listings for seasonal discounts at area businesses are offered at the center and on its website. Additional information about Red Bank is available at the Red Bank Train Station at Bridge and Monmouth Streets. Open Mon through Fri.

Count Basie Theatre. 99 Monmouth St.; (732) 842-9000; www.countbasietheatre.org. Named for Red Hook's most famous resident, this vaudeville-era theater situated in the center of downtown Red Bank was first built in 1926 and renamed in 1984 after briefly going dark for a time in the 1970s. As Count Basie's childhood home on Mechanic Street is no longer standing, this serves as the town's best monument to the jazz great. Over the years the building has undergone continuous renovations but it hosts an impressive lineup of jazz, classical, vocal, comedy, children's, theatrical, and musical performances year-round.

Sandy Hook Lighthouse. Gateway National Recreation Area; Sandy Hook, NJ; (732) 872-5970. A 20-minute drive northeast of Red Bank, this lighthouse dates to 1764, making it the oldest operating beacon in the US. It was the first landmark visible to sailors approaching the New York Harbor and was later occupied by British soldiers during the Revolutionary War, serving as a sanctuary for royal sympathizers. Because of a lack of erosion, the tower, which was once 500 feet from the water, is now a mile and a half removed. Climb to the top for a stunning view of Manhattan. Nearby are the Gateway National Recreation Area's visitor center, Fort Hancock, and the Sandy Hook Bird Observatory. Tours are available but limited. Open noon to 4:30 p.m. on weekends during the warmer months.

where to shop

CoCo Parì. 17 Broad St.; (732) 212-8111; www.cocopari.com. This 3-level Art Deco–style showroom gives some department stores a run for their money, with a wide swath of women's clothing, from swimsuits to evening gowns. Labels run from the (relatively) affordable

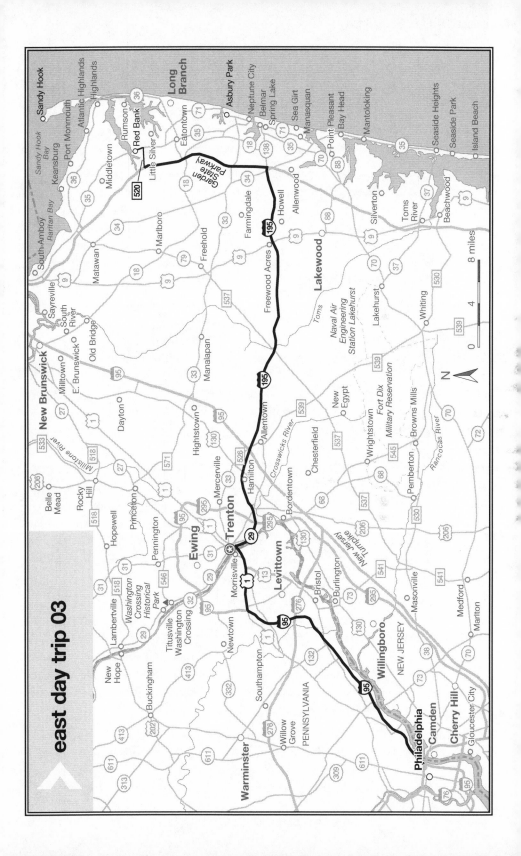

Juicy Couture to the more exclusive Catherine Malandrino and Robert Rodriguez. The swank footwear and handbag collection includes such notables as Jimmy Choo, Christian Louboutin, and Yves Saint Laurent. The store aims for a South Beach Miami feel, with club music, a personal shopper's attention to detail, and late-night hours. Open daily.

Jack's Music Shoppe. 30 Broad St.; (732) 842-0731; www.jacksmusicshoppe.com. A frequently filmed star of Kevin Smith movies, Jack's Music Shoppe is a local institution going strong after more than 4 decades. New and used CDs, DVDs, and vinyl line the aisles at the 6,000-square-foot-plus store. Listening stations give visitors an earful of new releases and staff picks. Going beyond the recorded note, Jack's also sells a large selection of sheet music, turntable equipment, and new and used musical instruments. Both touring and local bands have been known to stop here for in-store appearances. Open daily.

Jay and Silent Bob's Secret Stash. 35 Broad St.; (732) 758-0508; www.viewaskew merch.com. As Red Bank's other famous son, filmmaker Kevin Smith has remained a steadfastly loyal citizen, shooting and setting many of his movies here and opening this store in 1997. Billed as a "geek-free comic book outlet," Jay and Silent Bob's is named for the popular characters of Smith's movies. Besides the comic books, of which there are plenty of new releases and back issues, there's comic-related merchandise and Smith-centric memorabilia, much of which is signed. The store itself has been featured in the films *Chasing Amy* and *Jay and Silent Bob Strike Back.*

where to eat

No Joe's Cafe. 51 Broad St.; (732) 530-4040; www.nojoescafe.com. A full-service restaurant serving up soups, creative sandwiches, salads, and quesadillas, No Joe's is open all day long for casual eats. Contrary to the name, there *is* plenty of joe behind the wooden bar at this neighborhood staple. Choices include a slate of drip brews from local roaster Booskerdoo and Italian espresso drinks, plus chai, tea, and hot chocolate. Homemade sweets might include almond tea cookies and Frosted Flakes marshmallow squares. $.

Red. 3 Broad St.; (732) 741-3232; www.rednj.com. Plush banquettes and a casual yet sophisticated atmosphere characterize this urban bistro in the Broad Street business district. The menu is a globally inspired mix of flavors that bounces seamlessly from Asian tuna tartare with yuzu vinaigrette to Mediterranean citrus-herb chicken roulade with pesto bulgur and confit grape tomatoes. A sushi bar turns out creative rolls like the Pearl Street (lobster salad, tempura shrimp, mango, and spicy mayo), while the bartenders shake up seasonal cocktails that keep the lounge area bumping. Open daily. $$–$$$.

Restaurant Nicholas. 160 NJ 35 South; (732) 345-9977; www.restaurantnicholas.com. Red Bank's preeminent fine dining restaurant frequently tops national best-of lists. All dinners are served from a multicourse tasting menu that keeps patrons guessing with creations like seared foie gras over swiss cheese pain perdu with concord grape puree; filet mignon with carrot mille-feuille, roasted shallots, and new potatoes; and dark chocolate mousse with red wine cake, roasted figs, and crème fraîche ice cream. Seating at the chef's table is available on request for an even more exclusive experience. To accommodate budget-constrained diners, Chef Nicholas Harary has expanded to open Bar N, a more casual eatery, in the same building. $$$.

where to stay

Molly Pitcher Inn. 88 Riverside Ave.; (800) 221-1372; www.themollypitcher.com. This historic hotel, named for the nurse who became an American Revolutionary heroine, was built in 1928, and the handsome brick facade speaks to its grand past. Inside, the old-world decor is polished to a modern gloss. The rooms and suites have contemporary comforts like wireless Internet, cable TV, hair dryers, and wake-up service. There's a pool and fitness room on the premises and a marina for docking boats. The restaurant, bar, and many rooms overlook the Navesink River. Be sure to ask for a water view. $–$$$.

Oyster Point Hotel. 146 Bodman Place; (800) 345-8484; www.theoysterpointhotel.com. Befitting the stylish sensibility of Red Bank, this boutique luxury hotel and younger sibling to the Molly Pitcher Inn is outfitted in minimalist-chic decor. The suites and rooms include iPod docks, wireless Internet, cable TV, and valet and laundry service. Oyster Point maintains a fitness center and a marina for guests arriving by boat. Turndown service comes with chocolate chip cookies, and there are complimentary coffee and muffins in the morning. Some rooms have river views, and the hotel's restaurant, Pearl, offers waterfront dining. $$–$$$.

worth more time
asbury park, nj

This beach town 10 miles south of Red Bank has had a wildly diverse past: Over the course of a few decades, the onetime Christian retreat morphed into a family resort, then a counterculture hangout, then a failed yuppie destination, and most recently a gay mecca. The revitalized downtown shopping district buzzes with boutiques, art galleries, restaurants and the intriguing Paranormal Museum. Stroll the boardwalk for the farmers' market, rides, and games. Or stop into the Silverball Museum, home of the Pinball Hall of Fame, and end the evening at the Stone Pony Club, home of Southside Johnny and the Asbury Jukes.

southeast

day trip 01

southeast

a gambling town:
atlantic city, nj

atlantic city, nj

One of the original Victorian-era vacation resorts, Atlantic City wears the imprints of American history—from its signature boardwalk, built in 1870 and one of the first of its kind, to its boom in the Prohibition era, symbolized by the game *Monopoly* and the HBO show *Boardwalk Empire,* to its postwar mall surge. Though Atlantic City is known as the "Gambling Capital of the East Coast," it wasn't until 1976 that casinos were legalized and the state government staked its economy on them. Since then the city has endured fits and starts of development—most recently by the luxury Borgata casino and hotel, the renovated Caesars, and an outdoor outlet mall. A new casino from the Hard Rock Hotel is expected soon. As a fantasy vacation spot and a symbol of decadence, AC's charms are both seedy and glossy, and it can be hard to turn away.

getting there

To get to Atlantic City from Philadelphia, take I-76 east to NJ 42 and then it's a straight shot southeast on the Atlantic City Expressway, for about 45 miles. Total travel time is about 1 hour and 5 minutes.

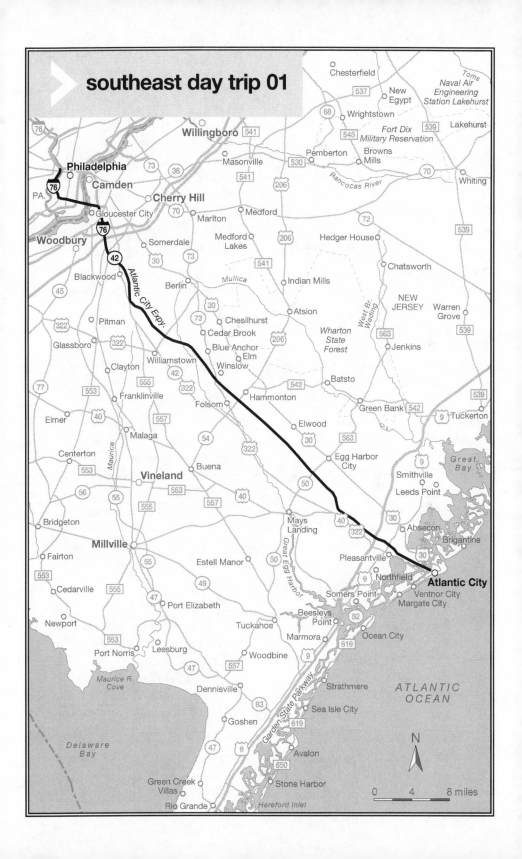

where to go

Atlantic City Aquarium. 800 N. New Hampshire Ave.; (609) 348-2880; www.acaquarium .com. The more than 19 tanks of sea creatures at this aquarium at the historic Gardner's Basin include the 25,000-gallon "Fish of the Mid-Atlantic" display with live diver feeding shows, stingrays, seahorses, nudibranchs, and sharks and rays. Visitors can learn more about live coral, observe the beautifully colored moray eels, or get up close and personal with crabs, snakes, spiders, turtles, and animals from the tropical rain forest. The aquarium is accessible by car or by boat; there's a courtesy dock at the neighboring marina for 4-hour visits. Open daily from 10 a.m. to 5 p.m.

Atlantic City Historical Museum. Garden Pier, S. New Jersey Ave. and the Boardwalk; (609) 347-5839; www.acmuseum.org. The primary attraction here is the permanent exhibit, "Atlantic City: Playground of the Nation," which showcases the borough's past, both innocent and decadent. Visitors are greeted by Mr. Peanut, the monocle-wearing legume, who leads the way to the miniature boardwalk and beach area with original sand art. Posters, costumes, photographs, Miss America memorabilia, and a documentary video tell the story of AC from the earliest Thomas Edison beach shots, to its historical amusement piers, to the legend of the infamous high-diving horse. Open daily from 10 a.m. to 4 p.m.

Boardwalk. Along the beach; www.atlanticcitynj.com. The first use of the postcard in America is credited to the Atlantic City boardwalk, and this stretch of wooden walkway has become an iconic symbol for summer leisure. While its planks have been degraded and rebuilt many times over in the years since it was first established, the boardwalk remains the cultural heart of the city. Vehicles have always been prohibited, so the best way to see it is on foot, by bicycle, or by "rolling chair," a manually pushed cart that allows the rider to take in the scenery at a leisurely pace. There are plenty of family amusements and plenty of kitsch, though the newer luxury Pier Shops at the Caesars offer a dramatically different alternative to the video arcades and humble souvenir vendors. At night the casinos and their high-end restaurants set the boardwalk aglow.

Casinos. Atlantic City; www.atlanticcitynj.com. The biggest draw to Atlantic City is its casinos, and many visitors, for better or worse, see the town only by the light of poker machines. There are currently 12 major casinos, with 1 more slated to open soon. Nine of the 12 are along the boardwalk. The remaining 3, Harrah's, the Borgata, and Trump Marina, are in the marina district, north of the boardwalk and bordering the Absecon Inlet. While each has its own distinct flavor, all of the casinos offer slots, poker, blackjack, roulette, craps, baccarat, keno, race books, and specialty game tables. With restaurants, shops, spas, and live entertainment on site, it's possible to spend an entire day in a single resort hotel. Open daily.

Ripley's Believe It or Not Museum. 1441 Boardwalk; (609) 347-2001; www.ripleys .com/atlanticcity. In keeping with Atlantic City's carnival atmosphere, this local outpost of an international chain of museums celebrates the amazing, the unusual, the odd, and the unbelievable. The Odditorium exhibits include a human shrunken head, the world's smallest production car, a life mask of Abraham Lincoln from 1860, a sculpture of Jimi Hendrix made from chicken wire, and many interactive exhibits and optical illusions. There's also a Laser Maze to navigate and special sideshow-esque events. Open 365 days a year.

where to shop

Pier Shops at Caesars. 1 Atlantic Ocean; (609) 345-3100; www.thepiershopsatcaesars .com. The high rollers need somewhere to spend their winnings, and the Pier Shops mall obliges with luxury goods from Salvatore Ferragamo, Gucci, Louis Vuitton, Burberry, Michael Kors, and Hugo Boss. For personal and beauty needs, there's M.A.C., Lush, and L'Occitane. And since not everyone wins at the casino, the first-floor "Boardwalk" is lined with more affordable shops, like Victoria's Secret, Levi's, and BCBG. The mall also houses 2 stylish eateries from Philadelphia restaurateur Stephen Starr: Buddakan and the Continental. A third-floor promenade is lined with Adirondack chairs set on a sandy "beach" overlooking the Atlantic. Open daily; hours change seasonally.

Quarter at Tropicana. 2831 Boardwalk; (800) 843-8767; www.tropicana.net. A 3-story streetscape designed to look like Old Havana—a tribute to the original Tropicana Casino and Resort in Cuba—the Quarter shelters over 30 shops. It's an eclectic mix, with Brooks Brothers, Caché, Chico's, Brookstone, and Swarovski standing side by side with the high-end makeup boutique and spa Blue Mercury, the gourmet food market Zeytinia, and the Old Farmer's Almanac General Store. The Quarter also has plenty of dining options, like Carmine's, P.F. Chang's, The Palm steak house, and the Russian-themed Red Square. The restaurant Cuba Libre appropriately serves mojitos, empanadas, and other Cuban specialties.

Tanger Outlets. 1931 Atlantic Ave.; (609) 872-7002; www.tangeroutlet.com/atlanticcity. With no sales tax on apparel in New Jersey, the shopping is always good. Just a few steps off the Boardwalk is this factory store mall set on The Walk. Designed like an open-air village, the 100 stores run along several blocks and include Nike, Calvin Klein, St. John, Kenneth Cole, J. Crew, and many others. Visit the website or the visitor center for specials, sales, and discounts. There's valet parking, self-park lots on Ohio/Baltic Avenue and Atlantic Avenue, and limited street parking. Open daily.

where to eat

Bobby Flay Steak. 1 Borgata Way; (609) 317-1000; www.bobbyflaysteak.com. Nestled in the Borgata Hotel, celebrity chef Bobby Flay's steak house opens into a red leather–lined entryway and a dramatic wood-paneled dining room with towering wine displays and lobster tanks. The steak-house fare is classic but updated: shrimp cocktail with smoked chile horseradish sauce; a Philadelphia strip steak with provolone cheese sauce and caramelized

atlantic city on the screen

Atlantic City's colorful indulgence has made it a popular setting for films and TV shows, starting as early as the beginning of the 20th century, when Thomas Edison Films captured parades and sunbathers in wool jersey suits on its beaches. The 1972 film The King of Marvin Gardens *evokes a pre-casino AC, while Louis Malle's* Atlantic City *was nominated for multiple Academy Awards in 1980. Most recently the HBO series* Boardwalk Empire, *set in the Prohibition era, has renewed interest in the tourist destination, though the show actually is filmed on a Brooklyn soundstage.*

onions; smashed baked potatoes with crème fraîche, goat cheese, and green onions. Traditional cocktails supplement an extensive wine list. Dinner only. Closed Mon. $$$.

Buddakan. 1 Atlantic Ocean; (609) 674-0100; www.buddakanac.com. A sibling to Stephen Starr's Buddakan restaurants in Philadelphia and New York, this pan-Asian eatery is overseen by a gilded Buddha. The modern cuisine is best appreciated family style: small plates of tuna spring rolls with chile mayonnaise and edamame ravioli in Sauternes-shallot broth; larger plates of lobster fried rice with Thai basil and wasabi-crusted filet mignon. The signature cocktails (Luck = Bombay gin, lime, ginger, and elderflower liqueur) are not to be missed. Open daily for lunch and dinner. $$$.

Teplitzky's Coffee Shop. 111 S. Chelsea Ave.; (609) 428-4550; www.thechelsea-ac .com/restaurants.php. In a nod to the original proprietors of this restored historic hotel, Teplitzky's Coffee Shop is a contemporary diner with a speakeasy bar. The original terrazzo floors, redwood walls, and cantilevered stools create an old-school ambience and the hearty, eclectic fare is served all day: eggs, waffles, and pancakes for breakfast; fried mac and cheese, matzo ball soup, and roasted chicken for lunch and dinner. Banana splits, monkey bread, and specialty cocktails finish things off. $$.

White House Sub Shop. 2301 Arctic Ave.; (609) 345-1564. They call them subs here but most Philadelphia vacationers will call them the best hoagies this side of the William Penn statue. The atmosphere is strictly no frills, and the service can be curt, but the sandwiches— monstrously huge fresh-baked rolls filled with Italian cold cuts, meatballs, or cheesesteak— are outstanding. There are only a few booths for seating. Prepare to wait in line and grab a number for take-out orders. Cash only. Open daily. $.

where to stay

The Chelsea. 111 S. Chelsea Ave.; (800) 548-3030; www.thechelsea-ac.com. Not every visitor to Atlantic City wants to stay within a quarter's throw of a casino, and the Chelsea, a resurrected hotel from the town's heyday, was the first non-gaming hotel to open here in decades. The midcentury modern property encompasses 2 signature restaurants, a spa, a fitness center, 2 pools, and a private beach. The Luxe Tower features 218 guest rooms and 5 suites, and the Annex houses 133 more, all with iPod docking stations, concierge services, and other amenities. Valet parking, bicycles, and in-room spa treatments are also available. $–$$$.

day trip 02

southeast

family getaway:
ocean city, nj

ocean city, nj

The population of Cape May County's largest city multiplies eightfold in the summertime, and no wonder—it's the best time to visit. Situated on the narrow finger of land surrounded by the Great Egg Harbor Bay and the Atlantic Ocean, Ocean City is at the halfway point between Atlantic City and Cape May, and it seems to embody the best of both worlds—or at least a happy-medium mixture of commercial attractions and wholesome pleasures. Like Atlantic City, Ocean City has a lively boardwalk with amusements and cheap souvenirs, but like Cape May, Victorian nostalgia lives on through a number of preserved buildings in the Historic District. And since its founding in 1879 by four Methodist ministers, OC has been a "dry" town, the sale of alcoholic beverages prohibited within its limits. Thankfully the blue laws that also nixed bathing, shopping, and recreation on Sunday were repealed in 1987.

getting there

Take I-76 East from Philadelphia and continue onto NJ 42 South, then the Atlantic City Expressway for 36 miles. From there take the Garden State Parkway to exit 25 for Ocean City. Take US 9 North to 34th Street and travel northeast into the city. Travel time without traffic is 1 hour and 20 minutes.

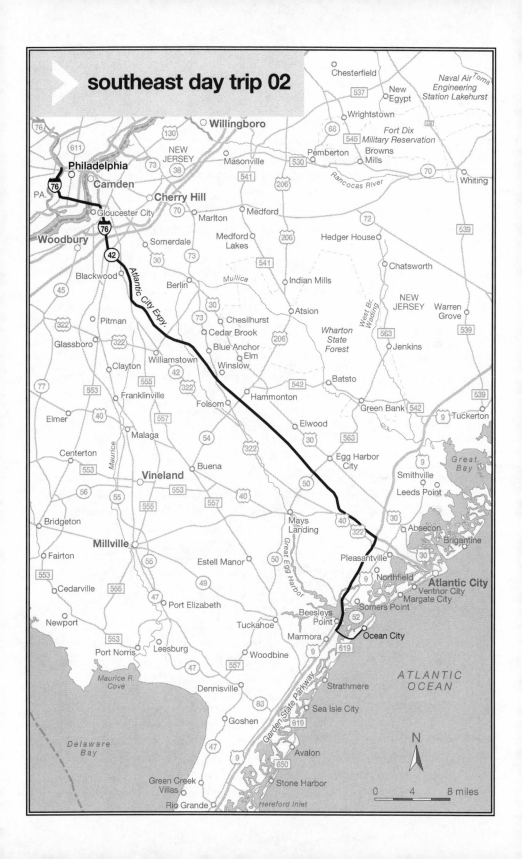

southeast day trip 02

where to go

Beach. Ocean City's eight miles of white-sand seafront is appealingly clean. During the summer season there are guards at several beaches and first-aid stations at 1st, 12th, 34th and 59th streets. Daily beach tags, required during the official summer season, can be purchased at City Hall, the 46th Street Post Office, the Welcome Center and the Information Center at the Music Pier. Surf chairs are available for handicapped visitors at the Ocean City Sports and Civic Center on the Boardwalk. There are restrooms at the Boardwalk at 1st, 6th, 8th, 12th and 34th streets; and showers and changing rooms available for a fee at 13th Street and Ocean Avenue.

Ghost Tour of Ocean City. 9th St. and Asbury Ave.; (609) 814-0199; www.ghosttour .com/oceancity. Every town has its spooky side, and this 90-minute candlelight walking tour showcases downtown Ocean City's paranormal past. The 8 sites include the town center, the boardwalk, the Flanders Hotel, a cemetery, and a haunted house. Tour guides share famous spirit-centric lore, like the story of the Jersey Devil and the shipwreck of the *Sindia,* a commercial sailing ship that sank 150 yards from the beach in 1901 — its pirate ghosts are thought to be guarding buried treasure from Asia. Tours run Apr through Nov; hours change seasonally.

Gillian's Wonderland Pier. 6th St. and Boardwalk; (609) 399-7082; www.gillians.com. The origins of this historic boardwalk amusement park stretch back to 1929, when it was first established with a Ferris wheel and merry-go-round. At its current location, Wonderland now has a 141-foot Ferris wheel and a host of indoor and outdoor rides, including bumper boats, roller coasters, a Tilt-A-Whirl, and much more. A minigolf course and water park are located on Gillian's Island, adjacent to the Wonderland complex. Pay as you go with tickets; books of tickets can be purchased ahead. Open seasonally.

Ocean City Historical Museum. 1735 Simpson Ave.; (609) 399-1801; www.ocnjmuseum .org. The 2 permanent exhibits here include "Sea View and Salt Air: A History of Ocean City," a time line integrating artifacts and photos from the museum's collection, and a glimpse into the story of the *Sindia,* the 4-masted barque that ran aground in 1901. The museum also mounts temporary exhibits, houses a gift shop and modern research library, and offers maps for a self-guided walking tour through the Historic District, stopping at Victorian landmarks and some of the original Tabernacle cottages of the religious vacationers. Open Tues through Sat. Free.

Ocean City Boardwalk. The 2.5 miles of boards in Ocean City are among the most wholesome of the Jersey resort towns, thanks to the lack of casinos and bars. The ocean breeze blows pleasantly over the car-free walkway, which is lined with a colorful array of souvenir shops, popcorn stands, saltwater taffy stores, and more. Family amusements — rides, go-karts, minigolf, arcades, and movie theaters — stretch from 6th Street to 14th Street. The Music Pier is a historic auditorium hosting a calendar's worth of events year-round, from pops to live theater. Every Thursday in July and August is Family Night with free entertainment. Bike traffic during summer hours is limited between 5 a.m. and noon.

where to shop

The Flying Carp. 939 Asbury Ave.; (609) 464-2608; www.theflyingcarp.com. Going beyond the usual summer-town trinketry, the Flying Carp is an eclectic gallery selling crafts to wear, to give, and to display, all made by American and Japanese artists celebrating a minimalist aesthetic. Among the goods are jewelry by noted designers Dana Kellin, Jane Diaz, and Catherine Weitzman; GurglePot ceramics; Bambu kitchen tools; Primal Elements soaps; Accents de Ville lamps; and stationery and candles. A second location at 745 Asbury Ave. sells clothing and accessories.

Gabrielle & Co. 810 Asbury Ave.; (609) 399-1008; www.gabrielleandco.com. Emphasizing the importance of proper underpinnings, the expert corsetieres at this lingerie and apparel boutique offer free professional bra fittings. Women shoppers are rewarded with luxury bath products, many of which are certified organic; cutting-edge women's apparel from casual to formal; and designer undergarments including bridal wear (Fantasie, Le Mystere, Felina). There's also gourmet food and home decor and accessories, such as aroma pearls and reed diffusers. Free facials are available by appointment.

Sun Rose Words and Music. 756 Asbury Ave.; (609) 399-9190; www.facebook.com/sunrosebooks. An independent selling books and music is a rarity in any town, let alone a beach town, but this store on the Asbury strip in the Historic District has survived on the quality of its carefully chosen stock and the personal service of its staff. In addition to books and CDs, Sun Rose carries office supplies, children's toys and arts and crafts kits, greeting cards, and stationery. The store also hosts author events. Hours change seasonally.

where to eat

Fractured Prune. 1225 Asbury Ave.; (609) 399-0482; www.fracturedpruneoc.com. A mid-Atlantic chain giving Dunkin' a run for its money, Fractured Prune specializes in "hand-dipped" doughnuts. Plain rounds are submerged in all manner of glazes and add-ons for specialty flavors like Dirty Banana (banana glaze and crushed Oreo), Pebble Beach (honey glaze, cinnamon sugar, and chocolate chips), and Coffee Crumb Cake (mocha glaze, graham cracker, and powdered sugar). Customers can venture into DIY doughnut design with mix-and-match toppings. The breakfast joint also serves egg sandwiches (in wraps, bagels, and, yes, doughnuts) and coffee. $.

Opa Gyros and Crepes. 944 Boardwalk; (609) 398-6188. Amid the curly fries, kettle corn, and funnel cakes of the boardwalk, this inexpensive, cross-cultural eatery offers some healthier nonfried options. The Greek fare includes traditional staples, like chicken souvlaki and hummus platters, spanakopita, villager salad, and well-stuffed gyro and falafel pita sandwiches. Dessert goes Franco-style with crepes filled with Nutella, bananas, jam, and many combinations thereof. There are picnic tables outside that can be covered in case of rain. $.

701 Mosaic. 701 4th St.; (609) 398-2700; www.701mosaic.com. Occupying an abandoned pizza parlor in Ocean City's North End, 701 Mosaic is an upscale bistro that creatively marries cuisine from the Caribbean and Mediterranean. (Breakfast, on the other hand, is a straightforwardly American affair.) Lunchtime brings cafe eats like jerk shrimp chicken wings, calamari Escovitch, and a surf-and-turf burger that's topped with grilled shrimp. The dinner menu features chicken Byzantine simmered with tomato, pepper, and leek over couscous with pine nuts, and crab cakes served over rice and peas. Seasonal hours. $–$$.

where to stay

Forum Motor Inn. 800 Atlantic Ave.; (609) 399-8700; www.theforuminoc.homestead .com. A block away from the beach and boardwalk, the Forum is Ocean City's best bet for inexpensive, unpretentious lodging. The rooms could use a facelift but they are clean and spacious and include turndown service, refrigerator, microwave, and cable TV. There are also 2 one-bedroom suites with kitchenettes. There's a washer-dryer room, game room, and pool on the premises, and the inn's 8th Street Cafe is open for breakfast and lunch. Beach tags are included. Open seasonally. $–$$.

Northwood Inn. 401 Wesley Ave.; (609) 399-6071; www.northwoodinn.com. One of the earliest homes built on the island, the Northwood Inn is a prominent landmark in Ocean City's Historic District. The 3-story building was renovated by the innkeepers to include air-conditioning, whirlpool suites, and a rooftop oasis with hammock and hot tub. Rooms are homily decorated in country style. Full breakfast is served on weekends, and a continental breakfast is offered on weekdays. Other amenities include free Wi-Fi, complimentary bikes, a DVD library, and beach tags. In-room spa services can be arranged. $$–$$$.

Plymouth Inn. 710 Atlantic Ave.; (609) 398-8615; www.plymouthinn.com. First established in 1898, this handsome inn 1 block off the beach has been restored with modern conveniences. The sunny, Victorian-decorated rooms are equipped with air-conditioning, cable TV, and wireless Internet. Beach tags, parking, and housekeeping service are included. Two-bedroom family suites are available and the inn allows children. A full breakfast buffet is served daily and can be eaten on the front porch or in the formal dining room. $–$$$.

south

day trip 01

south

victoriana by the sea:
cape may, nj

cape may, nj

Follow the Garden State Parkway to exit 0 for the city on the southern tip of the Cape May peninsula—and one of the nation's oldest summer vacation destinations. A family-friendly beach resort with a historic, wholesome flavor, Cape May is situated where the Delaware Bay meets the Atlantic Ocean. The town was first named for the Dutch captain Cornelius Jacobsen Mey, who charted the area in 1611, and it was later settled by New Englanders. The well-preserved Victorian homes dating back to the borough's incorporation are a magnificent sight to behold and there are guided tours and horse and carriage rides from which to view the colorful gingerbread "painted ladies" that line the streets and shoreline. The town, from top to bottom a National Historic Landmark, has steadily attracted birders, bicyclists, antiques seekers, and beach dwellers, but Cape May, inspired by the reinvigorated Congress Hall Hotel, has also evolved into a more sophisticated destination over the years, becoming a hub for chic lodging, dining, and shopping.

getting there

Take I-76 from Philadelphia onto the Atlantic City Expressway for nearly 37 miles, then follow the Garden State Parkway for an additional 26 miles to Cape May. Travel time is 1 hour and 40 minutes.

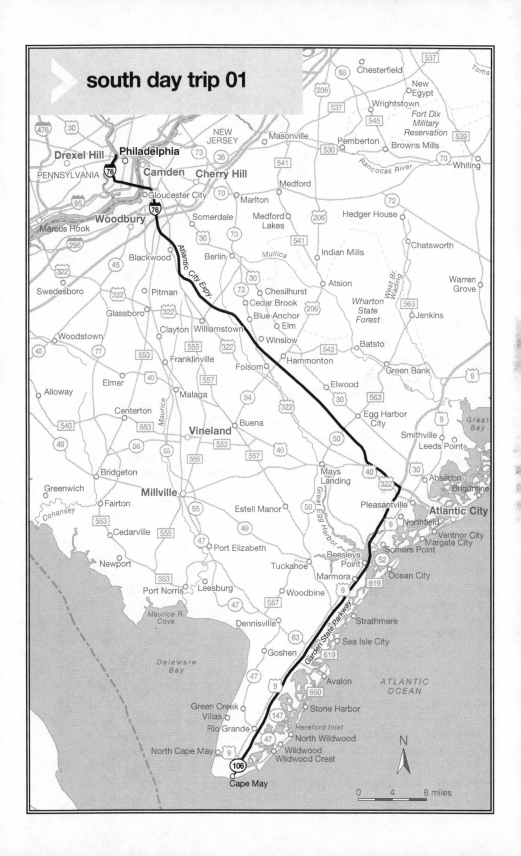

where to go

Cape May Welcome Center. 609 Lafayette St.; (609) 884-5508; www.capemay.com/visitors-center.html. Volunteers from the Mid-Atlantic Center for the Arts and the chamber of commerce man this tourist center and help visitors orient to the town. Maps and brochures are available and there's free 30-minute parking on site.

Beach. Multiple locations, Beach Ave. Among Cape May's many attractions, the clean, sandy beaches are at the top of the list. Among the choices are the farther-flung state-run Higbee Wildlife Area, with its beautiful scrub-covered dunes and Sunset Beach, the understated Cape May Point and its adjacent state park, and the city beaches, with their livelier, bikini-wearing crowds, which are in the center of the action. Geared Up Rentals (www.geareduprentals.com) hires out umbrellas, chairs, and other equipment by the day. There are daily fees for beaches during the season and tags can be purchased at City Hall or at any beach entrance. Children under 12 are free. Metered parking is available at many locations. There are showers along the beachfront for rinsing sand.

Cape May Bird Observatory. 701 E. Lake Dr.; (609) 884-2736; www.birdcapemay.org. The bird-watching season in Cape May hits its peak in early fall when migrating hawks, songbirds, shorebirds, waterfowl, and other flying creatures hover around the region's forests, marshes, and beaches. Visit the observatory for maps, books, and other information to help track and identify the various species. While there are no trails in the immediate area, there are plenty of places to spot warblers and songbirds, and the observatory also has information about birding at the Higbee Beach trails and other natural areas.

Cape May County Park and Zoo. 4 Moore Rd., Cape May Court House; (609) 465-5271; www.capemaycountyzoo.org. This 80-acre zoo is one of Cape May's many surprises—it's home to more than 200 species of wildlife and nearly 550 animals total. The expansive park, tucked away near the county courthouse off the Garden State Parkway, contains a reptile and amphibian house, primates, an exotic bird sanctuary, and an African savannah with roaming lions, leopards, and cougars. There are also a host of cuddlier creatures to meet up close in the Children's Zoo, and trains and carousel rides for kids. Open daily. Free.

Cape May Lighthouse. Lighthouse Ave.; (609) 884-5404; www.state.nj.us/dep/parksand forests/parks/capemay.html. Cape May's 157-foot navigational tower was built in 1859 and is still in operation today. The iconic landmark stands proudly over Cape May Point State Park. Climb the 199 steps for a view overlooking the entire peninsula, and on a clear day, to Delaware. Inside the tower, information displays tell the history of the lighthouse—actually the town's third—and about the lives of lighthouse keepers. In the Oil House is a visitor orientation center and museum shop. Tours are available. Hours change seasonally.

Cape May Wine Trail. (800) 275-4278; www.capemaymac.org. With its perfect grape-growing conditions, Cape May is a burgeoning region for wine production. A tour organized

eye on the sky

Cape May is a birder's paradise, and fall, spring, and summer bring great rewards to visitors toting binoculars. All bird-watching trips here should begin with a stop at the Cape May Bird Observatory (701 E. Lake Dr.; 609-884-2736; www.birdcape may.org) for a general orientation. The following are some great places for observing birds in their natural habitat.

- **Cape May Migratory Bird Refuge.** Sunset Blvd., West Cape May; (609) 861-0600; www.tnc.org. Known as Cape May Meadows, this area is great for viewing rare shorebirds in spring and summer; fall brings the hawk migration, songbirds, and owls.

- **Cape May National Wildlife Refuge.** 24 Kimbles Beach Rd., Cape May Court House; (609) 463-0994; www.fws.org. Foot trails here are devoted to songbird and woodcock viewing; the Dune Trail is a great place for spotting songbirds; and the Cedar Swamp Trail often yields owl sightings.

- **Cape May Point State Park and Hawk Watch.** Lighthouse Ave., Cape May; (609) 884-2159. Considered the best place in North America to view migrating hawks, the platform here is a popular spot in late September and early October.

- **Higbee Beach.** New England Rd., Cape May. Visit in fall (through early October) to view hawks and a bit later (through early November) to view warblers; in spring for songbirds.

by the Mid-Atlantic Center for the Arts and Humanities covers at least 3 of the 4 major operations (Cape May Winery, Turdo Vineyards, Hawk Haven Vineyard, and Natali Vineyards). The tour starts with lunch at a local restaurant, then sets off via trolley, stopping for tastings along the way. Tickets include glasses to take home. Tours are scheduled on select dates year-round.

Emlen Physick House. 1048 Washington St.; (609) 884-5404; www.capemaymac.org/attractions/physick. Visiting the Physick House is one of the best ways to explore Cape May's Victorian past. Exemplifying the "Stick style," this 18-room mansion was designed by acclaimed architect Frank Furness for Philadelphia native Dr. Emlen Physick and his widowed mother and aunt. The exterior is distinguished by oversized corbelled chimneys, hooded dormers, and porch brackets. The Mid-Atlantic Center for the Arts and Humanities runs guided tours exploring its distinctive architecture and gardens, interior decor, and

Victorian customs. In the Carriage House are changing exhibits, and the Twinings Tearoom serves lunch and afternoon tea. Open daily.

Historic Cold Spring Village. 730 US 9; (609) 898-2300; www.hcsv.org. A living-history museum, Historic Cold Spring Village is spread out over 30 acres of farmland north of Cape May. Costumed craftspeople showcase their tinsmithing, blacksmithing, bookbinding, and basket-making skills as they were applied in the age of "homespun" (1789–1840). Artisan crafts, such as wool, jams, toys, and candy, are sold at the Village Country Store. Heritage crops are grown on the village farm, and a children's activity area allows young visitors to engage in interactive projects and games. On-site eats are available at the Old Grange Restaurant, the Ice Cream Parlor, and the Bakery. Closed Mon. Seasonal hours.

where to shop

Washington Street Mall. Washington St.; www.washingtonstreetmall.com. Cape May's charming town center is anchored by this open-air, car-free promenade with its brick-paved walkways and old-fashioned ambience. The stores here are entirely small and independent, and many have been family-owned for multiple generations. There's the fashionable women's apparel at Free Store, eclectic gifts at Splash and Kaleidoscope, sweet souvenirs at Fralinger's Salt Water Taffy, and plenty of art galleries.

West End Garage. 484 Perry St.; (609) 770-8261; www.thewestendgarage.com. The finds are always eclectic at this covered marketplace in West Cape May. A relative newcomer to the local shopping scene, the Garage is filled with over 60 shops and stalls featuring local art, antiques, crafts, jewelry, clothing, sports memorabilia, books, and local food specialties. Winding through the aisles with their ever-expanding nooks can take a few hours. The cooperative's vendors are friendly without being pushy. Hours change seasonally.

where to eat

Blue Pig Tavern. Congress Place and Perry St.; (609) 884-8422; www.congresshall.com. A historic tavern in Congress Hall is the setting for this cozy gastropub serving up homey American eats. Breakfast includes malted waffles, eggs benedict with truffled hollandaise, and brioche blueberry French toast; lunch brings Cape May–style clam chowder with bacon and thyme, pulled pork sandwiches with Jack Daniel's barbecue sauce, and the house fish and chips; dinner specialties might include Yankee pot roast or crab-stuffed scallops, and a finish of pineapple cinnamon cheesecake. The Pig has both fireplace and patio seating, depending on the elements. $$–$$$.

Ebbitt Room. 25 Jackson St.; (609) 884-5700; www.virginiahotel.com/ebbitt.html. The refurbished dining room of the Virginia Hotel is one of Cape May's most elegant dining options. The farm-to-table cuisine changes seasonally but recurring favorites on the menu are the house crab salad with romaine, radish, manchego cheese, applewood bacon, and green goddess dressing; rare ahi tuna over buckwheat noodles with zucchini flower pesto; and filet mignon over potato-fennel gratin. The hotel's front porch has a more casual menu of small plates, sandwiches, and classic cocktails, and it's a great place for a lighter snack. $$$.

George's Place. 301 Beach Ave.; (609) 884-6088. Located in a former luncheonette, the elevated diner George's is an easygoing choice for a pre-beach breakfast or post-beach dinner. Greek-inflected fare like grilled fish or pork medallions with yogurt sauce and egg-plant orzo is simple and fresh. All entrees come with a choice of Greek or Caesar salad, making it a great value. Breakfast gets a little more creative with Nutella and tiramisu waffles, the meat lover's pita served with hash browns, and more than 10 types of omelets. BYO. Cash only. Open daily. $$.

Louisa's. 104 Jackson St.; (609) 884-5882. In a well-touristed place like Cape May, long-standing favorite restaurants can be hard to come by, but Louisa's has earned that distinction for both locals and summer vacationers alike. The diminutive, cheerily painted BYOB posts its daily selections in the window, and these are based on the day's harvest and catch. The homey, unpretentious cuisine favors off-the-boat fish and seafood, like baked cod plated with garlic aioli and house-made desserts like Mississippi mud pie. Reservations recommended. Hours change seasonally. $$.

foodie finds

With its local restaurant and wine scene, Cape May is a food-lover's dream. The following are some additional must-see stops for gastronomically inclined visitors.

- ***Beach Plum Farm.*** *140 Stevens St., West Cape May; (917) 797-0676. The supplier for the Ebbitt Room, Blue Pig Tavern, and the Rusty Nail is open for tours seasonally on Tues, Thurs, and Sat.*

- ***LeGates Farm Market.*** *3400 Bayshore Rd., Cape May; (609) 886-8500. Open daily during the growing season, offering local produce and pick-your-own pumpkins.*

- ***Love the Cook.*** *404 Washington St., Cape May; (609) 884-9292. Kitchen wares and gourmet food items abound at this well-curated shop.*

- ***Seaside Cheese Company.*** *600 Park Blvd., West Cape May; (609) 884-8700; www.seasidecheesecapemay.com. Artisanal cheese from around the world, gifts, and gourmet items.*

Mad Batter. 19 Jackson St.; (609) 884-5970; www.madbatter.com. There's nothing too exotic about the fare at this funky little eatery but the familiar flavors make it a good bet for a mixed group. Corned beef hash or eggs Benedict with lump crabmeat start the day off, while a blackened grouper sandwich or Waldorf chicken croissant provide midday sustenance. Dinner offerings might include grilled pork tenderloin with corn cakes and maple butter sauce or marinated Chilean sea bass with Asian slaw and sweet soy drizzle. $$–$$$.

where to stay

Eldredge House. 417 Broadway; (609) 884-5936; www.capemayeldredgehouse.com. The oldest operating inn in Cape May was built by Mayflower descendants in 1780. The 3-story colonial home has a wide range of rooms at different price points, but all feature private baths, queen-size beds, air-conditioning, cable TV, wireless Internet, DVD players, and bathrobes. Free off-street parking, access to beach chairs, and breakfast at partnering restaurants are all included in the nightly fee. The Cove Beach, the Historic District, and the Washington Street Mall are each a 10-minute walk away. $–$$$.

Mission Inn. 1117 New Jersey Ave.; (800) 800-8380; www.missioninn.net. Its Spanish tiled roof, pergola veranda, and Flemish gables make it something of an outlier in Cape May, and the Mission Inn is the only bed-and-breakfast in town that isn't banking on Victorian nostalgia. Located a block from the ocean, the inn offers 8 bright and simple guest rooms with headboards that are replicas of California missions, plus fireplaces and private baths, some with spa showers and jet tubs. The 2-course breakfast can be served in the dining room, solarium, or veranda. The inn's owners lend out bicycles and beach gear to guests. $$$.

Virginia Hotel. 25 Jackson St.; (800) 732-4236; www.virginiahotel.com. There are 24 rooms in the main building and 5 outlying cottages on this restored 1879 property updated with fresh neo-Victorian decor. Among the comforts are European linens, Bulgari bath products, wireless Internet, and continental breakfast. For summertime vacationers, there's free access to the Congress Hall swimming pool and a private beach area with chair and towel setup plus optional food service. Packages can include dinner at the hotel's Ebbitt Room restaurant. Children under 12 are not allowed. $$–$$$.

day trip 02

south

from polished stones to rock 'n' roll:
avalon, nj; stone harbor, nj;
wildwood, nj

A trip along the barrier islands of Cape May County reveals the rich and varied character of the Jersey shore—much of it nothing like its reality-television portrayal. This trip starts at the Seven Mile Island at the tony resort of Avalon and works south to Stone Harbor, a similarly quiet community. Farther south still is Wildwood—technically part of a collective of four towns called the Wildwoods—which is, true to its name, a bit rougher around the edges with a livelier, kitschier atmosphere. Visit all three or find the perfect beach spot and hunker down in the sand for the day.

avalon, nj

With an average home price topping $1.5 million, Avalon represents the swankier side of the Jersey shore. Once a thriving juniper forest, this stretch of coastal land was purchased in 1722 by the Learning family and developed as a resort in 1887, effectively leveling its hills and eliminating all traces of forest. A train connected the town to Philadelphia in the early 20th century, increasing the tourist trade, but it's currently accessible only by boat or car. The main recreation here is relaxation: Avalon's white sand beaches are bordered by prominent dunes; sailboats and yachts hug its back-bay coastline; and the short boardwalk encourages strolling and bike riding.

getting there

From I-76 in Philadelphia, travel east on the Atlantic City Expressway (36.6 miles) and then south on the Garden State Parkway for about 22 miles, until exit 13 for Avalon. Travel time is just under an hour and a half.

where to go

Avalon Free Public Library History Center. 215 39th St.; (609) 967-0090; www.avalon historycenter.com. An informational and cultural gateway to Avalon, the History Center is an educational institution that partners the free library and the historical society. Exhibits and public programs explore the town's past through access to archives of individuals and businesses. On display are dozens of publications, photographs, postcards, and other ephemera. Collected artifacts trace Avalon's deeply intertwined connection to the sea, such as an early 20th-century hollow wooden paddleboard used by town lifeguards. Closed Sun.

Beach. Avalon Ave.; www.avalonbeach.com. Of the 30 miles of Jersey shoreline, Avalon's beach was voted the best by the *Washingtonian* magazine—a major point of pride for the town's residents. The surf is gentle, the sandy stretch of beach is wide, and the picturesque dunes and small boardwalk only enhance its beauty. Beach tags are sold by the day and can be purchased on summer weekends at the booth at Community Hall. Surf chairs designed for visitors with mobility impairments can be reserved at the lifeguard station or at Community Hall.

Hollywood Bicycle Center. 2522 Dune Dr.; (609) 967-5846; www.hollywoodbikeshop .com. One of the best ways to explore Avalon and nearby Stone Harbor is by bike. Stop into this well-stocked rental shop before hitting the beach or boardwalk. Bike rentals include cruisers, trailers, hybrids, tandems, jog strollers, and for true old-fashioned charm, bright yellow surrey carts. There's also beach gear for hire—chairs, carts, and umbrellas, all available by the day. ID is required for rentals. Delivery is available with an extra charge.

where to shop

Boutique Bellissima. 264 21st St.; (609) 967-4343; www.bellissimaavalon.com. Fashionistas flock to this style-conscious purveyor of shoes, handbags, and accessories. Outfitted like a European salon, Bellissima's cozy couches and minimalist displays inspire luxury-minded selections. Inventory runs the gamut from rain boots to stilettos, with knee-high boots, flats, and wedges thrown in for good measure. Collections include Tory Burch, Kate Spade, Stuart Weitzman, Cynthia Vincent, Ted Rossi, Dolce Vita, and BCBG. Owner Danielle O'Hara also stocks children's shoes and apparel, jewelry, and lingerie.

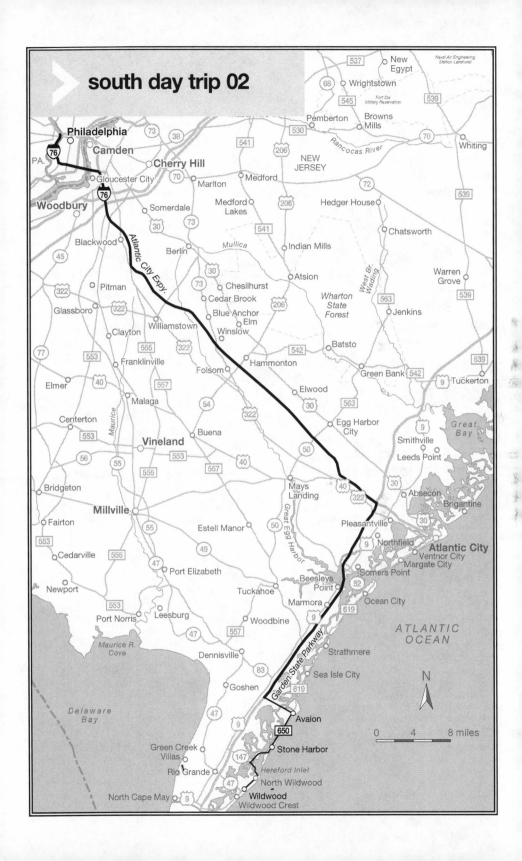

south day trip 02

where to eat

The Diving Horse. 2109 Dune Dr.; (609) 368-5000; www.thedivinghorseavalon.com. This shabby-chic BYO from a Philadelphia restaurateur brings city sophistication to beach eating. Fried oysters are given an upmarket twist with house-cured pancetta mayo and smashed potatoes; steamed clams are served up with braised pork belly, oregano, and heirloom corn; scallops are nested in toasted pearl pasta with preserved lemon and vermouth *nage.* Reservations are recommended for the cozy dining room but outdoor seating is first-come, first-served. Open nightly. $$$.

Oceanside Seafood. 2489 Dune Dr.; (609) 368-2114; www.oceansideseafoodavalon .com. A local summertime institution, Oceanside is open from April to October, with off-the-boat meals for takeout or dine-in. The ultra-casual atmosphere encourages down-and-dirty, lobster-bibbing, crab-cracking eating. As such, the fare is straightforward seafood-shack cookery—New England clam chowder, deviled crab cakes, and platters of broiled scallops and shrimp piled high with coleslaw and fries. Pasta dishes, fish sandwiches, and a kids' menu offer additional options. Open daily during seasonal hours for lunch and dinner. $$.

where to stay

Concord Suites. 7800 Dune Dr.; (609) 368-7800; www.concordsuites.com. The Concord combines the efficiency and privacy of a motor inn with the hospitality of a B&B. Its 90 suites were renovated in 2010. Designed for beaching families, each one includes a private bedroom with 2 queen beds, a living room with queen-size sofa bed, and a kitchenette with microwave, coffeemaker, and table settings for 6. Also included are two TVs with cable and DVD player, complimentary coffee, free beach tags, two pools, and free parking. A family-friendly tavern is located on the property. $–$$$.

stone harbor, nj

South of Avalon on the Seven Mile Island, Stone Harbor has been a beach resort community since the end of the 19th century. Like Avalon, it's a well-heeled town that attracts vacationers from all along the East Coast. And like Avalon, too, it's a quiet, less commercial sort of destination with protected beaches and an emphasis on outdoor activities, like boating and fishing. People come here to relax and lounge. Drive along the coastal edge to glimpse multimillion-dollar homes.

getting there

From Avalon, travel south on Ocean Drive for 3 miles, then turn left into Stone Harbor. Travel time from Avalon is 12 minutes.

where to go

Beach. Stone Harbor. The quiet, well-kept beaches of Stone Harbor, stretching along the Atlantic coastline from 81st Street through the 100s, are the focal point of this town. To maintain the safe, family-friendly atmosphere, Stone Harbor sets strict rules for beach use. Swimming, rafts, and surfboards are permitted only at designated lifeguarded beaches. Alcohol, pets, glass containers, picnics, and hardball are prohibited. All visitors age 12 and over must display beach tags during the summer season. They can be purchased for the day at the Stone Harbor Beach Patrol Building.

Stone Harbor Bird Sanctuary. 112th St. and Second Ave.; (609) 368-7447; www.stone harborbirdsanctuary.com. Meander along one of the 4 trails at this 21-acre coastal enclave and explore its microhabitats: an old-growth maritime forest, ancient dunes, freshwater ponds, and saltwater tributaries. Signature birds include great white egrets, great blue herons, night herons, and glossy ibis, but hundreds of migratory species stop here on their twice-annual migrations. It's also easy to spot frogs, river otters, and turtles here. Tours are available.

Stone Harbor Museum. 245 93rd St.; (609) 368-7500; www.stone-harbor.nj.us/museum .asp. Stone Harbor's genteel history is preserved in this small museum. While the emphasis here is on archiving rather than displaying, there are a handful of permanent exhibits, such as "On the Street Where You Live," which showcases current and vintage photographs of the town's oldest buildings. An audio/video display explores the history of the beach and boardwalk, while another installation looks at the storms that have come through Stone Harbor over the years. The gift shop sells a small array of souvenirs. Hours are seasonal.

Wetlands Institute. 1075 Stone Harbor Blvd.; (609) 368-1211; www.wetlandsinstitute.org. Founded by Herbert Mills in the late 1960s, the Wetlands Institute is a leading organiza- tion in coastal environmental education and a must-visit for anyone interested in nature or the shoreline ecosystem. The English cottage–style Marion's Gardens contain hundreds of native plants, while the Diller Coastal Exhibit is an aquarium with hands-on displays about wetlands life. Marshview Hall showcases wildlife art and carvings, and the Observation Tower provides a view of the surrounding area—on clear days, from Sea Isle City to Wild- wood. In summer there are back-bay boat rides, kayaking, live animal shows, and guided beach and dune walks. In the winter visitors can embark on a self-guided tour of the facility. Hours change seasonally.

where to shop

James Salt Water Taffy. 255 96th St.; (609) 368-0505; www.jamescandy.com. Enoch James discovered the perfect non-teeth-breaking recipe for saltwater taffy in the 1880s, and its success led to the development of other variations—chocolate-dipped taffy, filled- center taffy, and taffy pops. James's legacy lives on in all the Jersey boardwalks. The Stone

Harbor store sells paper-wrapped confections in nostalgic boxes and tins in flavors like banana, molasses, peanut, and of course, vanilla and chocolate. Also available are fudge and other confections.

Skirt. 272 96th St.; (609) 948-4912; www.shop-skirt.com. A sibling to a suburban Philadelphia boutique, Skirt is all about feminine style—from the candy-striped awning to the cabana dressing rooms swathed in Trina Turk–designed fabric. Individual pieces range from glamorous to casual: Theory separates, J Brand jeans, Shoshanna swimwear, Bettye Muller heels. But the emphasis in Stone Harbor is definitely on the preppy, beachy aesthetic of its summer residents, including Diane von Furstenberg flip-flops, cashmere knits, and basics from Petit Bateau. Open daily.

where to eat

Bread & Cheese Cupboard. 246 96th St.; (609) 368-1135; www.breadandcheesecupboard.com. What began as a neighborhood cheese shop has expanded into a full-service bakery serving sweet buns, muffins, croissants, scones, doughnuts, and other breakfast treats. The morning rush sees the crowds stocking up and toting away cups of espresso and cappuccino. Lunchtime shoppers come for the picnic goodies: baguettes and boules plus some of the Cupboard's international cheeses and gourmet condiments. When in doubt, go for the pepperoni bread—a baguette stuffed with pepperoni and cheese. $.

Jay's on Third. 9836 3rd Ave.; (609) 368-1000; www.jaysonthird.com. Jay's sets the bar high for a small-town restaurant and manages to provide a first-rate experience in its cozy dining room. The ingredient-focused, seasonally inspired fare at this contemporary white-tablecloth bistro borrows from all sorts of ethnic cuisines, with always-interesting results. Witness the confit duck, wrapped in a flour tortilla with jicama slaw and jalapeño jam, or the duck breast with yam puree, crushed pistachio, and cardamom-spiced lingonberries. All food products are humanely produced. BYO. Hours change seasonally. $$$.

Mack's Pizza. 83rd and 3rd Avenues; (609) 368-6224; www.mackspizzaofstoneharbor.com. Part of a family of down-home Jersey shore pizzerias owned by the Mackrone clan, the no-frills Stone Harbor outlet is all about the pie—there's pizza and nothing but on its menu. They're baked in a rotating brick oven, and come with locally inspired combinations of toppings: Ocean City (chicken, mushrooms, garlic, and tomato) and Wildwood (sausage, onion, green pepper, and extra cheese), to name just two. The thin, evenly crisped crust makes it a consistent winner of best-of-shore awards. BYOB. Open daily. $.

Yvette's Cafe. 221 96th St.; (609) 368-1855; www.yvettescaffe.com. Fresh ingredients transformed by simple preparations is the MO at Yvette's Cafe. The selection consists mostly of salads and sandwiches, the perfect fare for refueling during a day at the beach, and the atmosphere is pleasantly relaxed. Nothing is exotic—mixed greens with apples and blue cheese, grilled chicken panini with goat cheese, and a niçoise-style tuna sandwich are among the offered items, but the nightly dinner specials change it up. Open daily. $.

where to stay

Lark Motel. 9800 2nd Ave.; (609) 368-2500; www.larkmotel.com. The efficiency and 2-room units at this classic motel are certainly basic but they offer some nice comforts for a good value: wireless Internet, cable TV, maid service, beach tags, and free parking. The motel has a pool and a sundeck with a barbecue. Just a block away from the beach and close to Stone Harbor's 96th Street strip of restaurants and shops. Open Apr through Oct. $–$$.

wildwood, nj

While other Jersey shore towns preserve a Victorian past and quiet present, Wildwood is a very flashy, very 20th-century sort of place. The over 200 motels constitute the Wildwoods Shore Resort Historic District, and this stretch of 1950s and 1960s space-age "populuxe" architecture offers a neon-lit focal point. Nearby, the Doo Wop museum celebrates the town's history as an early epicenter for rock 'n' roll. The 38-block boardwalk, home to the Morey's Piers amusements and water parks, comes alive at night with a carnival atmosphere.

getting there

From Stone Harbor, take Ocean Drive across the Stone Harbor Bridge and then turn left on North Wildwood Boulevard, following it for about 1.5 miles to enter Wildwood, about 14 minutes total travel time.

where to go

Doo Wop Preservation League Museum. 3201 Pacific Ave.; (609) 729-4000; www.doo wopusa.org. At present this neon-tastic museum is really more of a shrine, though it's a work in progress, resurrecting the space-age Surfside Restaurant. The display inside celebrates 1950s and 1960s culture with memorabilia, furniture, art, photos, and pop culture ephemera. Outside is the Neon Sign Garden with restored signs from defunct local motels. A bus tour takes riders on a music-laden midcentury modern architecture tour through Wildwood, North Wildwood, and Wildwood Crest. Tours leave from the front of the museum. Hours change seasonally.

Wildwoods Boardwalk. Boardwalk. The center of all the action is here, on this 1.5-mile stretch of Americana. Beyond the rides and amusements—of which there are more here than at Disneyland—are souvenir shops, vendors hawking henna tattoos and hair wraps, and eateries serving up traditional Jersey shore favorites like cotton candy, cheesesteaks, funnel cake, and ice cream. If the 38 blocks seem too big to span by foot, hop on a battery-operated tramcar—originally built for the 1939 World's Fair in New York City—or rent a bike.

Morey's Piers and Beachfront Waterparks. 3501 Boardwalk; (609) 522-3900; www.moreyspiers.com. This seaside amusement park, family-owned and -operated since 1969, is a Wildwood landmark. There are over 100 rides and attractions for families and kids spread out over 3 parks: Mariner's Landing, Surfside, and Adventure Piers. Morey's also operates 2 water parks and Ocean Oasis, a beach club getaway with private cabanas, hammocks, massage services, and family activities; plus the Raging Waters park, which has the 1,100-foot Endless River, drop slides, a rope swing, a fountain pool, and many other play areas. Open seasonally.

where to shop

Hooked on Books. 3405 Pacific Ave.; (609) 729-1132; www.hookedonbooks.info. Two blocks off the Wildwoods Boardwalk might seem like an unlikely place for an excellent bookstore, but this shop, open May through September, fulfills every summer reading need and then some. The primary focus is secondhand books—both fiction and nonfiction, best sellers, and back titles—but Hooked on Books also stocks just-released titles, and they're usually discounted. Staff can offer personal recommendations. Check the website for the latest coupons. Open during the summer only.

Sand Jamm Surf Shop. 2701 Boardwalk; (609) 522-4650; www.sandjamm.com. Every beach town needs a good surf shop and Sand Jamm is Wildwood's altar to the impact zone. Catering to surfers and those who just want to look like them, this boardwalk outlet has it all: girls' and guys' apparel for both adults and children (North Face, Billabong, Roxy, Volcomm, Quiksilver), resort wear, sandals, hoodies, bathing suits, and gear for both surfing and skating. Sand Jamm also sells beach blankets, souvenirs—and even "coastal home" accessories. Open year-round; check for hours.

where to eat

Goodfish Grill. 3805 Pacific Ave.; (609) 729-2232; www.goodfishgrill.com. A few steps above the usual seafood shack, Goodfish Grill aims for a more satisfying dining experience. The expansive menu covers crab cake sliders and raw-bar appetizers, wraps, and sandwiches; a panoply of seafood served broiled or blackened with a choice of sauces; and—if that weren't enough—house specialties such as seared day-boat scallops over penne with sun-dried tomatoes and pesto. There's a large wine list and a children's menu. $$–$$$.

Jersey Girl Bar and Restaurant. 3601 Atlantic Ave.; (609) 523-1800; www.jerseygirlwild wood.com. When the boardwalk's fried eats wear thin, this unfortunately named casual restaurant and bar, located just a few blocks away, has more serious meals to offer. Hearty

American cuisine is the specialty: steaks, chops, burgers, and of course, seafood. The full bar features a martini menu and 15 wines by the glass. Al fresco seating options are available on the patio and some weekend nights feature live music. Closed Tues. $$.

Uncle Bill's Pancake House. 4601 Pacific Ave.; (609) 729-7557; www.unclebillspancake house.com. There are now 8 locations of this family-owned breakfast-centric restaurant spread throughout the Jersey shore, and each one has its loyal following. Family-friendly chow is the dominant theme, with a paper place-mat menu of inexpensive munchies. There are 14 varieties of pancakes (from peach to potato) as well as all manner of omelets and waffles, served all day long. For the uninitiated, this is a good place to try the Jersey specialty Taylor pork roll, which can come as a side order or on a sandwich. Cash only, but an ATM is on site. $.

where to stay

Sea Gypsy B&B. 209 E. Magnolia Ave.; (609) 522-0690; www.theseagypsy.com. While many of Wildwood's motels are decked out in midcentury neon, this restored manor dates from 1900. Set a few blocks off the hustle and bustle of the beach and boardwalk, the turreted home features 5 eclectically decorated guest rooms named for poets. An Arts and Crafts bungalow nearby expands the options with 6 additional suites and a private cottage. Rooms come with hot breakfast, shuttle service, a heated Jacuzzi on the front veranda, bicycle use, and complimentary candy from the stocked cabinet. $$.

southwest

day trip 01

southwest

the fruits of prosperity:
chadds ford, kennett square & the
pennsylvania brandywine valley

pennsylvania brandywine valley

Since its first European settlers recognized the natural beauty of the Brandywine Valley, the region has symbolized wealth and refinement: Witness its lavish estates, wineries, and remarkable landscapes immortalized by the Wyeth family of painters. Technically the valley spans southeastern Pennsylvania and northern Delaware, though this day trip focuses on the Pennsylvania segment. Follow the winding, lazy Brandywine River deep into Chadds Ford, visiting its famous attractions before exploring the charming town of Kennett Square, also known as the "Mushroom Capital of the World."

getting there

From Philadelphia, travel south on I-95 for 14 miles and exit at US 322 West. Continue on US 1 South/Baltimore Pike to get to Chadds Ford. Kennett Square is 7 more miles west on US 1. Travel time without traffic is 40 minutes.

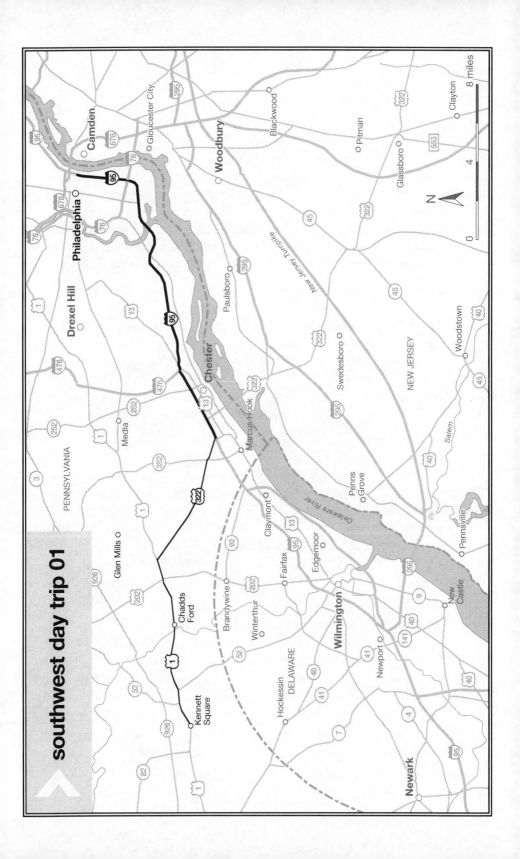

where to go

Brandywine Battlefield. 1491 Baltimore Pike, Chadds Ford, PA; (610) 459-3342; www
.brandywinebattlefield.org. Brandywine was the site of the largest engagement of the Revolutionary War, which took place on September 11, 1777, between George Washington's
Continental army and British forces led by General William Howe. The visitor center is just off
US 1/Baltimore Pike and houses historical exhibits of uniforms, weapons, and artifacts. An
18-minute film tells the story of the battle. From there, explore Washington's headquarters
at the Ring House and Lafayette's quarters at Gideon Gilpin's farmhouse. In September
there's an annual reenactment of the battle. Hours change seasonally, and historic house
tours are offered during some seasons.

Brandywine River Museum. 1 Hoffman Mill Rd., Chadds Ford, PA; (610) 388-2700; www
.brandywinemuseum.org. There were artists in three generations of the Wyeth family, and
this small, lovely museum celebrates their work. Set in a converted 19th-century gristmill,
the building literally sits over the Brandywine River, and the glass-walled lobby offers a scenic vista of the landscape that inspired famous works like *Christina's World*. In addition to
the Wyeth family art, the museum's permanent collection focuses on American illustration,
still-life works, and landscapes from artists such as Maxfield Parrish, Howard Pyle, and
Harvey Dunn. The museum also operates tours of the Wyeth Family House and the Kuerner
Farm, historic landmarks each. Open daily from 9:30 a.m. to 4:30 p.m. and for extended
hours in the week between Christmas and New Year's.

Brandywine Valley Wine Trail. (610) 444-3842; www.bvwinetrail.com. Southern Pennsylvania is an up-and-coming region for wine growers, and this trail, stretching from the
Brandywine Valley to just outside of Lancaster, includes 7 wineries: Black Walnut Winery,
Chaddsford Winery, Kreutz Creek Vineyards, Paradocx Vineyard, Patone Cellars, Penns
Wood Winery, and Twin Brook Winery. Download the map from the website—the trail
organizers recommend visiting 2 to 3 wineries per day for those sampling alcohol. All are
open to visitors, but check the website for hours. The trail organization sponsors special
events around the year.

Kennett Underground Railroad Tour. Chester County Visitors Center, 300 Greenwood
Rd., Kennett Square, PA; (610) 347-2237; www.undergroundrr.kennett.net. Kennett
Square was a hotbed of abolitionist activity in the 19th century, with over two dozen underground railroad sites or stations in Chester County—which some experts believe constitutes
the largest concentration in the nation. The Kennett Underground Railroad Center is a nonprofit educational institution that sponsors tours of these sites. Driving tours are available
on summer weekends and by appointment, leaving from the visitor center at Longwood
Gardens, for a modest donation.

Longwood Gardens. 1001 Longwood Rd., Kennett Square, PA; (800) 737-5500; www
.longwoodgardens.org. This massive garden, stretching over 1,077 acres, was founded by

Pierre S. du Pont in 1906, when he purchased an existing arboretum to save its trees from being cut for lumber. Today Longwood is a major cultural attraction and education center, with over 11,000 plant types and a multitude of fountains. The indoor conservatory houses 20 gardens alone—a walk-through takes over an hour. The outdoor areas feature changing displays, a children's garden, an oak knoll, a topiary garden, and an arboretum. Of special interest is the winter holiday display, which changes annually but is always impressive. Open daily; hours are seasonal.

where to shop

Brandywine River Antiques Market. 878 Baltimore Pike, Chadds Ford, PA; (610) 388-2000; www.brandywineriverantiques.com. This covered market in a restored 14,000-foot barn houses 40 antiques dealers. Every style and era is covered: 18th- and 19th-century furniture, sterling silver, Christmas decorations, Wyeth prints and books, Williamsburg pewter, country and primitive furnishings, vintage textiles, Art Deco glassware and china, and much more. Visit the front room and third floor for the larger furniture selections. The Mushrooms Cafe in the adjacent carriage house sells gifts and serves breakfast and lunch featuring the famous local fungi. Open Wed through Sun, 10 a.m. to 5 p.m.

The Mushroom Cap. 114 W. State St., Kennett Square, PA; (610) 444-8484; www.the mushroomcap.com. Celebrating the mushroom is the mission for this gift shop started by a local farming family. Fresh and dried whites, portobellos, and exotics are for sale, as are preserved goods, such as mushroom salad, marinated mushrooms, and mushroom pâté. Growing kits, t-shirts and other souvenirs—even bottles of Kennett Square "potpourri" (aka mushroom soil)—are also on offer. Better still is the educational component here: When the local mushroom museum closed, the Cap inherited its exhibits, including historic relics and a 10-minute video on the industry. Hours change seasonally.

mushrooms

The Mushroom Capital of the World comes by its designation honestly—the 47 farms in the region produce over a million pounds of the underground vegetable a year—about 64 percent of what's consumed in the US. The mushrooms are grown in windowless cinderblock buildings with wooden beds stacked 3 to 5 feet high. White mushrooms, shiitake, portobello, cremini, and exotics like Puffball and Blue Foot are among the varietals. In early September the town celebrates with the Mushroom Festival, whose festivities include a parade, tours of area farms, and plenty of food and crafts.

Terrain. 914 Baltimore Pike, Glen Mills, PA; (610) 259-2400; www.shopterrain.com/styers. From the company that owns Anthropologie and Urban Outfitters comes this flagship garden store, located in a rustic barn just east of Chadds Ford. Terrain has built a slavish following for its online business and the Glen Mills outpost showcases stylish, vintage-style housewares, cookbooks, gifts, garden furniture, and accessories—all arranged with eye-catching appeal. The nursery grows and sells chemical-free plants, from exotic bulbs to succulents to organic herbs, and the on-site cafe serves local, sustainable light fare in a stunning greenhouse setting. Open daily.

Thomas Macaluso Rare and Fine Books. 130 S. Union St., Kennett Square, PA; (610) 444-1063; www.abebooks.com/home/macalusobooks. Open since 1973, this rare-book dealer is something of an antique itself. Macaluso has a collection of over 20,000 scarce books on a wide variety of subjects, and 5,000 antiqued or lithographed maps and prints from the 16th century to the present. Autographs and ephemera are also displayed in the cases spread across 6 showrooms, and there are 2 additional bookshops dealing used books on the block. Open Mon through Sat, and Sun by special appointment.

where to eat

Half Moon. 108 W. State St., Kennett Square, PA; (610) 444-7232; www.halfmoonrestau rant.com. Belgian-beer aficionados flock to this cozy tavern in historic downtown Kennett Square. The mahogany bar features some 27 beers on tap, plus a long list of boozy bottles. The onetime home to the Kennett Kandy Kitchen has character to spare, with a tin ceiling, porcelain tile floors, and a rooftop deck. The menu favors wild game, like kangaroo medallions with blueberry jam; gator gumbo; and buffaloaf, but there are also plenty of familiar items like burgers, crab cakes, and herb-roasted chicken with three-cheese mac. Open for lunch and dinner. Closed Sun. $$.

La Michoacana Ice Cream. 231 E. State St., Kennett Square, PA; (610) 444-2996; www .lamichoacanaicecream.com. This family-owned Mexican-style parlor dishes up homemade ice cream, sherbet, and water ice, plus *paletas* (Popsicles) in 50 flavors. The ice cream is the standout. Traditional flavors mingle with more intriguing varieties like corn sprinkled with cinnamon or chile powder, rice pudding, avocado, guava and cream, tamarind, cheesecake, and eggnog. There's even an earthy mushroom flavor for the true Kennett Square experience. Sugar-free options, *horchata,* sundaes in homemade waffle bowls, fruit smoothies, and milk shakes are available, too. Open daily. $.

The Orchard. 503 Orchard Ave., Kennett Square, PA; (610) 388-1100; www.theorchard byob.com. The farmhouse exterior of this BYO belies its sleek, modern interior. The seasonal menu changes but always relies on local, organic, and sustainably raised ingredients. Selections might include foie gras served on brioche with sweet pomegranate reduction, day-boat scallops served over spaghetti squash with creamed leek sauce, or brown butter cake with vanilla malt buttercream and vanilla ice cream. For big spenders (and eaters), there's a chef's table with a customized tasting menu. $$$.

Sovana Bistro. 696 Unionville Rd., Kennett Square, PA; (610) 444-5600; www.sovana bistro.com. Never mind the strip mall setting—Sovana Bistro is a fresh, contemporary bistro and bar with a casual atmosphere and exacting, elegant food. European and American flavors blend in the changing menu: pole bean and fig salad with cured salami and Chianti vinaigrette; fresh pasta with wild boar Bolognese, and roasted whole fish with chickpea fritters and olive-celery citronette. There are also to-die-for pizzas with inventive toppings. Wash it all down with seasonal cocktails, like the Sovana Mule (tarragon, ginger blossom soda, Mandarin Blossom vodka). Closed Mon. Open for lunch Tues through Sat and dinner Tues through Sun. $$–$$$.

Talula's Table. 102 W. State St., Kennett Square, PA; (610) 444-8255; www.talulastable .com. Part country market, part takeaway eatery, part fine dining restaurant, Talula's Table is a nationally lauded jewel of a spot on Kennett Square's main drag. Visit in the morning for fresh pastries and coffee; midday for the selection of more than 100 artisan cheeses, charcuterie, soups, pastas, and sandwiches. Or if you're lucky enough to reserve the coveted farm table a year ahead (reservations are first-come, first-served and taken only by phone starting at 7 a.m.), bring up to 11 friends and settle in for the 8-course, $100 tasting menu, which lasts 4 hours and makes the most of the season's bounty. BYOB: Visit the website for wine pairing suggestions. Open daily. $–$$$.

where to stay

Bancroft Manor B&B. 318 Marshall St., Kennett Square, PA; (610) 470-4297; www.bancroft manor.com. Explore the historic district of Kennett Square from this centrally located inn, built by the founder of the mushroom industry. The Queen Anne–style building has 3 guest rooms, including a suite, each appointed with private bath and antiques. Wireless Internet access, cable TV, and a 3-course breakfast served in the sunroom or formal dining room are included, as is afternoon tea service. Common areas include a wraparound front porch, a parlor with wood-burning fireplace, and a study filled with local history books. Two-night minimum for Fri and Sat nights between Apr and Dec. $.

Kennett House Bed and Breakfast. 503 W. State St., Kennett Square, PA; (800) 820-9592; www.kennetthouse.com. Visitors to Brandywine Battlefield can lengthen the history lesson by staying at Kennett House, an Arts and Crafts–style foursquare granite mansion on Hessian Hill, a Revolutionary encampment site. The 3 guest rooms and suite are decorated with antiques and oriental rugs and include bathrobes, toiletries, wireless Internet, free parking, complimentary beverages, and early morning coffee and tea. The full breakfast is made from local ingredients and the owners offer friendly concierge services. Children 10 and over are welcome. $$.

day trip 02

southwest

art meets commerce:
wilmington, de

wilmington, de

"The largest city in Delaware" is not the most impressive superlative, but Wilmington nevertheless packs quite a lot of history and character in its minimal square mileage. The area between the Christina and Delaware Rivers was first settled by Swedes in the 17th century, but control of Wilmington was wrested by the Dutch and finally the English, who chartered the borough in 1739. Wilmington boomed with industry during the Civil War as a shipbuilding town, and in the 1980s the city grew once again when it attracted many national and international finance and insurance companies with its liberal local laws. The small and tightly organized city center has a strictly business feel but it's surrounded by cultural attractions, world-class dining, and the naturally beautiful landscapes of the Brandywine Valley.

getting there

Wilmington is a 40-minute drive from Philadelphia—a straight shot on I-95 South.

where to go

Delaware Art Museum. 2301 Kentmere Pkwy.; (302) 571-9590; www.delart.org. Founded in 1912 in honor of the artist Howard Pyle, the newly renovated and expanded Delaware Art Museum boasts a collection of more than 12,000 works. Holdings include American art and illustration from the 19th century to the present (Dante Gabriel Rossetti, Frederic Church,

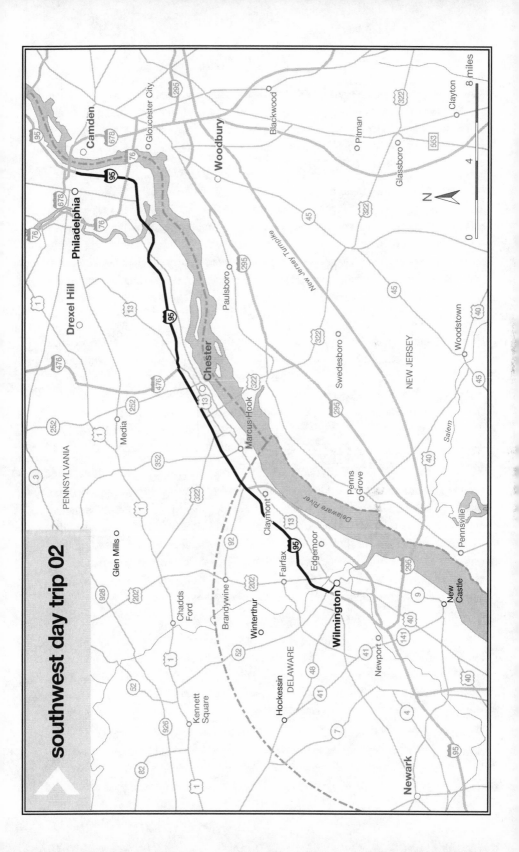

southwest day trip 02

Winslow Homer, Marsden Hartley, Edward Harper, and Louise Nevelson are just a few of the artists whose works are showcased here). There's also a 9-acre sculpture garden, and an interactive Kids' Corner. Summertime visitors can purchase a Brandywine Passport, which includes admission to 10 area attractions. Closed Mon and Tues. Sundays are free for visitors.

Delaware Children's Museum. 550 Justison St.; (302) 654-2340; www.delawarechildrens museum.org. Opened in 2010, the Delaware Children's Museum is the first of its kind in the state. The 37,000-square-foot facility is situated on the redeveloped riverfront. Permanent exhibits include ECOnnect, which delivers environmental education in the form of a walk-through sustainable home; Stratosphere, a 30-foot-wide climbing structure overlooking the lobby; Structures, a hands-on introduction to the building industry; a creative arts studio; and more. The DECafe serves healthy options for a light snack or lunch. Free parking. Open daily 9 a.m. to 4:30 p.m.

Delaware Museum of Natural History. 4840 Kennett Pike; (302) 658-9111; www.del mnh.org. The natural world and all of its wonders are on display at this modern museum founded by John Eleuthère du Pont. Galleries are devoted to Darwin and evolution, the Hall of Mammals, the Butterfly Garden, dinosaurs, and Delaware's fauna. Children can explore with their senses in the hands-on Nature Nook stocked with games, puzzles, experiments, fossils, and skeletons. A nature trail behind the museum is a mile-long path through wet-lands. Special changing exhibits and nature movies are also offered in rotation. Open daily, except for Christmas, Thanksgiving, Easter, Fourth of July, and New Year's Day.

Hagley Museum and Library. 298 Buck Rd. East; (302) 658-2400; www.hagley.org. A National Historic Landmark on the banks of the Brandywine River, the Hagley is the site of the original du Pont gunpowder company and the beginning of the family legacy. This museum, with its restored mills, workers' community, and ancestral home and gardens, was established in 1952 to honor the family and its contributions to Wilmington and the surrounding areas. The exhibits showcase early industrial technology from the 19th century as well as the personal stories of the people who worked there. Open daily from 9:30 a.m. to 4:30 p.m. Closed Thanksgiving and Christmas.

Nemours Mansion and Gardens. Powder Mill Dr. and Alapocas Rd.; (302) 651-6912; www.nemoursmansion.org. A little bit of Versailles in Delaware, Nemours is the 300-acre country estate created by Alfred du Pont in 1909–1910. The Louis XVI Rococo-style chateau has more than 70 rooms lavishly decorated with 18th-century French furnishings and artworks from European and American masters. The formal French garden mimics Versailles' grounds with its central axis, fountains, pools, and statuary. A walk through the boxwood collection, colonnade, maze garden, and classical Temple of Love is itself an amazing spectacle. Touring the home and gardens requires climbing several staircases, so

gardens of delaware

New Jersey may be known as the Garden State but Delaware, with its exquisite mansions and public parks, comes pretty close. The horticulturally inclined will be especially interested in visiting the following sites in and around Wilmington:

- ***Hagley Museum and Library.*** *DE 141, Wilmington; (302) 658-2400; www .hagley.org. Behind the du Pont ancestral home is a designated National Recreation Trail along the banks of the Brandywine and formal gardens.*

- ***Mt. Cuba Center.*** *3120 Barley Mill Rd., Hockessin; (302) 239-4244; www .mtcubacenter.com. Six hundred acres of rolling hills devoted to conservation of native plants of the Appalachian Piedmont include woodland and wildflower gardens. Tours are seasonal.*

- ***Rockwood Park and Museum.*** *610 Shipley Rd., Wilmington; (302) 761-4340. The gardenesque landscape surrounding this gothic mansion resembles a formal English park with exotic trees.*

- ***Winterthur.*** *5105 Kennett Pike, Winterthur; (800) 448-3883; www.winterthur .org. With 1,000 acres of streams, meadows, and gardens to explore, Winterthur offers natural beauty in all seasons.*

visitors must be physically fit and over 12 years old. Reservations are recommended. Open May through Dec, Tues through Sun.

Winterthur Museum, Garden, and Library. 5105 Kennett Pike, Winterthur, DE; (800) 448-3883; www.winterthur.org. The former country estate of Henry Francis du Pont (1880–1969) is another example of aristocratic splendor in the Brandywine Valley. The sprawling house and exhibition galleries now house the definitive collection of American decorative arts, with 90,000 objects made or used in America from 1640 to 1860. The surrounding 1,000 acres of woodlands, streams, and meadows are punctuated by an 8-acre spread of azalea bushes and the Enchanted Woods, a fairy-tale garden in bloom during the summer months. Open Tues through Sun, 10 a.m. to 5 p.m. Tours are offered daily. Tickets are valid for 2 consecutive days.

where to shop

Moore Brothers. 1416 N. DuPont St.; (877) 316-6673; www.moorebros.com. Bring your jacket to shop at this excellent wine store whose thermostat is always set to cellar temperature. The handpicked selections favor small production, family-run European wineries with which the sommelier proprietors have a personal relationship. They run from affordable ($10 per) to extravagant, but the quality is consistent across price point. Personnel eschew snobbery for education and assistance, and the in-store tastings are an eye- and palate-opening experience. There's a small selection of dessert wines and cognacs. Open daily.

Riverfront Market. 3 S. Orange St.; (302) 322-9500; www.riverfrontmarketwilm.com. Set inside a historic shipbuilding warehouse, this covered marketplace on the revitalized banks of the Christina River is lit with European charm and contemporary urban flair. The vaulted ceilings and exposed brick walls encase a first floor lined with independent merchants selling produce, meats, seafood, baked goods, pizza, sandwiches, sushi, and other takeaway cuisine. The second floor provides additional cafe-style seating overlooking the activity (especially bustling during weekday lunch hours) below. Closed Sun.

where to eat

Corner Bistro. 3604 Silverside Rd.; (302) 477-1778; www.mybistro.com. The easygoing, affordable meals at this neighborhood bistro are served 7 days a week, for lunch, dinner, and Sunday brunch, making it an anytime kind of place. Delicate crepes filled with mushrooms, zucchini, and bacon, fish tacos with avocado mousse, and roasted half chicken served over white truffle mashed potatoes with braised Belgian endive showcase the chef's range. And then there's the Banoffee tart or angel food cake frosted with whipped cream and crushed Heath Bar bits. All of the wines are inexpensive and available by the glass or bottle. $$.

Domaine Hudson Winebar and Eatery. 1314 N. Washington St.; (302) 655-WINE; www .domainehudson.com. Downtown Wilmington's wine bar befits the city it calls home—glossy yet unpretentious, Domaine Hudson serves nightly dinner with flavors that pop. There's a frisée salad with pickled mushrooms, celeriac, and warm bacon vinaigrette; braised duck leg over *pappardelle* pasta with ricotta *salata* and pan-roasted quail stuffed with foie gras and pear. The wine selection is vast and globe-trotting, representing a range of varietals and prices. The daily happy hour offers a good value for tasting wines. Open daily. $$–$$$.

Fresh Thymes Cafe. 1836 Lovering Ave.; (302) 656-2026. The best bet for healthy morning and midday eats in Wilmington is this Trolley Square cafe, a mother-daughter operation with an emphasis on local and organic ingredients. The cheerfully decorated brownstone packs in 10 cozy tables and serves fresh wraps, soups, omelets, pancakes, and French toast with plenty of vegan and gluten-free options. But hearty eaters need have no fear that it's all eggless brownies and quinoa—there are bison burgers, buffalo dogs, and pulled chicken sandwiches, too. Closed Sun. $.

Lucky's Coffee Shop. 4003 Concord Pike; (302) 477-0240; www.luckyscoffeeshop.com. An old-school diner goes new-school at Lucky's. Open every day from 6 a.m. until 10 p.m.,· this nostalgic-looking spot obliges all patrons with classics like creamed chipped beef on biscuits, tuna melts on English muffins and dense wedges of meatloaf. But there are also plenty of fresh ideas here, like the BBB Waffle (Belgian style, with bananas, vanilla ice cream, and butterscotch sauce), the Lucky Devil (a deviled ham and pepper jack panini), and ongoing raffles for fun prizes. $.

where to stay

Hotel du Pont. 11th and Market Streets; (800) 441-9019; www.hoteldupont.com. Like so many beautiful landmarks in the region, this luxury hotel in downtown Wilmington has its roots in the du Pont family's fortune. Pierre S. du Pont commissioned the 12-story Italian Renaissance building in 1910, and the gilded wonder continues to be the city's fanciest spot for lodging. The 206 guest rooms and 11 suites are outfitted with luxury bathrooms and spacious bedrooms. All come with wireless Internet and access to an on-site fitness center and business center. Valet parking, afternoon tea, and salon services are also available. $$$.

Inn at Wilmington. 300 Rocky Run Pkwy.; (302) 479-7900; www.innatwilmington.com. A clean, quiet boutique hotel removed from the city center, the Inn at Wilmington has recently been renovated. Rooms come in standard queen, double queen, and standard king denominations, and there are also 2-room king suites with kitchenettes. All feature amenities including cable TV, wireless Internet, housekeeping service, and complimentary newspapers and toiletries. There's a fitness room with free weights, cardio equipment, and yoga mats; a business center; valet service; and complimentary continental breakfast. $$.

worth more time
old new castle

Six miles south of Wilmington at the head of the Delaware Bay, New Castle was settled by the Dutch in 1651 and went on to have a tumultuous colonial history at the hands of competing European interests. The town's charming brick-lined historic district stretches across about 20 blocks and features several hundred buildings that date from 1700 to 1940, mingling Dutch, colonial, and federal architecture. Highlights include the Amstel House, Stonum, the Booth House, and the Old New Castle Court House, which was the first statehouse of Delaware. Stroll around to visit these buildings, and stop into the small antiques and collectibles shops along the way.

day trip 03

southwest

 **port of call:**
chestertown, md

chestertown, md

Situated on the Chester River, Chestertown became one of Maryland's major ports in the 18th century and it continues to offer an appealing window into America's past. The restored stately homes of the merchant class are clustered along the river's banks, giving off a majestic and patrician aura. The county seat of the largely rural Kent County, Chestertown is home to Washington College. Travelers here find a mix of maritime and colonial heritage, along with quality shopping and a fair bit of natural history.

getting there

From Philadelphia, travel south on I-95 and pick up DE 1 South beyond Wilmington. Head east on DE 299, then south on US 301 to enter Maryland. From there, head west on MD 291 to enter Chestertown. Total travel time is about 1 hour and 38 minutes.

where to go

Artworks. 306 Park Row; (410) 778-6300; www.artworkschestertown.org. A community nonprofit arts center and exhibition space, Artworks mounts monthly shows spotlighting local artists, from painters and ceramicists to sculptors and fiber artists. The gift shop stocks decorative and wearable art from area craftspeople. The organization also sponsors annual

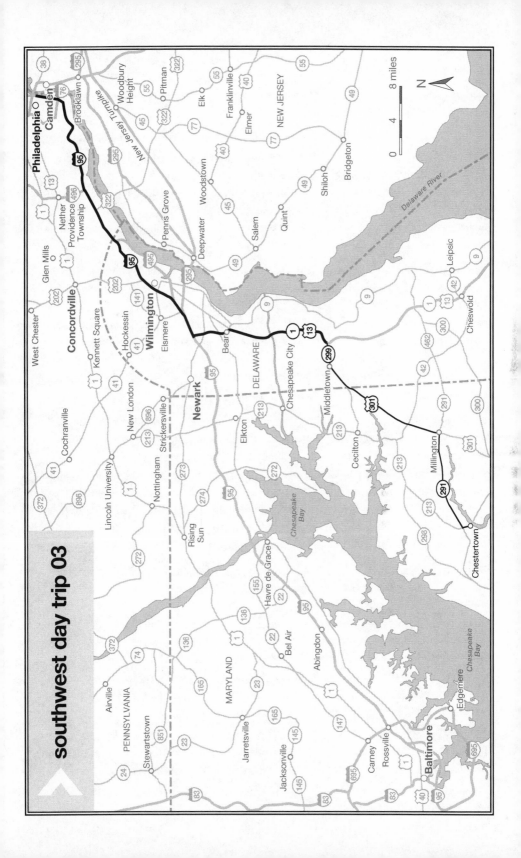

southwest day trip 03

studio tours in the fall. Openings are held on the first Friday of every month with a free reception from 5 to 8 p.m. Galleries are open Mon through Sat.

Chesapeake Farms. 7319 Remington Dr.; (410) 778-8400. This 3,000-acre research reserve with demonstration farm is open for self-guided driving tours from February through early October. Owned by the DuPont Corporation, the farms are devoted to advancing agricultural and wildlife management practices that are designed to be environmentally sound. The 16 stops include a waterfowl rest area, hedgerows, sunflower garden, cottontail rabbit habitat, and 40-acre marsh. The tour brochure is available on the Chesapeake Farms website. Free.

Farmers' Market and Artisans Market. High and Cross Streets; www.chestertown .com/market. Held on Saturday and Wednesday in the centrally located Fountain Park, the Chestertown Farmers' Market has been voted the top market in the state and its beginnings in the early 1980s long precede the current local-eating trend. Local farmers gather here to offer their plants, produce, and meats, plus value-added goods like natural beauty products, soaps, and fresh baked goods. The adjacent Artisans Market is set up by small local businesses and craftspeople, hawking everything from jewelry and clothing to painted furniture and pottery. Open Apr through Christmas.

Geddes-Piper House. 101 Church Alley; (410) 778-3499; www.kentcountyhistory.org. The brick federal building in the heart of Chestertown was the home of William Geddes, a regional customs inspector and possible owner of the brigantine *Geddes,* site of the Chestertown Tea Party. The town house was eventually purchased in the 20th century by the local historical society and now holds its archives and museum. The rotating exhibits are dedicated to Chestertown's merchant and maritime past. The society also holds special occasion tours and History Happy Hours on first Fridays. Open Tues through Fri from 10 a.m. to 4 p.m. and Sat from 1 to 4 p.m. from May through Oct.

Schooner *Sultana*. (410) 778-5954; www.schoonersultana.com. Recently constructed but modeled on an 18th-century design, this striking ship sails the Chesapeake, educating visitors on both the natural history of the watershed and the colonial history of the area. The original schooner was of mixed American and British heritage and it traveled between both coasts of the Atlantic until the American Revolution. The replica was built in 2001 and has been re-created with stunning detail. While it operates as a floating classroom for schoolchildren, the schooner also offers seasonal 2-hour sails to the public with ecology or musical themes. It's free to tour the ship when it's docked during occasional open houses.

where to eat

Fish Whistle. 98 Cannon St.; (410) 778-3566; www.fishandwhistle.com. Chestertown's only waterfront restaurant is also one of its best bets for round-the-clock eating. The house salad is strewn with red-wine poached pear, sliced apple, blue cheese, and spicy pecans;

the requisite crab dip is served on pretzel bread; and there are plenty of hearty entrees, like meatloaf and mashed potatoes, pork ribs with slaw, and oyster pot pie. Open daily, Fish Whistle has a late-night bar menu offered until 11 p.m. and Sunday brunch, plus daily food and drink specials. $$.

Lemon Leaf Cafe. 117 S. Cross St.; (443) 282-0004. This light and airy dining room demonstrates home-style cooking with plenty of local ingredients: Maryland crab cakes, oyster stew, and chicken and dumplings showcase regional traditions while flannel cakes with apricot syrup, omelets, and steaks come from a broader slate of American cuisine. Homemade desserts, like lemon pie and peach cobbler, are not to be missed. BYOB. Open for breakfast and lunch daily, and for dinner Thurs through Sat. Cash only. $$.

where to stay

Brampton Bed and Breakfast Inn. 25227 Chestertown Rd.; (410) 778-1860; www .bramptoninn.com. Listed on the National Register of Historic Places, this former plantation house is located a mile outside of Chestertown. The rooms of the 19th-century estate feature historic trappings such as working fireplaces and period antiques. They range from modest queen-size rooms to the Mulberry Cottage, replete with an infinity tub, breakfast nook, outdoor shower, porch swing, and hammock for two. The complimentary a la carte breakfast is crafted from ingredients from the estate's organic garden, and daily tea is served buffet style with fresh baked goods. $$$.

Great Oak Manor Inn. 10568 Cliff Rd.; (877) 502-6892; www.greatoak.com. The manor here is an enormous Georgian brick affair, situated on a 12-acre expanse along the Chesapeake waterfront. The 11 rooms on offer—decorated in period themes—include 2 two-room suites. Seven have water views and 5 have working fireplaces; some also have soaking tubs. Visitors can borrow bikes and kayaks, and in winter and springtime, the inn offers dinners with live jazz performances. Breakfast is a multicourse meal with the owner's signature crab quiche. Children are not allowed. $$–$$$.

day trip 04

southwest

bay city:
baltimore, md

baltimore, md

The largest seaport on the mid-Atlantic coast, Baltimore is a major metropolitan center with an interesting patchwork of neighborhoods and eclectic architecture. Founded in 1729, the cultural center of Maryland was named for the Irish Lord Baltimore, one of the founders of the original colony. The city sits on the Patapsco River, just above the mouth to the Chesapeake Bay, and its skyline is distinguished by what was once the tallest building in the US (the Phoenix Shot Tower) and what is currently the tallest equilateral pentagonal building in the world (I. M. Pei's World Trade Center). While the busy downtown with its famed Inner Harbor sees the most travelers, the charming neighborhoods of Fells Point, Charles Village, Mount Vernon, and Little Italy are worth checking out, too.

getting there

From Philadelphia, travel south on I-95 for 88 miles, then continue onto I-895 for almost a mile before exiting at Moravia Road. US 40 West goes into downtown Baltimore. Total travel time is just under 2 hours.

where to go

American Visionary Art Museum. 800 Key Hwy.; (410) 244-1900; www.avam.org. Opened in 1995, this unconventional museum on the south shore of the Inner Harbor

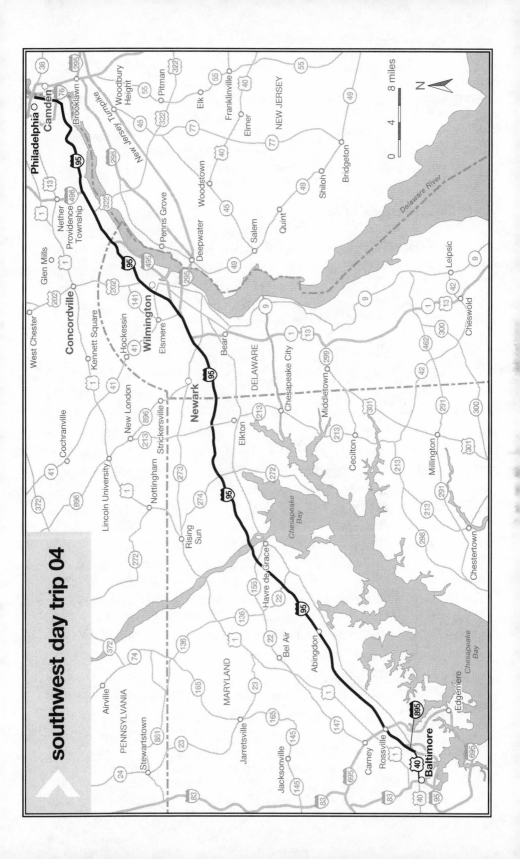

southwest day trip 04

highlights the work of self-taught, intuitive artists. The museum maintains a permanent collection of over 4,000 pieces and hosts changing exhibits organized by guest curators. Mr. Rain's Fun House is the on-site restaurant, and the cuisine is about as original as the artwork (which is to say very). There's also a Sideshow Shop with colorful displays of books, jewelry, scarves, toys, and original art. Open Tues through Sun, 10 a.m. to 6 p.m. Closed Christmas Day and Thanksgiving.

Babe Ruth Birthplace Museum. 216 Emory St.; (410) 727-1539; www.baberuthmuseum .com. Just north of Camden Yards, this row house was the home of the legendary baseball player Babe Ruth. The home and 3 adjoining houses were saved by the city in the 1970s, and an exhibit was installed there to honor the life and times of its famous son and his first official team, the Orioles. The nearby Sports Legends Museum was added on in 2005 to accommodate a wider scope of sports history. In the Babe's house, his original bedroom has been re-created—other displays showcase film portrayals of Ruth, his personal life, and the 500-home-run club. Both museums are open Tues through Sun from 10 a.m. to 5 p.m.

Baltimore Museum of Art. 10 Art Museum Dr.; (443) 573-1700; www.artbma.org. Founded in the aftermath of the great fire of 1904, the Baltimore Museum has a world-class collection of 19th-century, modern, and contemporary art from Europe and the US, plus ancient American, Pacific Island, and Asian works. A vast African art collection includes more than 2,000 objects from across the continent. American masters represented include Charles Willson Peale, John Singer Sargent, Thomas Eakins, Jacob Lawrence, and Henry Ossawa Tanner. Audio tours, cell phone tours, and podcasts are available. Closed Mon and Tues. Free, except for special ticketed exhibitions.

Historic Ships in Baltimore. Pier 1, 301 E. Pratt St.; (410) 539-1797; www.historicships .org. This maritime museum is actually a collection of military vessels: the US sloop-of-war *Constellation,* the US submarine *Torsk,* the US Coast Guard cutter *Taney,* and the lightship *Chesapeake.* Stroll the pier and tour the boats to learn about life at sea from the mid-19th century to the 1980s. Especially interesting is the *Constellation* Civil War ship that performed antislavery patrol, and the Seven Foot Knoll Light, a screw-pile lighthouse museum. Tickets are available outside of the ships, and there are discounts for multiple visits. Most of the walking is outside, so check the weather and plan accordingly. Hours change seasonally.

Maryland Historical Society. 201 W. Monument St.; (410) 685-3750; www.mdhs.org. The oldest continuously operating cultural institution in the state, Maryland Historical Society is the keeper of all things Maryland. The permanent collection includes over 2,200 paintings and miniatures; 900 pieces of furniture including many from Baltimore's "Golden Age"; Revolutionary and Civil War uniforms and flags; plus pottery, glass, and thousands of Native American and maritime objects. Special exhibitions focus on the region's evolution from colonial to modern times. Open Wed through Sat 10 a.m. to 5 p.m., and Sun noon to 5 p.m. Free on the first Thurs of every month.

Maryland Science Center. 691 Light St.; (410) 685-2370; www.mdsci.org. One of the oldest scientific institutions of its kind in the US, the Maryland Science Center is located in the Inner Harbor. First built in 1976, the current building was renovated in 2004 with a new addition. Exhibits span a collection of 2 dozen dinosaur skeletons, Maryland's aquatic life, and a view into outer space, with plenty of hands-on activities for kids in between. An IMAX theater and planetarium schedule regular shows. Open daily except Mon, Columbus Day, Thanksgiving, and Christmas.

National Aquarium in Baltimore. 501 E. Pratt St.; (410) 576-3800; www.aqua.org. More than 16,500 specimens live inside 2 million gallons of water contained within this public aquarium. Opened in 1981, it's the greatest symbol of the city's urban renewal and draws more tourists than any other attraction. There are 3 pavilions, each with several exhibits. Some of the highlights include Maryland's native fish, the tropical rain forest, and jellyfish. The glass pavilion is dedicated to Australian wildlife, and the walk-in aviary displays a river gorge inhabited by pythons, lizards, and barramundi. There are also dolphin shows, a shark tank, and coral reef displays, plus hands-on exhibits for children. Admission is by timed intervals; arrive early or buy tickets online to ensure getting in promptly. Open daily except Christmas and Thanksgiving.

where to shop

Antique Row. 800 block of N. Howard St.; www.shopantiquerow.com. This street in the downtown section of the city is lined with sellers of valuable and collectible wares and is

john waters's baltimore

*Baltimore native John Waters has memorialized his city in numerous films, and in his own twisted way, he has done quite a lot to bring attention to his hometown. An entire day trip might be devoted to a Waters-esque journey, starting with a stop at **Atomic Books & Atomic Pop** (3620 Falls Rd.; 410-366-1004), the unofficial Waters fan club headquarters, selling an assortment of the filmmaker's favorite things. Next stop: **Killer Trash** (602 S. Broadway; 410-625-2449), the quirky outfitter where Waters sources his characters' costumes. End, if you dare, at the biker bar **Holiday House** (6427 Harford Rd.; 410-426-6794), a central setting in the 2004 film A Dirty Shame. For more information on Waters's favorite spots, visit www.baltimore.org.*

itself an American antique. Between Drusilla's Books and R. Mark Mitchell's clock emporium, the stores run the gamut, including jewelry, art pottery, 19th-century silver, and chandeliers. While there aren't too many bargains, there are plenty of rare objects to peruse and ogle. Antique Row Stalls is a 2-floor, multi-dealer gallery featuring period furniture, modern designs, decorative objects, and fine art. Many stores are by appointment only.

The Book Escape. 805 Light St.; (410) 504-1902; 10 N. Calvert St., Baltimore; (410) 929-7653; www.thebookescape.com. This used and new bookstore with locations downtown and in the historic Federal Hill neighborhood carries over 40,000 volumes. The stock is well organized with large selections of all genres and chairs for browsing. Because space is at a premium, there are regular sales with very reasonable prices. Used books can be traded in for credit. The Book Escape also maintains an online business. The Calvert Street location is closed Sun.

Harborplace Mall and the Gallery. 200 E. Pratt St.; www.harborplace.com. The Inner Harbor harbors this shopping mall, a complex of 2 pavilions and a 4-story glass building, filled with a mix of national and locally owned shops. Familiar names include Ann Taylor, Banana Republic, Nine West, Coach, and H&M. This is the place to indulge in blue crab, Orioles and Ravens merchandise, Edgar Allan Poe memorabilia, and other local goodies. There's even a psychic/astrologer on the premises. The Gallery Garage offers affordable parking rates. Valet parking is also available. Open daily.

Patapsco Dutch Farmers' Market. 3321 Annapolis Rd.; (443) 682-9738; www.patapsco amishmarket.com. Known to the locals as the "Amish Market," this indoor marketplace is across from the Patapsco Flea Market, southwest of downtown Baltimore. The wares, as the name suggests, represent the culinary traditions of the Pennsylvania Dutch of Lancaster County—pickled salads, ham loaf, whoopee pies, shoofly pie, and hand-rolled pretzels, but there's pizza and Caribbean eats for a little more spice. Vendors also sell indoor and outdoor furniture. Open Thurs through Sat.

where to eat

B&O American Brasserie. 2 North Charles St.; (443) 692-6172; www.bandorestaurant .com. Named for the Baltimore & Ohio Railroad, this affable gathering place is located in its original headquarters, a Beaux Arts building in the Hotel Monaco. The inventively modern American cuisine is served all day from the demonstration kitchen. Breakfast and brunch items include slow-roasted pork belly hash and blueberry goat cheese pancakes with ginger syrup and cashew streusel. Lunchtime brings a falafel burger with spicy aioli and sweet pea ravioli with crawfish. Dinner goes all out with a mix of small and main plates: duck confit flatbread; rockfish with pumpkin seed "risotto"; and lemongrass crème brûlée. $$–$$$.

Charleston. 1000 Lancaster St.; (410) 332-7373; www.charlestonrestaurant.com. An upscale eatery in the waterfront neighborhood of Harbor East, Charleston has all the hallmarks of excellent dining, from its cushy dining rooms to its fine-tuned service. Dinner is a series of tasting menus, ranging from 3 to 6 courses, each of which can be paired with wine. With a French foundation and South Carolina flair, Chef Cindy Wolf's food is alternately rich and delicate: lobster soup with curry oil, grilled veal sweetbreads over potato puree, panroasted turbot over fresh artichoke and basil salad. Complimentary valet parking is available. Dinner only; closed Sun. $$$.

Nick's Fish House. 2600 Insulator Dr.; (410) 347-4123; www.nicksfishhouse.com. No visit to Baltimore is complete without a sampling of blue crab. Nick's Fish House is a good place to indulge, with both indoor and outdoor seating and a lively, family-friendly atmosphere. The fare is casual, even whimsical—witness the Forrest Grump Shrimp and the Hangover Grilled Oysters. And there's plenty of the coveted crustacean to spare, from the four-cheese crab mac to the traditional Maryland soup made with ham hocks and barley, and, of course, the crab cake dinner. $$.

Tapas Adela. 814 S. Broadway; (410) 534-6262; www.tapasadela.com. Fells Point's authentic Spanish restaurant is full of zesty charm. The neo-Moorish bar area is covered in bright tiles, while a courtyard offers extended seating in warm weather. The shareable small plates represent cooking traditions from across the Iberian Peninsula: garlicky shrimp in a *cazuela, manchego* croquettes with Arbequina olive oil, traditional blood sausage stew with pancetta and white beans. There's even a Spanish spin on the Baltimore crab cake. End with a classic plate of *churros y* chocolate and a glass of cava. Open daily for lunch and dinner. $$–$$$.

where to stay

1840s Carrollton Inn. 50 Albemarle St.; (410) 385-1840; www.1840scarrolltoninn.com. A series of interconnected row homes dating back to the 19th century form this lovely, luxurious inn at the center of the Heritage Walk in historic Jonestown. The decor is strictly luxe, with four-poster beds, in-room fireplaces topped with marble and oak, and oriental carpets. Many rooms feature whirlpools and separate showers. All have wireless Internet, flat-screen TV, refrigerator, and microwave. Breakfast is served in the first-floor parlor, the garden courtyard, or the guest rooms. Military discounts are available. $$–$$$.

Hotel Brexton. 686 Park Ave.; (877) 380-6708; www.brextonhotel.com. Brexton's Queen Ann–style brick castle first opened in 1881 and served as the childhood home of Wallis Warfield Simpson, Duchess of Windsor. The building was abandoned for two decades before being restored to its former elegance in 2010. Now one of the city's chicest boutique hotels, Brexton features 29 rooms with unique floor plans, ranging from queens to kings with sitting rooms and twin-bed nanny suites. Included in the daily rate is continental breakfast, afternoon tea, and wine and cheese reception. $$–$$$.

Inn at 2920. 2920 Elliott St.; (410) 342-4450; www.theinnat2920.com. Located just off O'Donnell Square in the Canton section of the city, Inn at 2920 has a chicly urban feel with exposed brick walls and tastefully minimal furnishings. The 5 guest rooms include a two-room suite. Each features a Jacuzzi tub and shower, free Wi-Fi, Gilchrist & Soames toiletries, and a flat-screen TV, plus access to the business center, free parking, and concierge services. Breakfast is included and friends and family can join at no additional charge. Romantic add-ons like wine, flowers, and spa services are also available. Children under 13 are not allowed. $–$$$.

day trip 05

southwest

small-town americana:
havre de grace, md; bel air, md

Northeast of Baltimore is Harford County, stretching from the shores of the Chesapeake Bay to an inland area dotted with horse farms and hillsides. Often overlooked by travelers who head straight for Baltimore or Annapolis, this largely agricultural area is just right for a short but leisurely visit to its cultural sites and well-preserved towns. This trip begins in the waterfront community of Havre de Grace, then winds westward to bustling Bel Air.

havre de grace, md

On the mouth of the Susquehanna River and the head of the Chesapeake Bay, Havre de Grace (aka HdG) was one of the earliest settlements in Maryland. The name, which means "harbor of mercy," reportedly was bestowed by General Lafayette, who said it reminded him of the French seaport of Le Havre. The pronunciation has since been Anglicized and much of the original town was destroyed during a shelling in 1813 by the British forces. Nevertheless, it was rebuilt with fine brick Victorian mansions that still line the streets of the pleasant downtown. HdG regularly attracts seafaring tourists with its marinas and yacht basin, and landlubbers with its recently rebuilt promenade and boardwalk bordering the bay.

getting there

From Philadelphia, head south on I-95 for 55 miles, then travel south briefly on MD 222 and west on US 40 to reach Havre de Grace. Total travel time without traffic is 1 hour and 16 minutes.

where to go

Concord Point Light & Keeper's House. Concord and Lafayette Streets; (410) 939-3213; www.concordpointlighthouse.com. The oldest continuously operated lighthouse in Maryland was built in 1827 to warn boats away from the currents and shoals at the mouth of the Susquehanna. The conical tower is topped with a 9-sided lantern that is still lighted nightly; the spiral staircase leading to the top is made of granite. Surrounding the lighthouse grounds is a tree-lined park. The restored keeper's house offers interpretive exhibits about lighthouse-keeping life and a gift shop. Open Apr to Oct on Sat and Sun from 1 to 5 p.m., weather permitting. Free.

Havre de Grace Decoy Museum. 215 Giles St.; (410) 939-3739; www.decoymuseum .com. Situated as it is between 2 major bodies of water, Havre de Grace has been a center for waterfowling for centuries, and locals have taken the art of decoy-making to great heights. This museum celebrates that historic and cultural legacy with a series of exhibits that explore the use and purpose of decoys and the evolution of waterfowling on the Susquehanna. On display are over 1,200 decoys from across the ages. Open daily except New Year's Day, Easter, Thanksgiving, and Christmas.

Havre de Grace Maritime Museum. 100 Lafayette St.; (410) 939-4800; www.hdgmaritime museum.org. Located on the intersection of the Chesapeake and the Susquehanna, the Maritime Museum is dedicated to preserving Havre de Grace's seafaring history, from the Native American inhabitants to the European colonists to the current population of the town. The museum's permanent exhibit tells the story of the colonists who left Jamestown and landed at the Upper Chesapeake, setting the stage for modern-day Maryland. Temporary exhibits showcase the art and culture of the region. Visitors can also stop into the Chesapeake Wooden Boat Builders School to watch students building and repairing vessels. Hours change seasonally.

where to shop

Arts by the Bay Gallery. 500B Warren St.; (410) 939-1818; www.artsbythebaygallery .com. This mixed-media gallery is a cooperative venture devoted to the best in local art. Work is submitted to a jury and rotated every few months, but at any given moment it might feature a selection of painting, jewelry, photography, ceramics, mosaic, works on paper, and sculpture. All of the pieces are for sale. Open Thurs through Sun, and during first Friday from 5 to 8 p.m., when the gallery offers special discounts. Appointments can be arranged during nonbusiness hours.

Bahoukas Antique Mall and BrewMania MuZeum. 408 N. Union Ave.; (410) 942-1290; www.bahoukas.com. Six dealers are gathered under one roof at Bahoukas, a whimsical 6,400-square-foot emporium for all things vintage and collectible. Among the goodies are toys, pop culture ephemera, jukeboxes, European oil paintings, Civil War items, and art

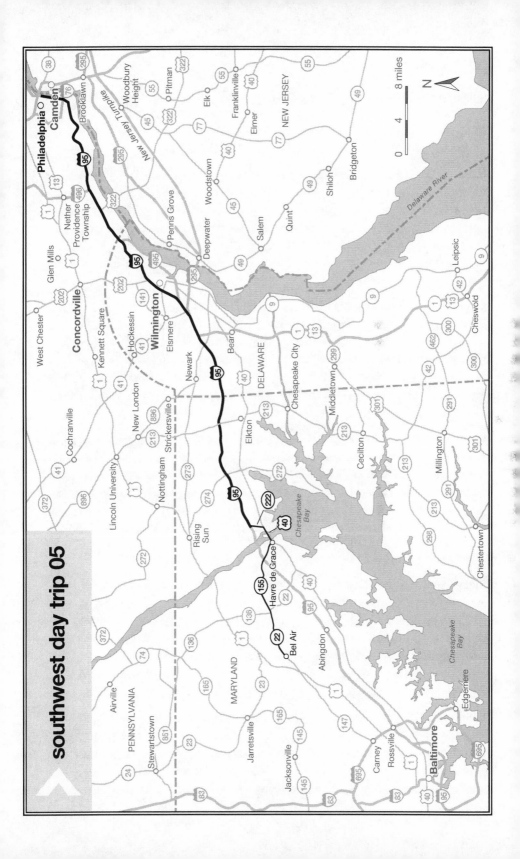

glass. Featured areas include the Man Cave, with NASCAR and sports memorabilia, and the BrewMania MuZeum, a major collection of beer- and alcohol-related items, from mirrored signs and furniture to taps and steins. Open Sun through Thurs from 10 a.m. to 6 p.m. and Fri and Sat from 10 a.m. to 8 p.m.

Havre de Grace Farmers' Market. Pennington Ave. and Washington St. Reaping Harford County's agricultural bounty, the Havre de Grace Farmers' Market stretches out along the town's Main Street on Saturday morning with an array of meats, fresh-cut flowers, plants, produce, and honey from local farms, plus alpaca products, soaps, and homemade ice cream. Live music adds to the festive atmosphere, and master gardeners are on-site the first Saturday of the month to offer advice and answer questions. Open Sat from May to the end of Oct, from 9 a.m. to noon.

Seneca Cannery Antique Mall. 201 St. John St.; (410) 942-0701; www.antiquesinhavre degrace.com. This 20,000-square-foot brick building was originally a tomato-canning factory, and later a hosiery mill, before becoming a large multi-dealer mall. In a town rich with antiques, Seneca Cannery is exceptional for its selection, along with a wide variety of stock. On view here are 2 floors' worth of furniture, pottery, vintage linens, pottery, costume jewelry, art, and more. Price points vary but there are some real bargains to be found. Open daily.

Washington Street Books. 131 N. Washington St.; (410) 939-6215; www.washington streetbooks.com. What was once an antiques shop with a few books has morphed into a major destination for book collectors. The 60,000 titles include rare books dating to the 16th century, first editions, out-of-print selections, comic books, military history titles, and an extensive general stock of new books. There still are also plenty of antiques on offer as well as fossils and crystals, jewelry, maps and prints, toys, and military items. Closed Tues.

where to eat

Price's Seafood. 650 Water St.; (410) 939-2782; www.pricesseafood.com. Price's promises the authentic Maryland crab house experience, bib and crackers included. Open since 1944, the ever-popular eatery is situated on the water. The atmosphere is bare bones—the better to make a mess in. All the regional suspects are on the menu: Maryland crab soup, crab cake sandwiches and platters, plus hot steamed crabs by the bushel. There's a children's menu and plenty of chicken and steak entrees for pickier eaters. Closed Mon. Open for lunch and dinner. $$.

Vancherie's. 419 N. Union Ave.; (443) 502-2465; www.vancheries.com. A Main Street institution since 1943, Vancherie's offers diner cuisine for breakfast and lunch, and an appealing dose of small town flavor. Crab omelets and crab eggs benedict are local specialties served with potatoes or grits. For lunch, there's a straightforward selection of salads, sandwiches and burgers, no menu descriptions needed and all reasonably priced.

Occasional specials like pumpkin-stuffed French toast or caramel apple topped waffles liven up the choices. Open daily 7 a.m. to 2 p.m. $.

where to stay

Vandiver Inn. 301 S. Union Ave.; (800) 245-1655; www.vandiverinn.com. This Victorian gingerbread mansion has been converted into a beautifully detailed bed-and-breakfast with 8 spacious rooms decked out in modern country decor. (An additional 9 rooms are located in the nearby Murphy and Kent guest houses.) While it's not a luxury inn, Vandiver offers a great value for the money. Each chamber has a unique floor plan—some feature claw-foot tubs, Jacuzzis, and/or fireplaces; others have private entrances. All include air-conditioning, cable TV, Wi-Fi, and breakfast. Monday evening features family-style suppers for added cost. $$.

bel air, md

Since its founding in 1780, the county seat of Harford has been more or less on the upswing—and it shows. The attractive small town is rich in green space, Victorian housing stock, and a picturesque Main Street lined with pubs and boutiques. While Bel Air functions quite well on its own, it's accustomed to visitors, as the annual Chocolate Festival, Farm Fair, and Maryland State BBQ Bash bring tourists to town.

getting there

From Havre de Grace, take MD 155 West for 7.7 miles to MD 22, then turn right onto Hickory Avenue and left onto Courtland Place. Total travel time is about 29 minutes.

where to go

Visitor Center at Bel Air Armory. 37 N. Main St.; (410) 838-0584; www.belairmd.org. Start your exploration of Bel Air at this information center, which provides the lowdown on local attractions, restaurants, lodging, and special events, as well as local merchant goods and gifts for sale. Open Mon through Fri.

Hays House Museum. 325 Kenmore Ave.; (410) 838-7691; www.harfordhistory.net. Named for Thomas Archer Hays, a prominent Bel Air landowner, the Hays House was built in 1788 and expanded in the 1800s. The small frame structure is the oldest in Bel Air and demonstrates the lives of rural gentry in the region during the 18th and 19th centuries, with period furnishings. The whole thing can be seen within an hour. Tours are given every Sun year-round from 1 to 4 p.m. or by appointment.

where to eat

Brooms Bloom Dairy. 1700 S. Fountain Green Rd.; (410) 399-2697; www.bbdairy.com. This creamery and dairy store serves light daytime fare in its rustic farm-room atmosphere: soups with warm biscuits or corn bread; quiche paired with yogurt and apples; sandwiches; and salads. Save room for dessert. The old-fashioned hand-dipped ice cream is made from fresh cow's milk in a wide variety of flavors, and customers have been known to line up for it. The store sells the farm's cheese, eggs, and sausage, as well as many other farm products from around the region. Hours are seasonal. Closed Mon. $.

Pairings Bistro. 2105 Laurel Bush Rd.; (410) 569-5006; www.pairingsbistro.com. The concept at this handsome restaurant is unique: Belgian cuisine is crossed with Mediterranean flavors, with some Chesapeake Bay flair thrown in for good measure. Menu items might include Belgian mussels with shallots, bacon, and blue cheese; coriander-rubbed duck breast over wild mushroom risotto; and/or maple crème brûlée. The kitchen emphasizes local and organic ingredients and each dish is designed to be paired with wine. In fact, there's a wine shop on-site from which to choose selections for dinner or for takeout. Open for lunch and dinner; closed Mon. $$.

Sean Bolan's Pub. 12 S. Main St.; (410) 803-1173; www.seanbolans.com. Main Street's Irish watering hole has roots in County Tipperary, and as such it offers a true Gaelic experience. The dark wood interior, pressed tin ceiling, and soccer matches on the overhead television set the stage for the traditional cookery: ploughman's lunch, shepherd's pie, bangers and mash, and fish and chips. For the less orthodox, there's Irish nachos and steak with Jameson whiskey cream sauce. The 16 taps feature a mix of Irish, English, Belgian, and American brews, supplemented by a long list of import and craft bottles. Open daily 10 a.m. to 2 a.m. $$.

where to stay

Country Inn and Suites. 1435 Handlir Dr.; (800) 596-2375; www.countryinns.com. This chain hotel has a surprising pastoral charm—with a fireplace, front porch, hardwood floors, and fresh-baked cookies, it's the closest Bel Air has to a B&B. The guest rooms are outfitted with cherry furnishings, microwave, refrigerator, and free Wi-Fi. The complimentary breakfast buffet is loaded with both hot and cold items, and there's a weeknight social hour with free hors d'oeuvres. The hotel is equipped with a fitness center, pool, lending library, and business center. Suites are available. $.

west

day trip 01

west

quilts, buggies & shoofly pie:
lancaster, pa; bird-in-hand, pa

The southeastern swath of farmland inhabited by German settlers was dubbed "Pennsylvania Dutch Country" in the mid-20th century, reflecting an archaic term for the immigrants. These days the population has changed and "Pennsylvania Dutch" is a descriptor used by tourists. The towns of Lancaster and Bird-in-Hand (as well as surrounding towns such as Ronks, Blue Ball, Paradise, and Intercourse) house the world's largest Mennonite population and second-largest Amish population, offering a rare glimpse into preindustrial, agrarian life, with working farms, exquisite handicrafts, hearty eats, and, yes, horse-drawn buggies. Scrappy downtown Lancaster is constantly undergoing revitalization, and though many visitors skip over the city in favor of the outlying areas, our day trip combines the best of both worlds: museums and urban dining, along with farm-dotted stretches of land and winding roads made for day-trip driving.

lancaster, pa

Lancaster is one of the oldest inland cities in the US, carved out in the bends of the Susquehanna River in 1734. Architecturally the buildings run the gamut, from the Germanic/colonial buildings of the 18th century through to the Art Deco structures of the 1930s. Around historic Penn Square with its Civil War Soldiers and Sailors Monument, it's possible to see Georgian townhomes, a federal mansion, an Italianate villa, and postindustrial storefronts. Like Philadelphia's, Lancaster's streets are arranged in a grid, and it's an easy city to

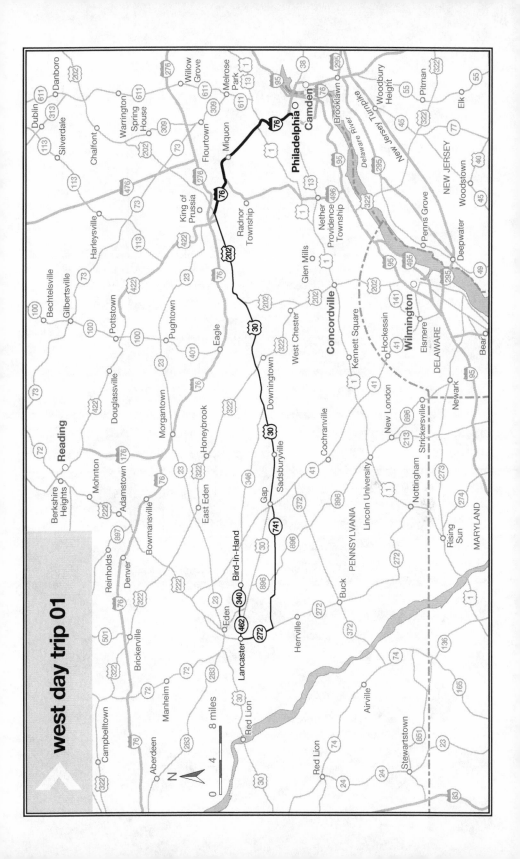

navigate. In recent years the city has hedged its bets on arts and culture, and there are many galleries, museums, and shops to explore.

getting there

From Philadelphia, travel west on I-76 toward Valley Forge for almost 17 miles, then take US 202 South to US 30. Stay on 30 for 24 miles, and then travel along PA 741 West for 9 miles. Head north on PA 272/US 222 to enter Lancaster. Total travel time is about 1 hour and 32 minutes.

where to go

Pennsylvania Dutch Country Visitors Center. 501 Greenfield Rd.; (800) PA-DUTCH; www.padutchcountry.com. The rural backgrounds of Lancaster can be confusing. Stop off here to orient and plan your itinerary. The well-established visitor center is staffed by helpful guides armed with stacks of brochures, maps, coupons, and tickets. They can also help with restaurants and lodging reservations, and a short film provides extra context. A 90-minute Amish Countryside Tour leaves from here periodically throughout the day, except Sunday. Center is open daily except Thanksgiving, Christmas, and New Year's.

Heritage Center Museum of Lancaster County. 13 W. King St.; (717) 299-6440; www .heritagecentermuseum.com. Located in downtown Lancaster in 2 buildings from the 1790s, the Heritage Center maintains a permanent collection of items typifying regional history and the arts, including furniture, portraiture, and decorative items. For the uninitiated this museum provides background on Amish culture including common misconceptions. On-site is a working 1920s print shop, where volunteers will help visitors print their own souvenirs. Hours change seasonally. On first Fridays, the museum stays open until 9 p.m. Free.

Lancaster Quilt and Textile Museum. 37 N. Market St.; (717) 397-2970; www.quiltand textilemuseum.com. The sister museum to the Heritage Center is housed in a dramatic Beaux Arts bank with a 64-foot barrel-vaulted ceiling. Inside the galleries is one of the most extensive collections of 19th- and 20th-century Amish quilts from the area, originally amassed by the founder of Esprit clothing. Special exhibits explore connections between traditional art forms and contemporary textiles. The museum store is full of heirloom crafts, including quilts, carvings, and weavings. Open on first Fridays until 9 p.m. Mar through Dec. Closed Sun and Mon.

Landis Valley Museum. 2451 Kissel Hill Rd.; (717) 569-0401; www.landisvalleymuseum .org. Lancaster's living-history village and farm reenacts Pennsylvanian German life from 1740 to 1940. Brothers Henry Kinzer Landis and George Dilelr Landis opened the museum at their family homestead in 1925. It has since been expanded to 100 acres with more than 40 buildings. Visitors can walk through the artisan craft shops, heirloom gardens, and farmsteads, led by costumed guides who explain Pennsylvania Dutch traditions. The

Weathervane Museum Store carries local crafts, including folk art painting, tinware, leather goods, wooden cabinetry, and more. Open daily until 5 p.m.

Mennonite Information Center. 2209 Millstream Rd.; (717) 299-0954; www.mennonite infoctr.com. To many in the modern world, the Mennonite and Amish ways are more than a little mysterious, and visitors to the region may find it difficult to interact in public with these notoriously private people. This information center sets out to demystify both religious sects. The theater has regular screenings of the 30-minute film *Who Are the Amish?* as well as the 17-minute film *Postcards from a Heritage of Faith* about the Mennonites. The center operates a store and regular tours to further acclimate curious visitors. Open Mon through Sat; closed Thanksgiving, Christmas, and New Year's Day.

Wheatland. 230 N. President Ave.; (717) 392-4633; www.lancasterhistory.org. The home of James Buchanan, the 15th president of the US, is a brick federal-style estate about 1.5 miles outside of downtown Lancaster. After purchasing it from its second owner, Buchanan lived here for 2 decades. It was declared a National Historic Landmark in 1961, and in 2009 the foundation that operates the house and the Lancaster Historical Society merged. Inside, the Victorian decor has been preserved, including the library where Buchanan wrote his inaugural address and presidential memoirs. Behind the home are a carriage house, ice house, privy, gardens, and pond visitors can tour. Closed Sun, Christmas, New Year's, and all major holidays. Tours are offered hourly most months of the year and by appointment from Jan to Mar.

where to shop

Angry, Young and Poor. 356 W. Orange St.; (717) 397-6116; www.angryyoungandpoor .com. Quilts and hexes are not everyone's aesthetic, and for those people there is this independent "punk shop," founded in 1995 by 2 locals. It seems almost inevitable that a store like this might crop up in Lancaster, and it's proven to be quite successful. The inventory covers just about anything the titular shopper might want, including 7-inches, CDs, and LPs; band-logo bags; studded leather; body jewelry; hair dye; sunglasses; books; and posters—not to mention a full line of clothing for girls and guys with an anti-anything attitude. Closed Sun and Wed.

Building Character. 342 N. Queen St.; (717) 394-7201; www.buildingcharacter.biz. Inside 10,000 square feet of historic warehouses are the 35 stores that make up Building Character. Most of the vendors are eco-conscious and use recycled materials; the wares include handmade jewelry, secondhand clothing and shoes, hand-painted furniture, soaps, vintage goods, local crafts, indie fashions, and collectibles. An entire store, Salvage Chic, is devoted to repurposed items made from architectural salvage materials. The building is tucked away behind a brick archway and down an alley. There's parking in a lot off Market Street. Open daily.

Central Market. 23 N. Market St.; (717) 735-6890; www.centralmarketlancaster.com. The true heart of Lancaster, Central Market has a long and storied history. The site has seen several buildings come and go, but the current market house was built in 1889 in the Romanesque revival style. Inside is a veritable smorgasbord of selections, from Pennsylvania Dutch staples like scrapple, headcheese, and meadow tea, to ethnic eats like pad thai, hummus, and baklava, to homemade fudge and ice cream. In between are vendors selling fresh-cut flowers, crafts, produce, meats, and bath and body products. Open Tues and Fri from 6 a.m. to 4 p.m. and Sat from 6 a.m. to 2 p.m.

where to eat

Gibraltar. 931 Harrisburg Ave.; (717) 397-2790; www.kearesrestaurants.com/gibraltar. A fine dining restaurant emphasizing Mediterranean seafood, Gibraltar is elegant enough for a special occasion but relaxed enough for a spur-of-the-moment meal. The house Bibb salad tosses gruyère cheese brioche croutons and pumpkin seeds with organic lettuces. Seared diver scallops are set atop black truffle mashed potatoes with porcini mushroom sauce. Rack of lamb is studded with a pistachio crust and drizzled with cherry port wine sauce. There's also a tapas menu for smaller bites. Open daily. Serves lunch and dinner on weekdays; dinner on weekends. $$$.

John J. Jeffries. 300 Harrisburg Ave.; (717) 431-3307; www.johnjjeffries.com. This cozy highbrow bistro, named for a tobacco inspector whose stamp was found on the floor beams, brings food trends full circle, marrying the sustainable ingredients and farm-fresh cooking of Lancaster County with big-city flavors. The menu changes seasonally but might include a crispy pork belly loin served over johnnycake with poached pear and maple syrup, pork and beef chili with sunnyside eggs, crème fraîche, and local cheese, or pastured chicken with cocoa mole sauce. $$–$$$.

Mr. Sticky's Homemade Sticky Buns. 501 Greenfield Rd.; (717) 413-9229; www.mr stickys.net. When stopping into the Pennsylvania Dutch visitor center, it's nearly impossible to resist the lure of Mr. Sticky's, which has taken this local confection to a whole other level. Varieties include the original sticky bun (dubbed the Extremely Addictive), the walnut sticky, the cinnamon bun slathered with cream cheese icing, and the cinnamon bun topped with peanut butter and milk chocolate curls. At $2 per, they're a little pricey, but worth both the caloric and the financial splurge. $.

where to stay

Lancaster Arts Hotel. 300 Harrisburg Ave.; (866) 720-2787; www.lancasterartshotel .com. A brick tobacco warehouse has given way to this urbane boutique hotel that's within walking distance of the city's galleries, restaurants, and shops. The 63 guest rooms and suites feature industrial-chic design, with exposed beams, brick walls, and plenty of original artwork. The room fee includes continental breakfast, Wi-Fi, taxi service, and access to the business and fitness centers. Some additional amenities are an iPod docking station, flat-screen TV, Turkish bathrobes, and wine refrigerator. The in-house John J. Jeffries restaurant (see above) is a standout. $$–$$$.

Lovelace Manor Bed and Breakfast. 2236 Marietta Ave.; (717) 399-3275; www.lovelace manor.com. With its ornate bracketed porches and 12-foot ceilings, this impressive building is an example of Second Empire domestic architecture and it's now home to a classic and comfortable B&B. The 4 rooms, named for poems by Richard Lovelace, have an old-fashioned feel but they're hardly fussy. All include TVs with DVD players, robes, en suite bathrooms, and free Wi-Fi. Common spaces include the Victorian parlor, billiards room, and business center. Spa services can be arranged. Hot breakfast is served in one of the dining areas. $–$$.

bird-in-hand, pa

The total population of this Amish and Mennonite community is 300 but Bird-in-Hand seems to loom much larger. Named for the old saying "a bird in the hand is worth two in the bush," the town was the basis for a 1955 musical called *Plain and Fancy,* which is sometimes credited for starting the region's tourist boom; motor inns, shops, and family-style restaurants followed, making Bird-in-Hand an ideal place for outsiders to soak in the slow pace of Dutch country life.

getting there

From Lancaster, head northeast on PA 462 East and turn left on PA 340 East/Old Philadelphia Pike, driving for 5 miles to arrive in Bird-in-Hand. Total travel time is about 16 minutes.

where to go

Abe's Buggy Rides. 2596 Old Philadelphia Pike; (717) 392-1794; www2.abesbuggyrides .com. Travel through the Amish country as the Amish do, by horse-drawn buggy. This company obliges with guided tours offered year-round on roads where cars rarely dare to go. There are 5 tours to choose from: 2.3 miles (20 minutes); 3.5 miles (30 minutes); 4.5 miles (45 minutes); 4.75 miles (1 hour); and 5 miles (1 hour 15 minutes). All are scenic views of the countryside; some ride over an 18th-century railroad bridge, others to a 1-room schoolhouse, and the longer excursions stop at an Amish home or Mennonite craft store and bake shop. Tours offered Mon through Sat 9 a.m. to 5 p.m., weather permitting.

Bird-in-Hand Farmers' Market. 2710 Old Philadelphia Pike; (717) 393-9674; www .birdinhandfarmersmarket.com. Proffering a mix of touristy souvenirs and authentic crafts from Bird-in-Hand's industrious citizens, the farmers' market encompasses 30 vendors.

Shoppers will find dolls and glider rockers, quilts and quillows, moccasins and sandals, and T-shirts and caps. The edible options include hand-rolled pretzels, pecan buns, old-fashioned candy, caramel corn, pickled relishes, locally grown produce, and smoked meats and cheeses. Open 8:30 a.m. to 5:30 p.m. Fri and Sat year-round; Wed Apr through Nov, and Thurs July through Oct.

Plain & Fancy Farm. 3121 Old Philadelphia Pike; (717) 768-4400; www.plainandfancyfarm .com. It's possible to create a whole day trip out of a single site in Bird-in-Hand: A truly one-stop shop for area visitors, Plain & Fancy Farm operates a tourable Amish Country Homestead, the Amish Experience Theater, Aaron & Jessica's Buggy Rides, and van-driven country tours. There's also a store with local crafts, bakery items, canned goods, and other souvenirs, and a snack stand with soft pretzels and hand-dipped ice cream. Rounding out the offerings are the Plain & Fancy restaurant, the Miller's Smorgasbord restaurant, and the AmishView Inn and Suites for lodging.

where to shop

Bird-in-Hand Village Antique Market. 2705 Old Philadelphia Pike; (717) 397-6820. Don't be fooled by appearances. This expansive showcase set in a red barn off an old filling station looks deceptively small from the outside. Inside there are 40 dealers, and while there are quilts and hexes to be found within, the wares go beyond local crafts. Collections include motor memorabilia, redware, glassware, jewelry, books, primitives, linens, holiday decorations, kitsch, magazines, and vintage pop culture items. Open daily from 10 a.m.

Log Cabin Quilts. 2679 Old Philadelphia Pike; (717) 393-1702; www.lcquiltshop.com. This decidedly new-school quilt shop was opened in 2007, but its owner comes from a quilt-making family that sold its wares directly from the farm to buses filled with tourists. The stores of handmade quilts, pillows, and crafts reflect traditional designs and techniques in a wide range of colors. Also on offer are patterns, fat quarters, charm packs, and dozens of fabrics sold by the yard and precut for the DIY type. Open Thurs through Mon from 9 a.m.

Lost in the Country Rustics. 3027 Old Philadelphia Pike; (717) 682-0399; www.litcrfarm tables.com. Those trawling for locally made farm tables will want to make a stop at this custom cabinet and furniture maker. Drawing from the rich store of ancient barns in the region, Lost in the Country exclusively uses reclaimed wood (old-growth pine, oak, fir, and American chestnut) as its starting point. Pieces are designed by Amish craftsmen, then decorated with milk paint and hand-rubbed finishes. The beds, cabinets, shelves, hutches, benches, tables, and chairs are simple and timeless. Hours are seasonal.

where to eat

Bird-in-Hand Family Restaurant. 2760 Old Philadelphia Pike; (717) 768-1550; www .bird-in-hand.com. Three generations of the Smucker family have perfected the recipes

pennsylvania dutch food

Dining in Amish country is one of its chief pleasures, as the lush farmland can inspire cravings for hearty, fresh food. Pennsylvania Dutch food is characterized by its European influences as much as the thrifty, homesteading culture of its settlers. Potato salad, soft pretzels, breaded cutlets, and pork and sauerkraut come straight from German cuisine. Pickled vegetable salads like chowchow, dried corn, and scrapple (a kind of sausage made with cornmeal and buckwheat) are the inventions of transplants and farmers stretching their resources. The smorgasbords can be a good place to sample many specialties in one go, though often these restaurants are a rushed, noisy affair. And be warned: This food is heavy, as it was designed to be enjoyed by people who work the fields and churn their own butter. Nevertheless, diners tasting their way through Lancaster County should not leave without having tried a slice of gooey, molasses-filled shoofly pie.

at this casual, convivial eatery, and they're banking on the fact that the country air makes tourists hungry. The menu features nonregional fare like burgers, club sandwiches, and crab cakes, plus local items like pork and sauerkraut and ham loaf with pineapple sauce. The smorgasbord includes a soup, salad, and bread bar, entrees such as pot roast and fried chicken, and a dessert bar laden with cobblers, cakes, pies, puddings, and brownies. There's also a children's menu and a buffet for kids. Closed Sun. $–$$.

Plain & Fancy Restaurant. 3121 Old Philadelphia Pike; (800) 669-3568; www.plainand fancyfarm.com. "Farm-to-table" before it was fashionable, this restaurant dates to the 1960s. The food is as down-home and hearty as one might expect. A la carte options include iced raisin bread, chicken corn chowder, ham steak with cider sauce, egg noodles with browned butter, pepper cabbage, and apple crumb pie. There's also an Amish Farm Feast, a 3-course, family-style meal served with sides, fresh-baked breads, and complimentary beverages. Open daily for lunch and dinner. $$.

where to stay

Bird-in-Hand Village Inn and Suites. 2695 Old Philadelphia Pike; (800) 914-2473; www .bird-in-handvillageinn.com. Four 19th-century buildings on the National Register of Historic Places have been preserved to offer visitors 24 guest rooms and suites overlooking neatly manicured grounds. All are decorated with period furnishings and include private baths, complimentary continental-plus breakfasts, tours of area farmland, evening snacks, use of nearby pools, hot tubs, athletic courts, and Wi-Fi access. Many also have whirlpool baths, fireplaces, and kitchenettes. Children under 16 not permitted. $$–$$$.

Orchard Inn. 44 S. Harvest Rd.; (717) 768-3644; www.orchardinnpa.com. Tucked away on a back road and surrounded by fields and fruit orchards, this motel emphasizes simplicity in a modern-country setting with just enough personal attention to set it apart from the chains. The no-frills rooms are clean and quiet and rates include a very basic continental breakfast, plus cable TV, coffeemaker, microwave, refrigerator, and bottled water. The modern conveniences keep travelers comfortable but the clip-clopping of passing buggies adds to the rural ambience. One of the best values in the area, and good for families. $.

day trip 02

west

vintage finds:
adamstown, pa

adamstown, pa

Straddling Berks and Lancaster Counties, Adamstown is a tiny borough that was settled by William Addams on the site of a Native American village. The village of less than 2,000 people is best known for its antiques trade. With scores of shops, marketplaces, and flea markets here, the moniker Antiques Capital, USA, is well earned and there's enough merchandise to keep any shopper busy for hours on end. While Sundays net the best cross section of open stores, visiting on the weekend means dealing with crowds—many day-trippers travel from as far away as Washington, D.C., and New York City. Either way, come early for the best selection, especially at the outdoor markets, which tend to close up by midday.

getting there

From Philadelphia, travel west on I-76. Take exit 286 toward US 222. Turn right on PA 272 North. The majority of stores and markets are along PA 272. Total travel time is about 1 hour and 20 minutes.

where to go

Mad Hatter Antique Mall. PA 272 and Willow St.; (717) 484-4159; www.antiquescapital .com. A former hat factory has been repurposed into a gigantic antiques mall with booths and showcases, featuring the goods of over 100 active dealers. Specialties here include wall hangings, dolls, advertising, vintage clothing, glassware, ceramics, retro modern goods, and linens. The sheer volume and depth of each collection promises great finds. The mall is air-conditioned and offers ample parking and clean restrooms. Open Thurs through Mon, 10 a.m. to 5 p.m.

Renninger's. 2500 N. Reading Rd.; (717) 336-2177; www.renningers.com. With 3 locations (the others are in Kutztown and Mt. Dora, Florida), Renninger's is something of a juggernaut in the antiques world. The original market was agricultural, but the owners transitioned to antiques in the 1960s as local tourism grew. Today the indoor portion alone boasts 300 booths with specialties like sports memorabilia, toys, 19th-century furniture, vintage kitsch, prints, tableware, and jewelry. The outdoor portion is more of a hodgepodge, but the finds are affordable. Special weeks bring "extravaganzas" focusing on themes. Open Sun only. Outdoor market hours are 5 a.m. to about midday. Indoor hours are 7:30 a.m. to 4 p.m.

Shupp's Grove. 607 Willow St., Reinholds, PA; (717) 484-4115; www.shuppsgrove.com. Situated in a lovely shady grove off of the main Adamstown drag, Shupp's was the original antiques market in the area, opened in 1962. It's still one of the premier stops here. Browse under the acres of trees for toys, furniture, vintage tableware, linens, books, records, advertising, and jewelry. Making the outdoor market a bit less rustic are a snack bar, coffee stand, and bathrooms on-site. Visit on theme weeks for special collections of political memorabilia, textiles, military gear, or holiday decorations. Open Sat and Sun from 7 a.m. to 4 p.m., Apr through Oct.

Stoudtburg Village. PA 272 and Stoudtburg Rd.; www.stoudtburgvillage.com. Adamstown lacked a proper village center, so the Stoudt family, owner of the Stoudt Brewery, has re-created a northern European hamlet here, replete with clock tower and living quarters. There's a plaza to stroll through with a fountain and scores of shops to browse—some selling antiques, but others offering wine, stationery, dolls, crafts, and cupcakes. There's a coffee bar and an old-fashioned soda fountain on the premises. Hours vary.

Stoudts Black Angus Antiques Mall. 2800 N. Reading Rd.; (717) 484-4386; www .stoudts.com. This expansive (70,000-foot) indoor antiques mall is one of the newer complexes in the area, and the 300 dealers tend to cater to the well-heeled shopper. For those not necessarily looking for a bargain there's a treasure trove here: Amish redware reproductions, clocks, Bakelite jewelry, Americana, folk art, midcentury modern furniture, toys, maps, art, and much more. There's also a deli and bakery in the complex. Open Sun 7:30 a.m. to 4 p.m.

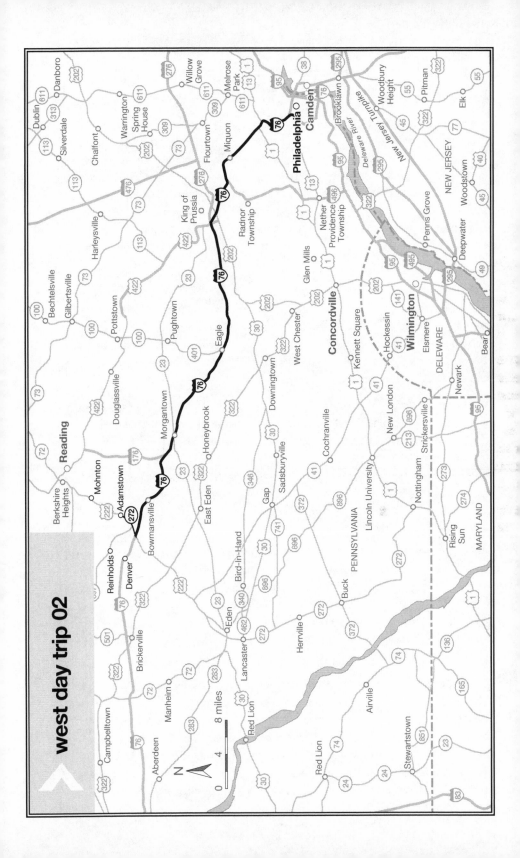

where to eat

Black Angus Restaurant and Pub. 2800 N. Reading Rd.; (717) 484-4386; www.stoudts beer.com. The Black Angus has been around for a half century, right at home along the strip of Adamstown malls, as it's decorated with antiques and political memorabilia. Settle into the homey dining room with one of Stoudt's flagship beers—there are usually at least 6 on tap, plus an engine-pumped cask—and some substantial pub fare (pulled pork and cheddar sandwich, German sausage platter, beef stroganoff). Open Mon through Thurs for dinner; Fri and Sat for lunch and dinner; and Sun for brunch and dinner. $–$$.

Black Horse. 2170 N. Reading Rd., Denver, PA; (717) 336-6555; www.atblackhorse restaurant.com. This 1730 tavern, part of the same-named inn, has gone modern with geometric platings, a bylined chef, and a menu of microbrews. The Philly cheesesteak pierogies are stuffed with braised short rib and cheddar. Parsley-and-horseradish-crusted salmon comes with tempura asparagus, shaved fennel, and whole-grain mustard sauce. Chocolate *pots de crème* is turned into a modern s'more with caramelized marshmallow and graham cracker crumbs. There's also a children's menu, and the tavern menu with happy hour specials has plenty of casual options. $–$$.

Boehringer's Drive-In. 3160 N. Reading Rd.; (717) 484-4227. When the antiquing is done, feet are tired, and wallets are lighter, fast food appeals. Open April to September, this classic "drive-in" serves homemade ice cream (lemon custard, butter brickle, and the usual favorites), milk shakes, sundaes, and root beer floats. The savory fare is mostly of the sandwich variety: barbecue burgers, hot dogs, cheesesteaks. Prepare for long lines during the height of the season. Grab a picnic table by the creek or take it to go. $.

where to stay

Amethyst Inn. 144 W. Main St.; (800) 594-4808; www.adamstown.com. Surrounded by balconies and gardens, this violet-hued gingerbread Victorian from the 1830s makes for a photogenic getaway. The Amethyst bed-and-breakfast belongs to a larger complex that includes a fleet of vacation cottages and a "vacation home." The main building has been converted to offer 6 guest rooms (2 are suites) freshly outfitted with antique heirlooms, handmade quilts, and lace curtains. All feature gas fireplaces, whirlpools, and a multicourse breakfast. $$.

Living Spring Farm Bed and Breakfast. 1737 Alleghenyville Rd., Mohnton, PA; (888) 329-1275; www.livingspringfarm.webs.com. Tucked into 32 acres 1 mile from Adamstown's antiques row, Living Spring has 3 rooms plus a cottage for guests, all with a distinctive farmhouse atmosphere. The rooms are country cozy, with fireplaces for added romance. All have private baths, and the Rose Room features a claw-foot tub. Amenities include complimentary snacks and beverages, cable TV, and bathrobes. Full breakfast is served on weekends; continental breakfast is served on weekdays. $.

day trip 03

west

revolution & royalty:
king of prussia, pa

king of prussia, pa

Though the name Valley Forge is used loosely to refer to the national park and surrounding areas, Valley Forge is more accurately a small town set on the Valley Creek. (The historic village has been partially re-created inside the park for visitors' edification.) Of course, this area is best known as the site where the Continental army spent the winter of 1777–1778 during the Revolutionary War, and the 3,500-acre expanse of history is a major draw (about 1.2 million people visit every year). Nearby King of Prussia had its own share of Revolutionary history—George Washington visited its eponymous inn during the encampment. The inn was moved during modern development and is now listed on the National Register of Historic Places; King of Prussia is currently more famous for its mega mall. Start your day trip at the park and finish with retail therapy.

getting there

From Philadelphia, travel west on I-76. Take exit 328A and merge onto US 422 West, driving for nearly 3 miles. Exit on PA 23 West and continue onto North Outer Line Drive to enter the park. Total driving time without traffic is 30 minutes.

where to go

Valley Forge National Historic Park. 1400 N. Outer Line Dr.; (610) 783-1099; www.nps .gov. Founded in 1976, this 3,500-acre park commemorates the winter encampment of George Washington and his army in 1777. Today it's equally popular among history buffs and outdoor enthusiasts. On the history side, start at the visitor center for a map and a list of the day's ranger-led tours. On weekends during spring and fall and daily during the summer, the park holds reenactments of soldier life. Trolley tours around the grounds also are available seasonally. DIY types can avail themselves of the cell phone tour. Sporty visitors can take advantage of the park's many trails for hiking, biking, bird watching, and horse riding. The park is open daily from 7 a.m. to dark; individual buildings have their own hours.

King of Prussia Mall. 160 N. Gulph Rd.; (610) 265-5727; www.kingofprussiamall.com. East Coast America's largest mall (as defined by retail space), King of Prussia is actually 3 separate but interlinked malls. The original component, the Plaza, is a semi-enclosed shopping center anchored by JCPenney. The Court came next, with Macy's, Bloomingdale's, and fancier shopping. More upscale still is the new Plaza, with Neiman Marcus, Nordstrom, and designers such as Kate Spade, Louis Vuitton, and Cartier. All told, there are more than 400 stores here to browse, plus dozens of restaurants, ranging from the food-court staples like Taco Bell and TCBY to the more elegant Morton's and Sullivan's steak houses. Open daily. Store hours vary.

where to eat

Creed's Seafood and Steaks. 499 N. Gulph Rd.; (610) 265-2550; www.creedskop.com. One of the few independently owned restaurants in the area, Creed's is a white-tablecloth establishment that caters to eaters with traditional tastes. The raw bar covers a nice

hiking at valley forge

The historic monuments and sites at Valley Forge National Park are in and of themselves a major attraction, but active visitors will also want to take advantage of the park's vast recreational possibilities. The Joseph Plum Martin Trail offers 28 miles of designated hiking trails that connect the historic and interpretive sites. The Horseshoe Trail runs from Washington's Headquarters to the Appalachian Trail. The Mount Joy and Mount Misery Trails offer a hilly challenge, while the River and Valley Creek Trails are flatter. Hiking is also permitted in the open areas of the park. Every June brings National Trails Day, sponsored by the American Hiking Society, with guided excursions, birding, and other special events.

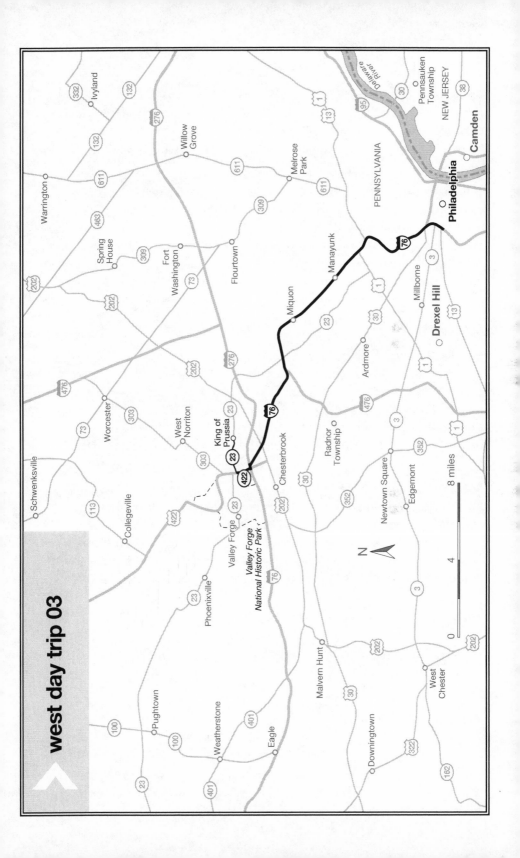

west day trip 03

selection of oysters from both coasts, and appetizers include wild mushroom soup with truffle croutons and a classic wedge salad. Fish is charcoal grilled and filleted; steaks and chops are pan-seared and served with a choice of sauces. Sit in the bar for lighter bites. Open for lunch and dinner Mon through Fri, dinner on Sat. Closed Sun. $$–$$$.

Seasons 52. 160 N. Gulph Rd.; (610) 992-1152; www.seasons52.com. A fast-growing chain emphasizing healthy eating, Seasons 52 is a welcome addition to the food-court cuisine of the King of Prussia Mall. The menu is sourced from seasonal ingredients and nothing is over 475 calories. The customizable flatbreads are a good place to start, as are the farmers' market vegetable soup and edamame with green-tea salt. Move on to a low-fat buffalo burger with guacamole and spicy sour cream, Sonoma goat cheese ravioli, or artichoke-stuffed shrimp. End the meal with one of the mini indulgences—pecan pie with vanilla mousse or classic red velvet cake. Open daily for lunch and dinner. $$.

where to stay

Crowne Plaza Valley Forge. 260 Mall Blvd.; (610) 265-7500; www.cpvalleyforge.com. Just across the way from King of Prussia Mall, the Crowne Plaza is an ideal overnight shelter for shoppers. Guest rooms include relaxation amenities, coffeemaker, refrigerator, premium TV, and Wi-Fi access. Club-level rooms are an upgrade, with courtesy bathrobe and umbrella, plus continental breakfast and evening reception. All guests have access to Bally Total Fitness Center. The contemporary American Stirling's Restaurant and Lounge is on the lobby level. $$$.

Dolce Valley Forge. 301 W. Dekalb Pike; (877) 851-5551; www.dolce-valley-forge-hotel .com. Situated on 9 acres of landscaped grounds, Dolce is a large hotel and conference center that has recently been updated. The 327 guest rooms range from deluxe king and double queen rooms to king junior and 1-bedroom suites. All are appointed with flat-screen TVs, Wi-Fi, and Aveda products. A 3-season heated outdoor pool, fitness center, billiards room, and complimentary shuttle service to the mall are available for guest use. $.

day trip 04

west

big small town:
west chester, pa

west chester, pa

Once known as Turk's Head, the borough of West Chester is the seat of Chester County, and it's the home of such varied phenomena as 19th-century clock-making, West Chester University, the Commodore computer company, the composer Samuel Barber, the shopping network QVC, and the television series *Jackass*. Unsurprisingly, there's a lot to see and do here. West Chester's compact downtown is rich in history from the Revolutionary War to the Civil War, and the entire area is listed on the National Register of Historic Places. Stroll along High Street to admire the Greek revival architecture or the 3,000 colonial structures scattered around. The walkable area around the university—particularly Gay and High Streets—is bustling with shops, restaurants, and bars that showcase this small town's sophistication. Encouraging visitors, the town keeps parking free on weekends in all garages and lots.

getting there

From Philadelphia, travel west on I-76, exiting at US 202 South toward West Chester. Travel for 16.7 miles, then take the Paoli Pike exit and continue onto Gay Street to hit the center of town. Total travel time without traffic is 45 minutes.

where to go

American Helicopter Museum. 1220 American Blvd.; (610) 436-9600; www.helicopter museum.org. The nation's premier aviation museum, library, and education center devoted to helicopters is, appropriately, based in the Philadelphia suburbs where 2 major manufacturers are headquartered. Within, the museum displays a narrative of aviation history as well as over 35 civilian and military helicopters, autogiros, and convertaplanes—some suspended, some climbable. Rides are offered on selected days throughout the year. The museum also features a gift shop. Open Wed through Sun until 5 p.m.; Mon and Tues by appointment only.

Chester County Historical Society. 225 N. High St.; (610) 692-4800; www.chesterco historical.org. Founded in 1682, West Chester has been remarkably well preserved, due to forward-thinking residents and no major fires in its past. Much of that ancient bounty can be found at the History Center, which contains a museum, library, photo archives, and an arts-promoting Cultural Center. The permanent collection, focused on the customs, traditions, and narratives of West Chester residents throughout the ages, is rotated through exhibits here. Expect to see locally made grandfather clocks, quilts, and furniture and clothing from the early 1700s. Open Wed through Sat 10 a.m. to 5 p.m. Closed Thanksgiving, Christmas Eve and Day, and New Year's Day.

QVC Studio Park. 1200 Wilson Dr., West Chester; (800) 600-9900; www.qvc.com. A major phenomenon of the late 20th century when it was founded and a still-thriving on-air and online business, the home-shopping network QVC opens its doors to the public. Guided walking tours reveal a behind-the-scenes look at multimedia retailing. Plan accordingly and you can also join the studio audience and watch segments being taped. This being an organization that's all about shopping, there's an extensive studio store with a sampling of items that are sold on-air and online, from cookbooks to beauty products. Tours are held throughout the day, 7 days a week. Closed on major holidays.

West Chester Railroad. 230 E. Market St.; (610) 430-2233; www.westchesterrr.net. One of the nation's earliest railroads, the West Chester Company operated out of the Market Street Station for 89 years, playing a vital role in the local economy and the region's growth. The recently (2009) revamped railroad offers pleasantly scenic 90-minute leisure trips along the Chester Creek between the towns of West Chester and Glen Mills, stopping at a set of historic stations on the way. Hours and theme trains change seasonally.

where to shop

Chester County Book and Music Company. 975 Paoli Pike; (610) 696-1661; www .ccbmc.com. One of the largest independently owned bookstores in the US, Chester County spans 28,000 square feet and serves as a de facto community gathering place. The extraordinary collection includes 125,000 titles, the area's largest children's department,

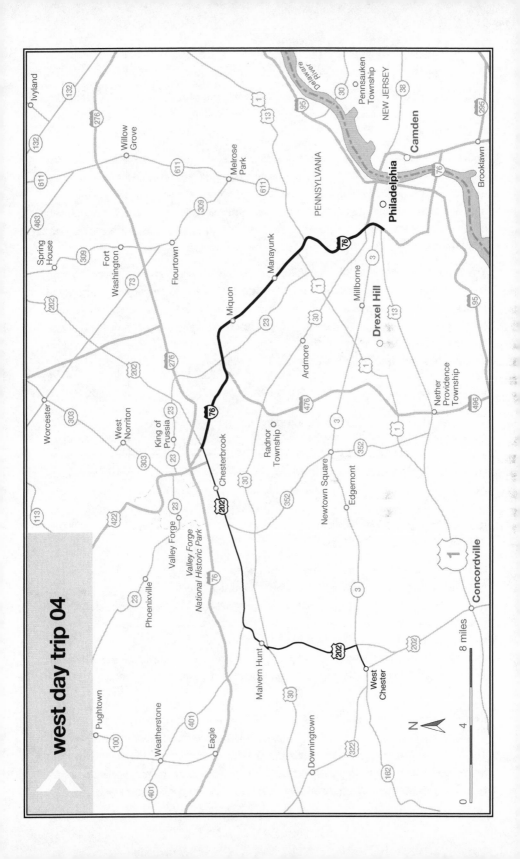

1,500 magazines, 25,000 recordings, and 5,000 DVDs. The staff is passionate about stock and actively hand-sells merchandise. There's even an in-store restaurant with a full menu of Cajun-style food, plus coffee, espresso, tea, and soft drinks. Closed Thurs.

Eclat. 24 S. High St.; (610) 692-5206; www.eclatchocolate.com. Foodies from all over flock to master chocolatier Christopher Curtin's boutique, which has gotten write-ups in *Vogue* and *Food and Wine* magazines. The selection is worldly and inventive: creative caramels in flavors like pear and calvados, single-origin mendicants, shiraz truffles, and bars with complements like toasted corn, caramelized hazelnuts, wasabi peas, and cacao nibs. Best of all, the staff offers free samples. Hours change seasonally.

The 5 Senses. 133 W. Market St.; (610) 719-0170; www.the5senses.com. Aiming for a shopping experience that can't be found in the mall, the 5 Senses specializes in unusual and affordable objects made by North American and regional artists. Hostess gifts like spiced nuts, funky wind chimes, and jewel-like soaps mingle with garden accessories and sculpture, glass and metal jewelry, cherry-wood kitchen utensils, fleece baby blankets, and block print cards. Open daily, and the store stays open late on first Fridays and third Thursdays.

where to eat

Dilworthtown Inn. 1390 Wilmington Pike; (610) 399-1390; www.dilworthtown.com. This historic tavern, set outside of downtown West Chester, has a convivial fire- and gas-lamp-lit atmosphere and plenty of charming colonial details in its authentically restored dining rooms. The chef offers elegant, internationally hued American cuisine—ginger crisp lobster over pound cake with pinot-cherry compote; lemongrass chicken breast with Kaffir lime *jus*; rack of lamb with merguez-stuffed olives and chimichurri sauce. Accompanying the fine food is a list of 800 wines, including the largest selection of port on the East Coast. Open daily for dinner. $$$.

Gilmore's. 133 E. Gay St.; (610) 431-2800; www.gilmoresrestaurant.com. An alum of Philadelphia's Le Bec-Fin, Peter Gilmore has taken his classic French training and transformed an 18th-century town house into a fine-dining destination in downtown West Chester. The dinner menu is divided into petite, *moyenne,* and *grande* portions, and the cookery is a mix of classic and nouvelle styles: seared ahi tuna with Asian pear and radish emulsion; panko-encrusted pig's feet with confit cabbage; fish served over creamed leeks with sauce Bordelaise; and butterscotch croissant bread pudding. Open daily for dinner and Sun for brunch and dinner. BYO. $$.

Iron Hill Brewery. 3 W. Gay St.; (610) 738-9600; www.ironhillbrewery.com. The West Chester branch of a local chain of brewpubs is a busy, occasionally noisy gathering spot. The craft beer selection includes a mix of house brews, monthly releases, and bottled reserves. (Samples are available on request.) The menu runs the gamut, from sports-bar-type snacks like nachos, sweet potato fries, and hearth-baked pizzas to quirkier choices like

Oktoberfest egg rolls and the Smoke House Burger with smoked gouda, barbecued onions, and bacon. There are plenty of gluten-free selections. In all, something for everyone. $–$$.

Nudy's Cafe. 300 W. Market St.; (610) 696-4550; www.nudyscafes.com. With 7 area locations, Nudy's is a local powerhouse of a diner, and it's no wonder. The menu of breakfast and lunch items treads the perfect line between familiar and enticing: gingerbread pancakes, grilled shrimp salad, crispy fried onion–topped filet mignon sandwich. The specials display more ingenuity, with build-your-own oatmeal and apple-cake French toast. The affordable prices, easy atmosphere, and solid service make it an appealing standby for students and their parents alike. $.

where to stay

Faunbrook Bed & Breakfast. 699 W. Rosedale Ave.; (800) 505-3233; www.faunbrook .com. Once the home of a Civil War–era congressman, Faunbrook is set in a 2-acre estate a few blocks from the downtown center. The 1860 home is embellished with period details like Monticello windows, mahogany millwork, and a wraparound porch, and it's surrounded by neatly manicured gardens, waterways, and a gazebo. The 6 rooms have a stately Victorian decor, with heavy wood furniture and drapery. Some have gas fireplaces and/or clawfoot tubs. The full breakfast can be served by candlelight or firelight. $$.

1732 Folke Stone Bed and Breakfast. 777 Copeland School Rd.; (610) 429-0310; www .bbonline.com/pa/folkestone. This stone farmhouse is named for its date of origin, and the owners have done as much as possible to retain its original character—evident in the open-beam ceilings and random-width flooring. Three guest rooms all feature private baths (not en suite), cable TV, and air-conditioning; each has its own style of period decor. Breakfast is served on heritage Wedgwood china by the fireside or on the veranda overlooking the pond. There's a 24-hour snack station for peckish guests. Great for a rural if not entirely private getaway. $.

day trip 05

west

capital cities:
hershey, pa; harrisburg, pa

Taken together, the two cities on this day trip into Dutch Country embody a world of contradictions. There's Hershey, Pennsylvania, a town built entirely around a chocolate factory at the turn of the 20th century, and whose industry still thrives on sweets and tourism. Farther west lies the state capital, Harrisburg, a relatively serious city that has played an important role throughout American history. This excursion starts at Hershey and moves on to the palate-cleansing Harrisburg.

hershey, pa

Chocolatetown, aka the "Sweetest Place on Earth," has a Willy Wonka sort of magical quality to it. After building a fortune with his chocolate factory, Milton Hershey decided to develop a community around it—what he considered a model town for his employees. He began with Hershey Park in 1907 and continued building through the Great Depression,· providing his own personal Works Progress Administration for the area. Today the town continues to flourish with more amusements, gardens, museums, and hotels, all catering mainly to families and the young at heart. Walk through the streets where the lights are shaped like Kisses and you'll still catch a whiff of the confections that paved them.

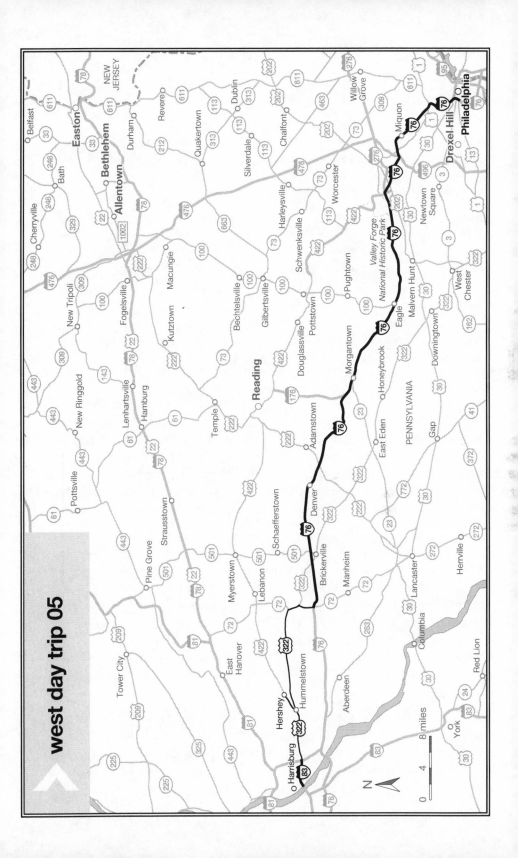

west day trip 05

getting there

From Philadelphia, travel west on I-76 for 60 miles, then pick up PA 72 on exit 266, and travel north for 2.6 miles. Continue on to US 322 West/Horseshoe Pike for 12 miles and turn right onto Cocoa Avenue to enter Hershey. Total travel time is 1 hour and 50 minutes.

where to go

Hershey's Chocolate World. 251 Park Blvd.; (717) 534-4900; www.hersheys.com. The visitor center in Hershey is the first place to stop and taste the town's chief export, learn about its history, and generally orient oneself to the area. Chocolate World offers an Omnimover dark ride tour through the chocolate-making process (not the actual production facility) with animatronic cows and other singing creatures. Visitors can create their own chocolate bars and experience the "factory" up close. There's also a 3D musical show, Hershey Trolley tours with singing conductors, and the Hershey's Chocolate Tasting Group experience, in which visitors can learn more about the nuances of the cocoa bean—all of which are offered throughout the day. Several shops and restaurants complete the world contained within. Hours vary seasonally.

Hersheypark. 100 W. Hersheypark Dr.; (800) HER-SHEY; www.hersheypark.com. This 110-acre complex started as a leisure park for factory employees but has since grown into a contemporary theme park with over 62 rides and attractions. The original carousel is still here, but there are also fast-whizzing roller coasters (11), a boardwalk area with water rides (seasonal), kiddie rides, shops, restaurants, strolling shows, and a concert auditorium that books major popular music acts. The ticket fee includes admission to ZooAmerica North American Wildlife Park. Hours vary and there are special events during Halloween, Christmas, and springtime.

Hershey Gardens. 170 Hotel Rd.; (717) 534-3492; www.hersheygardens.com. Once a simple rose garden commissioned by Milton Hershey as a gift for his wife, this 23-acre park and arboretum now encompass a Children's Garden with multiple play areas and a Butterfly House with more than 300 butterflies. There are 11 distinct theme areas that include perennials, herbs, seasonal displays, Japanese trees, and more. Open Fri through Sun from Apr 15 through late Oct, and select days in early Apr, Nov, and Dec.

where to shop

Crossroads Antique Mall. 825 Cocoa Ave.; (717) 520-1600; www.crossroadsantiques .com. Proving that Hershey's local treasure goes well beyond candy, Crossroads is a cooperative dealership set in a 2-story parabolic-arch barn on a former dairy farm that was used to supply milk for Hershey chocolate. Nine dealers offer an eclectic mix of wares: the Three Painters (framed paintings and photos); Homespun Heritage (quilts, primitives, and crocks); Toy Chest; Chocolatetown Memories; pottery; housewares; and automotive gear. Open daily during June, July, and Aug, and Thurs through Mon the rest of the year, 10 a.m. to 5:30 p.m.

Shops at the Hotel Hershey. 100 Hotel Rd.; (717) 533-2171; www.thehotelhershey.com/the_shops. Adding to the decadent ambience of the luxury Hotel Hershey is this set of 7 boutiques. The Jeweler sells rare Le Vian chocolate diamonds as well as an array of other precious and semiprecious designs—even some modeled after Hershey's Kisses. Other boutiques include Holidays (festive decor); Signatures (Hershey logo wear); A Storied Home (decor and gifts); Swing (golf items); Shine (swimwear); and the Spa Boutique (premium body care items made from chocolate). Hours vary; some shops are seasonal.

where to eat

Chocolate Avenue Grill. 114 W. Chocolate Ave.; (717) 835-0888; www.chocolateavenuegrill.com. Its name might suggest that this eatery is part of the Hershey chocolate empire, but it's actually an independently owned, family-friendly casual restaurant in downtown Hershey. The food is international and accessible, with burgers, sandwiches, and Philly-style hoagies dominating both the lunch and dinner menus. For bigger appetites, there's pork osso bucco, mango barbecue chicken, and crab cakes. Kids' menu available. Closed Sun. $–$$.

Hershey Pantry. 801 E. Chocolate Ave.; (717) 533-7505; www.hersheypantry.com. A warm and inviting spot, the Pantry has a mix of familiar and quirky bites for breakfast, lunch, and brunch: egg sandwiches on sun-dried tomato bread, homemade sticky buns, taco fries. Dinnertime brings Caprese-style rolled and stuffed chicken breast, broiled fish platters, and mushroom-stuffed pasta in garlic cream sauce. Afternoon tea and desserts (pies and cakes galore) available to go round out the offerings. On hotter days find a seat on the screened-in porch. Closed Sun. $–$$.

where to stay

Hotel Hershey. 100 Hotel Rd.; (717) 533-2171; www.thehotelhershey.com. The official resort of Hersheypark, the Hershey Hotel is designed to pamper grown-ups. The landmark building has 276 guest rooms decorated in tasteful brown hues and decked out with flat-screen TV, iPod alarm clock, coffeemaker, and luxury linens. On-site are a spate of boutiques, a full-service spa, and multiple restaurants. The hotel offers complimentary valet parking, shuttle service, concierge, babysitting, and a business center. Naturally, there's chocolate with the turndown service. $$$.

sweet pampering

Bringing every woman's fantasy to life, the Hotel Hershey's spa (717-520-5888; www.chocolatespa.com) offers a number of singular choco-tinged beauty treatments: cocoa massage, chocolate-bean polish, chocolate sugar scrub, chocolate fondue wrap, even a chocolate mani-pedi. The Everything Chocolate packages—Hershey Kiss, Hershey Hug, and Chocolate Escape—bundle the services into more affordable spa experiences. Proponents swear all of that cocoa has rejuvenating effects, but even if it doesn't, the spa offers some delicious-smelling relaxation.

harrisburg, pa

Set on the banks of the winding Susquehanna River, Harrisburg has been the capital of Pennsylvania since 1812, and the seat of Dauphin County for much longer. Its majestic capital building is an architectural marvel and there are plenty of historic sites amid the orderly streets and government buildings here. But unlike many capital cities, Harrisburg isn't all business—it's a living place bursting with arts, culture, and commerce. Second Street is the city's restaurant row, while Strawberry Square is its shopping epicenter. And at the heart of it all is City Island Park, a major hub for recreation.

getting there

From Hershey, travel on US 322 West for 7 miles to I-83. Travel an additional 2.5 miles, then exit at 17th Street to enter Harrisburg. Travel time is about 20 minutes.

where to go

City Island. 10 N. 2nd St.; (717) 233-7211. Within this municipal park set in the Susquehanna (and connected to the mainland by bridge) is a host of small, amusing attractions: minigolf, an old-time carousel, a kiddie train, batting cages, an arcade. Explore history with the replica of the John Harris Trading Post, take a paddleboat ride on the *Pride of the Susquehanna,* or stay ashore and tool around on a carriage ride. Or if it's the right season, watch a minor league baseball or soccer game at the stadium. Walking trails run the perimeter, and canoes and Jet Skis are available for rental.

National Civil War Museum. 1 Lincoln Circle at Reservoir Park; (717) 260-1861; www.nationalcivilwarmuseum.org. Founded by former mayor Stephen Reed, a Civil War enthusiast, this museum memorializes the conflict and its aftermath. A self-guided tour leads through the 10 galleries on the second floor and continues down onto the first-floor galleries and theater, where the video *We the People* is screened. Temporary exhibits take up the remaining gallery space on the first floor. On view are more than 24,000 artifacts, photos, documents, and manuscripts. Outside on the museum's grounds is the "Walk of Valor," a path laid with red bricks bearing the names of war veterans honored by their surviving descendants. Open Mon, Tues, and Thurs through Sat from 10 a.m. to 5 p.m.; Wed from 10 a.m. to 8 p.m.; and Sun from noon to 5 p.m. Closed New Year's Day, Easter, Thanksgiving, and Christmas.

State Capitol. N. 3rd St.; www.pacapitol.com. Actually the third capitol building for Harrisburg, this stunning Beaux Arts Renaissance revival dome is a National Historic Landmark and a regional treasure. The building was designed in 1902 by Joseph Miller Huston and is referred to as a "palace of art," for its stained-glass windows, murals, and sculptures. It was also dubbed "the handsomest building I ever saw" by then-president Theodore Roosevelt. The vividly painted rooms mix and mingle Greek, Roman, and Victorian aesthetics, and the dome is capped with green glazed terra-cotta tile. The building has been undergoing restoration since 2006 but tours are free and scheduled throughout the day.

State Museum of Pennsylvania. 300 North St.; (717) 787-4980; www.statemuseumpa .org. Part of the state capitol complex, this nonprofit museum honors the region's history and culture with 4 floors of exhibits and displays, plus a multimedia planetarium. From the prehistoric times through current events, and archaeology through zoology, visitors will find just about every era of Pennsylvania life covered. The 4 million objects include Susquehanna Indian pottery, rovers used at Three Mile Island, jerseys worn by famous athletes, and mid-century modern designs by Harry Bertoia. Open daily.

where to shop

Midtown Scholar Bookstore. 1302 N. 3rd St.; (717) 236-1680; www.midtownscholar .com. The nation's largest used academic bookstore takes up residence in a former 1920s theater building replete with neon marquee. Its 6 levels are stacked with over 100,000 used, rare, and discount books. Many are unavailable anywhere else, due to special arrangements with academic publishers. (The store's website offers 1 million volumes.) Browse the shelves and stop into the Famous Reading Cafe for an organic tea or Counter Culture espresso and check out the Yellow Wall Gallery featuring works by local artists. Open daily.

Plum Sport. 300 Market St.; (717) 737-4505; www.theplumclothing.com. Trendy fashionistas in Harrisburg flock to this boutique, which specializes in high-end designer sportswear for women and offers a one-on-one shopping experience with its helpful staff. Brands include Seven for All Mankind, Nicole Miller, Secondhand Yoga, Emu Australia, Michael Stars, and True Religion, among others. The pieces range from casual to dressy, all with a youthful flair. A sibling store, Plum, is located on Walnut Street and sells more exclusive brands. Closed Sun.

where to eat

Bricco. 31 S. 3rd St.; (717) 724-0222; www.briccopa.com. A collaboration between the Olewine School of Culinary Arts and Harrisburg Hotel Corporation, Bricco is a fine-dining restaurant with a sleek yet warm ambience that's good for romance as well as larger groups. Lunch consists of small plates of roasted vegetables, panini, and stone-oven pizza with toppings like Kennett Square mushrooms, *burrata,* and caramelized onions. The Capital City Lunch, which is $10 and includes beverage, is a great deal. Dinner gets more pricey, with raw-bar selections, house-made pastas, and entrees like day-boat cod with potato-leek hash and smoked olives. The wine list is extensive. Open daily, serving lunch and dinner Mon through Fri and dinner on weekends. $$-$$$.

Home 231. 231 N. St.; (717) 232-4663; www.home231.com. Off the main drag a block from the Capitol, this relaxed eatery is set in 2 converted row houses. The kitchen serves comfort food updated with local farm products and just enough twists to keep it interesting: smoked trout sandwich with hard-boiled egg and arugula, lump crab salad with curry vinaigrette, and fish and ricotta gnocchi with braised beef ragout. The dinner menu also has a hearty selection of small plates/bar snacks, such as chorizo corn dogs, polenta fries, and crispy rock shrimp with buffalo sauce. A small wine list is supplemented with creative and classic cocktails. Open daily. $$.

where to stay

City House Bed and Breakfast. 915 N. Front St.; (717) 903-2489; www.cityhousebb .com. Overlooking the river, this 4-room town house is the antithesis of the fluffy Victorian B&B. Grab a seat in the indoor garden room or exterior veranda for water views. The cleanly decorated guest rooms are furnished with king-size Westin Heavenly beds, private baths, LCD flat-screen TVs, iPod docking stations, and free Wi-Fi. Some also have river views and/ or fireplaces. Full breakfast, beverages, and sweets are also included. An easy walk to both the historic and downtown districts of Harrisburg. $.

northwest

day trip 01

northwest

mountaintop vista:
jim thorpe, pa

jim thorpe, pa

Often called the "Switzerland" of America because of its mountainous setting, Jim Thorpe serves as the gateway to the Poconos. The hillside town was originally given the Lenape name Mauch Chunk, or bear mountain, but it was later renamed for an Olympic athlete who was schooled nearby. In between it served as a major center for coal mining and the home base for a dangerous gang called the Molly Maguires. In marketing itself as a tourist destination, Jim Thorpe hasn't necessarily shied away from that dark but intriguing history. For skiers it's an obvious launching point—the Big Boulder, Blue Mountain, and Jack Frost resorts are nearby—but Jim Thorpe charms even nonsporting visitors with its steep and winding streets, its mix of intriguing architecture, and stunning scenery that promises beautiful views in all seasons.

getting there

From Philadelphia, take I-76 West and merge onto I-476 North toward Plymouth Meeting and travel for 60 miles. From there, take US 209 south to pick up Lehigh Avenue and enter Jim Thorpe. Total travel time without traffic is 1 hour and 47 minutes.

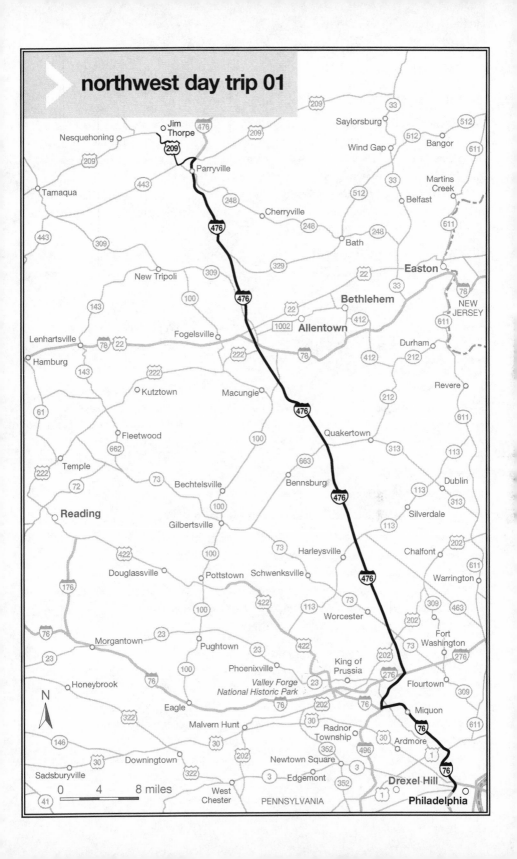

northwest day trip 01

where to go

Asa Packer Mansion. Packer Ave.; (570) 325-3229; www.asapackermansion.com. The home of Asa Packer, railroad magnate and the founder of Lehigh University, has been left virtually intact since Packer died in 1912. It's a marvel inside and out: The 1861 construction was designed by Philadelphia architect Samuel Sloan, and its cast-iron frame is capped by a red tin roof and belvedere. Tours run every half hour throughout the day. Tickets are sold on a first-come, first-served basis. Parking is at the train station lot. Hours change seasonally.

Lehigh Gorge Rail Trail. Lehigh Ave. (near the Carbon County Courthouse). This 26-mile multi-use rail trail traces the flow of the Lehigh Canal and connects Jim Thorpe and White Haven. The scenic path cuts through 4,500 acres of gorge with river and waterfall views, with some spottable wildlife (herons and beavers are often seen here). Leave from Jim Thorpe and you'll be riding uphill; many cyclists take a shuttle from Jim Thorpe to the opposite end for an easier ride. From the Jim Thorpe trailhead cross over the renovated iron railroad bridge to ride into downtown.

Lehigh Valley Scenic Railway. 1 Susquehanna St.; (570) 325-8485; www.lgsry.com. You don't need to be a train enthusiast to enjoy the dramatic scenery of the Lehigh Gorge from a passing vintage 1920s open-air coach. This 16-mile narrated route travels along the former mainline of Jersey Central Lines before passing onto the Lehigh Valley line, winding along the twists and turns of the Lehigh River. The diesel-powered trains have been updated with comfortable seats, and dogs are allowed on the 1-hour trip. Open May through Dec. Hours change seasonally.

Mauch Chunk Lake Park. 625 Lentz Trail; (570) 325-3669; www.carboncounty.com/park. This park on the outskirts of Jim Thorpe is designed to be enjoyed year-round. In summer the lake beach is open to sunbathers and swimmers, and fishing is permitted along the shoreline and from the pier. Canoes, kayaks, and rowboats can be rented from Boat Launch A. In the cooler months, there are trails to explore, by foot or by bicycle. Also contained within is the Carbon County Environmental Center, which features its own nature trails, butterfly gardens, and bird observatories. Campsites, cabins, and cross-country skiing are also available seasonally. Open daily 8:30 a.m. to 4:30 p.m.

Mauch Chunk Museum and Cultural Center. 41 W. Broadway; (570) 325-9190; www.mauchchunkmuseum.com. Jim Thorpe's colorful history is showcased in this Victorian-era church, from Lenape customs and culture, to the arc of the mining industry, to the life and achievements of its namesake athlete. A 30-foot working model of a switchback gravity railroad is one of the highlights. The museum also offers guided van tours of the town that leave from the train station at selected hours throughout the day. The museum store sells books and other media. Open 10 a.m. to 4 p.m. Closed Mon and holidays.

who was jim thorpe?

An unusual town with an unusual name could only be attributed to an unusual personage. Jim Thorpe was a part–Native American athlete born in Oklahoma and schooled in Carlisle, Pennsylvania, where he began his career in 1907. Thorpe played professional American football, baseball, and basketball. He also won Olympic gold medals in 1912 for the pentathlon and decathlon. The medals were taken away when it was discovered that he had been playing semiprofessional baseball for a salary before the Olympics, but were restored in 1983, 30 years after his death. The end of Thorpe's life was not particularly triumphant—he died of cancer after years of unemployment and alcoholism. But when the government of Oklahoma didn't build a monument to honor him, Thorpe's widow, Patricia, approached the government of Mauch Chunk, which bought his remains, erected a statue, and renamed the town after him, even though Thorpe himself had never been there.

Old Jail Museum. 128 W. Broadway; (570) 325-5259; www.theoldjailmuseum.com. The Carbon County Prison was occupied from 1871 to 1995, before it was converted into one of the town's most popular, albeit creepy, attractions. This is where the Molly Maguire coal miners controversially were hanged in the 1800s—touring visitors can still view the eerie handprint that one of the men placed on the wall as proof of his innocence, the gallows, and the dungeons used for solitary confinement. Regular tours are conducted every day but Wed from Memorial Day to Labor Day and on weekends only during Sept and Oct.

where to shop

Dreisbach House. 62 Broadway; (570) 325-2638. Set on the first floor of an imposing 1899 mansion on Jim Thorpe's major shopping strip, this gem of a vintage shop has been restored with gold ceilings and hand-stenciled walls. The specialty here is secondhand clothing and accessories—fur shawls, hats, scarves, purses, hats, and hatboxes. An entire room is dedicated to jewelry. The owner also maintains an interesting selection of dishware, books, and seasonal items, plus chenille bedspreads, table runners, and other home decor. Open weekends year-round.

Naturally Yours. 103 Broadway; (570) 325-8209; www.naturallyyoursorganics.com. Representing the newer, hippie-esque breed of Jim Thorpe resident, Naturally Yours is an eco-emporium that specializes in low-impact alternatives to everyday products. Fair-traded clothing for adults and infants is made from organic cotton, bamboo, alpaca, and hemp. Paper and jewelry are fashioned out of recycled materials. Also in stock here are natural personal care items, beeswax soaps, stainless steel bottles, and nontoxic cleaning agents. Closed Tues and Wed.

Pufferbellys Railroad Gift Shop. 36 Susquehanna St.; (570) 325-2528; www.pufferbellys .info. Already a magnet for railroad enthusiasts as a stop on the Lehigh Gorge Scenic Railway, Jim Thorpe indulges them further with this everything-trains store. On offer are both contemporary and nostalgic goods: model trains, license plates and tin signs, prints and posters, jewelry, logo caps, books, magazines, and DVDs. Visitors can also browse through aisles of toys, branded apparel (from Lackawanna, Reading, Jersey Central, Conrail, and other railroads), and plenty of other gift ideas. Hours are seasonal.

where to eat

Broadway Grille and Pub. 24 Broadway; (570) 732-4343; www.broadwaygrillepub .com. This affable restaurant in the Inn at Jim Thorpe was recently given an update but the exposed brick walls and gas fireplaces hearken back to Victorian times. The hearty breakfast menu includes maple vanilla French toast and huevos rancheros, while lunch and dinner offer equally accessible selections: nachos and spring rolls, bourbon-glazed meatloaf, and fire-grilled steaks. A decent beer and wine selection and homemade desserts like key lime pie finish things off. Open daily for breakfast, lunch, dinner, and late-night eats. $$.

Flow. 268 W. Broadway; (570) 325-8200; www.theccccp.org. Housed in a onetime factory from the 1800s, now a complex of art galleries and studios, this farm-to-table bistro aspires to big-city dining with local, seasonal ingredients. Plates come small (wild boar currywurst; bacon mac 'n' cheese; mussels in tomato ginger broth) and large (sea scallops with ginger carrot puree; vegetarian potpie; Asian pork noodle bowl). The desserts—blueberry lavender flan and chocolate-covered pretzel mousse—are one size fits all. Diners can look through a glass box to view the Mauch Chunk Creek flowing underneath the building. Open for lunch and dinner Wed through Mon. $$.

Moya. 24 Race St.; (570) 325-8530; www.jimthorpemoya.com. The brainchild of an Ecuadorian-born chef, Moya is named after his hometown. The fare, however, is contemporary American. The ever-changing menu might include goat cheese and asparagus salad with red beets and roasted almonds, roasted chicken with garlic and capers, and/or pork medallions with dried fruit balsamic chutney. The well-varied wine cellar stocks many affordable options, and Moya maintains a nice selection of Belgian and German beers. Hours change seasonally. Reservations recommended. $$.

where to stay

Angel of the Morning. 504 North St.; (570) 325-2961; www.angelofthemorningbb.com. Owner Rosemary Fauzio is a native to the Jim Thorpe area and has opened her personal home to guests. The inn, a half mile from the historic town center, offers just 3 rooms, all with private baths, cable television, and air-conditioning. Two have Jacuzzi tubs. Off-street parking is included and a full-course breakfast is served in the dining room. Tea and cookies are offered in the afternoon. Adults only. $.

Inn at Jim Thorpe. 24 Broadway; (800) 329-2599; www.innjt.com. This landmark building was erected in 1849, and the Inn at Jim Thorpe nicely balances its Victorian past with modern amenities. There are 45 rooms and suites in the main building, plus a recently refurbished building across the street and a small inn a few doors up. All have cable TV, Wi-Fi, and air-conditioning, and the suites also feature whirlpool baths and fireplaces. Spa services are also available. Overnight guests are given $7 vouchers toward breakfast at the Broadway Grille and Pub on the inn's ground floor. $–$$.

Times House. 25 Race St.; (267) 210-8130; www.timesjimthorpe.com. Set in the center of the historic district next to St. Mark's Church, Times House was once the home of Asa Packer's sons and later the home base of the *Times-News*. Its current incarnation is an upscale inn, conveniently located to the town's shops, galleries, and restaurants. There are 2 suites here, both with elegant high ceilings, antique furniture, queen beds, electric fireplaces, private baths, and sitting areas. Continental breakfasts with fresh-baked pastries are served en suite. No children under 12. $–$$.

day trip 02

northwest

the city the railroad built:
reading, pa

reading, pa

The seat of agrarian Berks County, Reading is perhaps best known for its railroad (made famous in the game Monopoly) and its outlet malls. And while the postindustrial era was not particularly kind to this small city, recent efforts are afoot to turn it into a cultural destination. Already there are two major art centers, a lively performing arts scene, and several annual festivals. Parts of this city look a lot like Philadelphia—Reading's streets are lined with 19th- and early 20th-century brick row houses. But then there's the Pagoda, a quirky and inimitable landmark that looms in the city's skyline on Mount Penn. Just across the Schuylkill River, West Reading is Reading's sibling city, with a revitalized Main Street along Penn Avenue. This day trip will take you to both.

getting there

From Philadelphia, travel west on I-76, then take US 422 West toward Pottstown, following Business Route 422 into Reading. Total travel time is 1 hour and 12 minutes.

where to go

Central Pennsylvania African-American Museum. 119 N. 10th St.; (610) 371-8713; www.cpafricanamericanmuseum.org. Set inside the Old Bethel African Methodist Episcopal Church—the oldest black-owned church building in Berks County and a stop on the

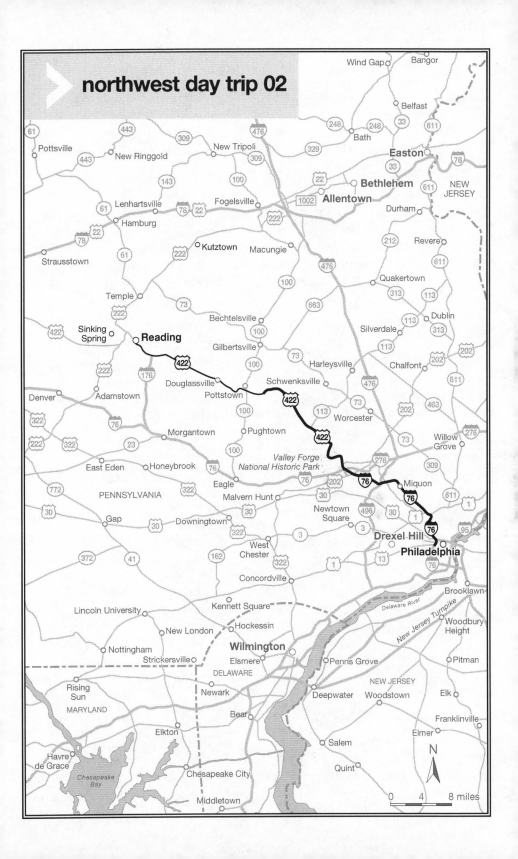

Underground Railroad—this museum celebrates African-American history and culture with an emphasis on the region. Exhibits display art, court documents, and artifacts from the 17th century to the present. Admission includes a guided tour of the museum and the cellar where runaway slaves were hidden. Open Wed and Fri 10:30 a.m. to 1:30 p.m., Sat from 1 to 4 p.m., and other days by appointment.

Goggle Works. 201 Washington St.; (610) 374-4600; www.goggleworks.org. Since 2005 Reading's community art center has taken up residence in a former eyeglass factory—in fact, the first optical glass factory in the world. Redeveloped in part by local businessman Albert Boscov of Boscov's Department Stores, the center has multiple galleries showcasing works by regional artists and beyond and has been a major part of the city's revitalization. A permanent exhibit is dedicated to the building's history and an art-house movie theater, cafe, and museum store are also part of the facility. Open daily from 11 a.m. to 7 p.m.

Historical Society of Berks County. 940 Centre Ave.; (610) 375-4375; www.berkshistory .org. The permanent collection here consists of some 20,000 items, including art by E. S. Reeser, Christopher Shearer, Victor Shearer, and Frederick Spang. The lower levels interpret local history with displays of a Conestoga wagon and 1902 Duryea, plus toys, furniture, musical instruments, and other household items. Changing temporary exhibits focus on other aspects of Berks County's history and culture, such as decorative arts. Open Tues through Sat 9 a.m. to 4 p.m.

Mid-Atlantic Air Museum. 11 Museum Dr.; (610) 372-7333; www.maam.org. Explore the history of aviation from hot-air balloons to classic airliners at this museum located at the Carl A. Spaatz Field, the area's regional airport. Inside the giant hangar are displays of military trainers, bombers, helicopters, experimental planes, and more. The museum also hosts public events, such as a World War II weekend air show, considered by some to be the best reenactment of its kind in the nation. Guided and self-guided tours are available. Open daily from 9:30 a.m. to 4 p.m.

Pagoda. 98 Duryea Dr.; (610) 655-6271; www.readingpagoda.com. Reading's oddest landmark is also its most recognizable—the Pagoda was commissioned in 1906 and built for $50,000 to cover a stone quarry. Originally intended to be a luxury resort, the Pagoda was abandoned when it was denied a liquor license and the bank foreclosed on the property. The building was sold to the city for $1 in 1911 and has belonged to its residents ever since. Notable features include 60 tons of terra-cotta tiles, the fireplace and chimney, and a Japanese cast bell made in 1739. Visitors can enjoy lunch and snacks in the Pagoda Cafe on the first floor. Call for hours.

Reading Public Museum. 500 Museum Rd.; (610) 371-5850; www.readingpublicmuseum .org. Combining art, science, nature, and culture in one fell swoop, the Reading Public Museum has a little something for every visitor. Three floors of galleries include both permanent and changing exhibitions. The fine art collection emphasizes painting and features such notables as N. C. Wyeth, Raphaelle Peale, Frederic Church, and Edgar Degas, plus a large number of works by Pennsylvania German artists. The natural-history collection includes insects, birds, mammals, and anthropologic specimens from Asia, Europe, and the Americas. A planetarium and 25-acre arboretum are also part of the complex. Open Tues through Sat from 11 a.m. through 5 p.m. and Sun from noon to 5 p.m.

where to shop

Fairgrounds Farmers' Market. 2935 N. 5th St.; (610) 929-3492. Philadelphia may have Reading Terminal Market but Reading has Fairgrounds Farmers' Market. This indoor wonderland for foodies is of the old-school variety—no fancy products here, just simple fresh produce, seafood, meat, cheese, grains, candy, local wines, spices, and baked goods. The restaurant vendors turn out Creole cooking, pizza, ice cream, doughnuts, sandwiches, smoothies, Polish delicacies, fresh pasta, and more. Go early to avoid the crowds. Open Thurs, Fri, and Sat.

Hello Bluebird. 609 Penn Ave., West Reading, PA; (610) 750-6642; www.hellobluebird .net. Part of West Reading's strip of independent boutiques, Hello Bluebird is a collective of artisans and crafters who sell socially conscious and affordable products on consignment. This means that shoppers are directly supporting the artists. Like Etsy come to life, the store consists of 2 floors of brightly painted galleries stocked with handmade cards, pillows, aprons, jewelry, baby gifts, tea towels, soaps, candles, and books. There's also a nice selection of vintage clothing. Closed Mon.

Tom Sturgis Retail Pretzel Store. 2267 Lancaster Pike; (610) 775-0335; www.tomsturgis pretzels.com. Located just outside Reading, the Tom Sturgis Pretzel bakery and store set up shop here in the 1920s, and it's the only major pretzel manufacturer left in the area. About 4 million pounds of the salty snack are produced here and sold at retail stores around the country. Nowadays the variations run beyond the classic Pennsylvania Dutch style to include chocolate-covered, low-sodium, and cheese-flavored pretzels, and in all manner of shapes and sizes. Store hours are Mon through Sat 8:30 a.m. to 5 p.m.

VF Outlet Center. 801 Hill Ave.; (610) 378-0408; www.vfoutlet.com. Reading's reputation as the "outlet capital" started here with the VF Outlet Store, an expansive all-purpose selection of products from Lee, Wrangler, Vanity Fair lingerie, Nautica, JanSport, and many more. In the ensuing years, a mall has sprung up around it, with factory outlets from Black & Decker, Jones New York, Dooney & Bourke, Reebok, Timberland, and others. Check the website or visitor center for additional savings and coupons. Open daily.

where to eat

Dan's. 1049 Penn St.; (610) 373-2075; www.dansrestaurant.com. Reading's preeminent fine-dining restaurant marries contemporary American cooking with French technique.

Located in the historic Penn's Common district, the restaurant maintains a spare and inviting atmosphere. The food is a bit more labored—vol-au-vent pastry stuffed with beef bourguignon, twin duck breasts finished with truffle honey, lemongrass crème brûlée—and the results are upscale if not groundbreaking. Gluten-free options are available. Open Wed through Sat for dinner and Sun for brunch and dinner. $$$.

Panevino. 25 N. 2nd St.; (610) 376-1101; www.panevinoreading.com. This Italian trattoria in downtown Reading emphasizes rustic regional cooking with some American accents. Steamed cockle clams are tossed with fregola pasta pearls and roasted zucchini. Hand-made pappardelle pasta is tangled up with braised prime rib and roasted pumpkin. And a double-cut pork chop is dusted with smoked paprika and fennel pollen. An expansive wine list includes over 150 selections. A menu of late-night bar fare is offered on Friday and Saturday evenings. Closed Mon. $$.

Tomcat Cafe. 2998 Penn Ave., Sinking Spring; (610) 678-1098. A funky, fun stop-off. Breakfast choices veer toward the unconventional with banana, peanut butter, marshmallow, and chocolate chip pancakes; Fruity Pebbles French toast; and an omelet stuffed with short ribs, crabmeat, roasted peppers, and blue cheese. Dishes are named for pop songs and singers (witness the Darling Nikki sandwich, with marinated portobello, roasted peppers, spinach, and mozzarella, and the Green Day crepes with spinach, asparagus, eggs, and goat cheese). Open daily for breakfast and lunch, and for dinner on Fri and Sat nights. $–$$.

where to stay

Bed & Breakfast on the Park. 1246 Hill Rd.; (610) 374-4440; www.parkbandb.com. This Queen Anne Victorian mansion was built in 1887 for a local merchant and a onetime owner of the Pagoda. Its historic character has been meticulously retained with original plaster ceiling medallions, chandeliers, and woodwork. There are 4 guest rooms with color themes—2 with private baths, 2 with shared bath—plus a carriage house suite. All are decorated with antiques in the Victorian style. Included are expanded continental breakfast, cable TV, and off-street parking. $$.

Overlook Mansion B&B. 620 Centre Ave.; (610) 371-9173; www.overlookmansionbed andbreakfast.com. A stately Victorian manor with formal decor, Overlook accommodates just 2 guests or 2 couples—though its owners insist that there could be some visitors of the paranormal variety lurking about. Both rooms are quite spacious and feature cable TV and mini refrigerators. The inn is situated in the Centre Park Historic District, about a 5-minute drive to downtown Reading. Light breakfast is served en suite and complimentary beverages and snacks are offered throughout the day. In-room massages can be ordered for an added fee. Children are not permitted. $$.

worth more time
kutztown

A half-hour drive northeast from Reading, the small borough of Kutztown is more firmly rooted in Pennsylvania Dutch Country and home to Kutztown University. The Crystal Cave is a natural wonder, known for its sparkling clusters of quartz, and visitors can take a 45-minute underground tour to see them up close. In summertime, the main attractions are the Kutztown Festival and the Kutztown Fair, held in July and August, respectively, both major events with live entertainment, food, amusements, and plenty of rural flavor. Also worth checking out are the Pennsylvania German Cultural Heritage Center and the Pennsylvania Dutch Hex Sign Tour, area wineries (Pinnacle Ridge and Blair Vineyards), and the excellent antiques shopping (Renninger's Market, Antique Complex, and a few smaller stores clustered around Main and Noble Streets).

day trip 03

northwest

cities along the lehigh:
allentown, pa; bethlehem, pa

Part of the limestone basin of the Great Appalachian Valley, this region northwest of Philadelphia is known to locals simply as the Valley—they take for granted the fact that the Lehigh River runs through it. But the river is the essence of this region, spurring its development from the 18th century on. At one time the Lehigh Valley produced the steel to build the Golden Gate Bridge and the New York City skyline. Its postindustrial slump well documented by the Billy Joel song "Allentown," the region has reemerged in recent decades with a focus on tourism and the arts. The major cities here—Allentown, Bethlehem, and Easton—each have their own distinct flavor.

allentown, pa

The third-largest city in Pennsylvania, Allentown began as a Pennsylvania Dutch community (Allenschteddel), then evolved into a market center and industrial hub in the 20th century. With most of the heavy industry gone, Allentown now thrives on the service sector. Visitors will find museums, historic sites, and arts events aplenty. The downtown area is a mix of nicely maintained Victorian and craftsman homes, high-rises, and converted industrial buildings. A holdover from its earliest days, the park system—the highest acreage of any American city—keeps the green spirit alive even in the midst of an urban downtown.

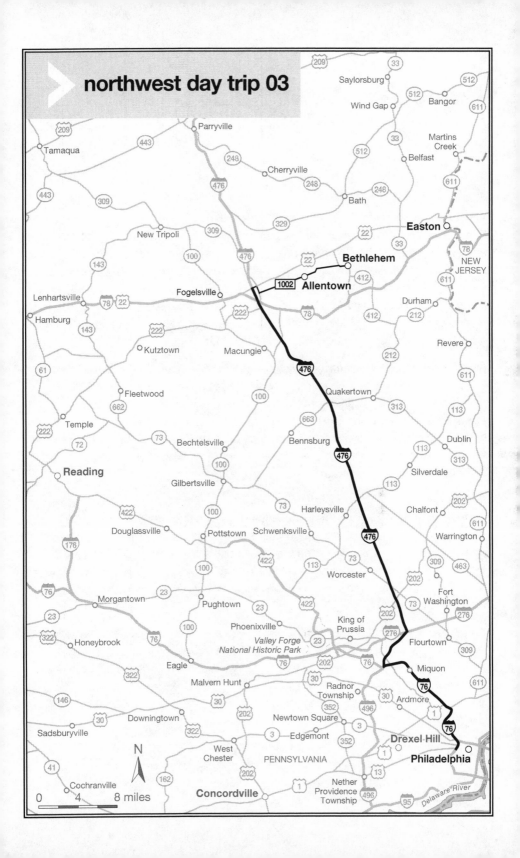

getting there

From Philadelphia, travel west on I-76, then north on I-476 for 41 miles. Pick up US 22 East for 4 miles and exit at 15th Street to enter Allentown. Total travel time without traffic is 1 hour and 19 minutes.

where to go

Allentown Art Museum. 31 N. 5th St.; (610) 432-4333; www.allentownartmuseum.org. Founded by Pennsylvania Impressionist painter Walter Emerson Baum, the Allentown Art Gallery quickly grew into this major cultural center, now housing 13,000 works of art spanning 700 years. Major holdings include the Kress endowment of 53 Renaissance and Baroque paintings and sculpture, a Frank Lloyd Wright–designed room, textiles, decorative arts, contemporary American painting and sculpture, and works on paper. A recent expansion designed by Philadelphia firm Venturi Scott Brown brought more gallery and educational space and a new gift shop. Closed Mon. Free on Sun.

America on Wheels Museum. 2 N. Front St.; (610) 432-4200; www.americaonwheels .org. One of the city's major redevelopment projects of the 20th century, this little boy's dream of a museum in a former meatpacking plant explores the ins and outs of over-the-road transportation. The 3 main galleries feature the permanent collection of over 75 bicycles, motorcycles, cars, and trucks, including the locally made Mack truck. The highlight for many visitors is the 1891 Nadig gas-powered carriage. Parking is available in a lot next to the building. Closed Mon and major holidays.

Dorney Park and Wildwater Kingdom. 4000 Dorney Park Rd.; (610) 395-3724; www .dorneypark.com. Allentown's hometown amusement park is one of the most prominent in the nation, initially founded in the Victorian era on a private estate. Over the years it has expanded with the addition of a water park featuring over a dozen rides and pools, 22 slides, 2 tubing rivers, 2 wave pools, and more. There are 9 roller coasters here among other rides. The Camp Snoopy kid's park area includes rides and activities for younger children. Hours are seasonal.

Lehigh Valley Covered Bridge Tour. (610) 882-9200; www.lehighvalleypa.org. There are just over 200 remaining covered bridges in Pennsylvania and 7 are in the Lehigh Valley. This tour is a self-guided drive covering 50 miles, from Allentown to Kreidersville, to view them. The oldest bridge dates to 1836. Many are closed to cars but all can be crossed by foot, and there are multiple sites for picnicking along the way. The map and brochure can be downloaded as a PDF from the website or mailed in advance.

Liberty Bell Museum. 622 W. Hamilton St.; (610) 435-4232; www.libertybellmuseum.org. While tourists in Philadelphia flock to see the Liberty Bell, many don't realize that it was actually hidden here in the Zion's United Church of Christ during the American Revolutionary War. This small museum honors that history with a replica, a hand-painted mural telling the story of the bell, Allentown's own "liberty bell," which was cast in 1769, and exhibits of the Revolutionary War and colonial America. Closed Sun and closed for the month of Jan. Hours change seasonally.

Museum of Indian Culture. 2825 Fish Hatchery Rd.; (610) 797-2121; www.museumof indianculture.org. The headquarters for Native American culture and history, this museum was founded in 1980. The Northeast Woodland Room displays Lenape (Delaware) tools, crafts, and trade, with displays of beadwork, pottery, and basketry from Northeastern tribes. Other collections include relics of the Little Bighorn and Custer's Last Stand, spirit dolls of the Hopi, and beadwork of the Great Plains tribes. The museum also hosts the Roasting Ears of Corn Festival—Pennsylvania's oldest—in August. Guided tours are available Fri through Sun from noon to 4 p.m.

where to shop

Allentown Fairgrounds Farmers' Market. 17th and Chew Streets; (610) 432-8425; www.fairgroundfarmersmkt.com. Hearkening back to Allentown's days as a Pennsylvania Dutch settlement, this farmers' market is the best local source for traditional foods such as ring bologna, scrapple, chowchow, kiffles, and more. Local farms sell their conventional and organic produce direct to consumers, while gourmet stands stock exotic horseradish, pierogies, New York–style deli sandwiches, southern-style ribs, and cheeses from around the world. Eat on the premises or take selections to go. Open Thurs, Fri, and Sat.

Merchants Square Mall. 12 S. Vultee Rd.; www.merchantssquaremall.com. A former production facility for US Navy torpedo bombers has since been transformed into a mega-store with multiple dealers. Antiques and vintage goods vendors sit alongside specialty shops featuring contemporary crafts, fashion, accessories, sewing materials, and a model train museum. Regular special theme shows in the 10,000-square-foot showroom might showcase records, comics and sci-fi memorabilia, sports collectibles, or antique toys. Open Fri, Sat, and Sun.

where to eat

Fat Boys House of BBQ. 652 Union Blvd.; (484) 240-1744; www.fatboyshouseofbbq .com. Started by a local couple with a serious barbecue hobby, this mobile truck serves what many consider to be the best smoked meat in the valley. Sandwiches include classic pulled pork and brisket, as well as some original inventions topped with coleslaw, fries, and barbecue sauce. The hefty platters include a choice of meat (chicken, pork, brisket, ribs, or combinations thereof) with 2 sides (the mac and cheese is a favorite) and a roll or hush puppies. Follow the Twitter feed (@fbhouseofbbq) for the latest location. $.

Yocco's. 625 Liberty St.; (610) 433-1950; 2128 Hamilton St.; (610) 821-8488; 1930 Cat-sauqua Rd.; (610) 264-1884; www.yoccos.com. With 3 area locations, Yocco's has the lock on local hot-doggery. The atmosphere is bare bones and the offerings here are simple and cheap: burgers, sausages, cheesesteaks, fish fillets and chicken sandwiches, crispy fried pierogies. The signature special is a frankfurter on a steamed roll with chopped onions, tangy mustard, and the meaty house chili sauce. Check individual locations for hours, but all are open daily. $.

where to stay

Glasbern Country Inn. 2141 Packhouse Rd., Fogelsville, PA; (800) 313-0885; www .glasbern.com. Just west of Allentown, this historic inn, named for a "glass barn" on the property, is set on a 130-acre estate, making it the perfect retreat for a city-country get-away. Most of the 19th-century buildings have been restored and there's a spa, heated swimming pool, and elegant restaurant with farm-to-table cuisine on the premises. With room for 34 guests, the Glasbern has a range of options, from 2-story suites with steam showers, patios, and 2-person whirlpools to simpler standard guest rooms. Breakfast is included. $$$.

bethlehem, pa

Originally settled by a group of Moravians, a Protestant sect persecuted in their native Germany and Czech Republic, Bethlehem supposedly was founded on Christmas Eve and thus, named for the biblical town where Jesus was born. The small city lies squarely in the middle of the Lehigh Valley, and for a time Bethlehem was its center for trade. While the town has since grown more diverse than its early population, holiday time remains a popular season to visit, with an annual Peace Pilgrimage from nearby Nazareth ending here. Despite the rise and fall of industry, much of the historic downtown has been left intact and is now inhabited by small boutiques, restaurants, spas, and nightclubs. Other local draws include a recently built Sands Casino and the annual summer gathering Musikfest.

getting there

From Allentown, take PA 1002 West/Tilghman Street for 5 miles into Bethlehem. Total travel time is about 16 minutes.

where to go

Historic Bethlehem Visitor Center and Museum Store. 505 Main St.; (610) 691-6055; www.historicbethlehem.org. As an umbrella organization for the city's multiple historic sites and museums, Historic Bethlehem operates this welcome center. Come here for tickets, information, and maps. Those with special needs planning to visit the city's 19th-century buildings are also accommodated here. All of the historic sites are within walking distance.

christmas in bethlehem (pa)

Dubbed Christmas City since its founding in the 18th century, Bethlehem has always been closely intertwined with Yuletide. For tourists December can be a special time to visit. The city burns bright with live arts performances, tours, horse-drawn carriage rides, and decorations and displays aplenty. Every December "peace pilgrims" walk 10 miles from Nazareth to Bethlehem to promote nonvio-lence. Another big event is the holiday bazaar Christkindlmarkt, held on weekends in November and December. See www.christmascity.org for the latest updates.

There's public parking at the garages on North Street and Walnut Street and metered parking on side streets. Closed Mon.

ArtsQuest Center at SteelStacks. 101 Founders Way; (610) 332-1300; www.artsquest .org. ArtsQuest is a community nonprofit that hosts annual events such as Musikfest and an arts and crafts bazaar at Christmastime. Most recently it has taken up residence in the former headquarters of Bethlehem Steel. This performing-arts campus features 3 outdoor performance venues, an art-house cinema, and a high-tech "connect zone" with video games and computers. There's also a bistro here, named for the local candy Mike and Ike. Open daily.

Banana Factory. 25 W. 3rd St.; (610) 332-1300; www.bananafactory.org. Bethlehem's other visitor center is housed in this repurposed warehouse and distribution center. Now an art center with 3 contemporary galleries, the Factory also shows a film about the city's history. The arts studios are open to the public on first Fridays with free demonstrations by glass blowers and ceramists and galleries offering works for sale. The gift shop is closed Sun and Mon, but the center is open daily.

Burnside Plantation. 1461 Schoenersville Rd.; (610) 691-6055; www.historicbethlehem .org. The homestead of James Burnside was set along the Monocacy Creek on a green stretch of land and known as the "farm in the city." It remains one of Bethlehem's major historic attractions. The property encompasses an 18th-century farmhouse, summer kitchen, garden, orchard, 2 barns, and other outbuildings. Buildings are not open to the public but the grounds are free for strolling. Self-guided visits and group tours are available. Open year-round, dawn to dusk. Free; donations are appreciated.

Kemerer Museum of Decorative Arts. 427 N. New St.; (610) 691-6055; www.historic bethlehem.org. This manor house is now used to display local history and aesthetics going back 300 years. Period rooms are embellished with furnishings, paintings, decorative arts, Bohemian glass, clocks, folk art, and textiles. The permanent collection of cast-iron toys, dollhouses, maps, and prints on display brings the past to life. Changing exhibits highlight design through selected eras. Open Fri through Sun from noon to 4 p.m. Admission for children under 6 is free.

National Museum of Industrial History. 530 E. 3rd St.; (610) 694-6644; www.nmih.org. With heavy industry as such a driving force in the Lehigh Valley's history, it makes sense that this newly opened Smithsonian-affiliated institution would be headquartered here, across from the former Bethlehem Steel facility. Exhibits explain how the Industrial Revolution and ensuing decades impacted American society through its economy, scientific advances, and worker relations. On view are textile machines, farm implements, and models of plants, many on loan from the Smithsonian. Call for hours. Free.

where to shop

The Attic. 516 Main St.; (610) 865-2210; www.atticclothes.com. The second location of a local mini chain, the Attic combines consignment, secondhand, and new clothing with a trendy flair. On sale are new and used items with labels such as Ann Taylor, Ellen Tracy, Free People, Nine West, Kensie, and Silence & Noise, plus racks of modern and retro accessories from jewelry to bags and belts. The store also sells vintage and new home decor items that veer toward the kitschy side of things. Open daily.

Seasons Olive Oil and Vinegar Tap Room. 504 Main St.; (610) 866-2615; www.seasons taproom.com. The owners of this very specialized store reason that by allowing customers to taste the high-end products, they will help them to cultivate an educated palate. Single-estate extra virgin olive oil from around the world and traditional light and dark balsamic vinegars are stored "on tap" in stainless steel Italian fustis and dispensed for sipping. Also available are infused oils and vinegars and other gourmet food gifts and homewares. Open daily.

Shuze. 530 Main St.; (610) 419-8655; www.shopshuze.com. The selection at this downtown boutique is, as its name suggests, partial to footwear. With an emphasis on stylish comfort, Shuze carries brands such as Naot, Alegria, Franco Sarto, and Desigual, plus nurse's clogs, Frye boots, and Hunter wellies. Even so, the other body parts don't go neglected here: Apparel options include trendy denim, designer purses, dresses, outerwear, accessories, knits, and locally made jewelry. Open daily from 11 a.m.

where to eat

Bethlehem BrewWorks. 569 Main St.; (610) 882-1300; www.thebrewworks.com. This industrial themed brewpub's most recent claim to fame was a visit from President Barack Obama. Open since 1998, the giant space seats 250 people and serves lunch, dinner, and brunch. The emphasis, of course, is on the signature beers: golden ales, oatmeal stout, weissbier, and others, including seasonal lambics. The bar-friendly food ranges from 10

lehigh valley wine

Designated an American Viticultural Area in 2008, the rich shale farmlands of eastern Pennsylvania are one of the region's newest frontiers for grape-growing and winemaking. The Lehigh Valley Wine Trail (see www.lehighvalleywinetrail.com) includes 8 vineyards and wineries. The downloadable map can serve as a guide for the tour.

- *Amoré Vineyards and Winery. 7054 Beth-Bath Pike, Bath; (610) 837-1334; www.amorewines.com. Call for hours.*

- *Big Creek Vineyard. Keller Road, Kresgeville; (610) 681-3959; www.bigcreek vineyard.com. Open daily from 1 p.m.*

- *Blue Mountain Winery. 7627 Grape Vine Dr., New Tripoli; (610) 298-3068; www.bluemountainwine.com. Open daily 11 a.m. to 6 p.m.*

- *Clover Hill Vineyards and Winery. 9850 Newtown Rd., Breinigsville; (610) 395-2468; www.cloverhillwinery.com. Open daily.*

- *Franklin Hill Vineyards. 7833 Franklin Hill Rd., Bangor; (888) 887-2839; www .franklinhillvineyards.com. Open daily.*

- *Galen Glen Winery. 255 Winter Mountain Dr., Andreas; (570) 386-3682; www.galenglen.com. Open weekends.*

- *Pinnacle Ridge Winery. 407 Old Route 22, Kutztown; (610) 756-4481; www .pinridge.com. Open daily.*

- *Vynecrest Vineyard and Winery. 172 Arrowhead Ln., Breinigsville; (610) 398-7525; www.vynecrest.com. Hours change seasonally.*

styles of wings, to pancetta mac and cheese, to Pennsylvania Dutch classics like pork schnitzel served with cabbage and potato salad. Open daily from 11 a.m. to 2 a.m. $$.

Blue Sky Cafe. 222 W. 4th St.; (610) 867-9390; www.theblueskycafe.com. Open for breakfast and lunch only, this casual eatery on the south side of town knows how to make the daytime meals interesting. Morning choices include a fried egg Reuben; the house omelet with lump crab, roasted red pepper, and avocado; and raspberry cream cheese–stuffed French toast. Lunchtime brings a menu of panini, quesadillas, burgers, and wraps, with plenty of vegetarian options and a killer grilled cheese. Closed Mon. $.

1741 on the Terrace. 437 Main St.; (610) 625-2219; www.1741ontheterrace.com. Housed in the historic Hotel Bethlehem, 1741—named for the building's inaugural year—charms with its Moravian tiled floor and floor-to-ceiling Palladian windows. The food is equally elegant and memorable, but not at all prissy: white truffle and chicken potpie; pan-seared halibut over mushroom pave; Meyer lemon flan tart. The award-winning wine list features vintages from around the world. Open daily for dinner, 5 to 9 p.m. $$–$$$.

where to stay

Historic Wydnor Hall Inn. 3612 Old Philadelphia Pike; (800) 839-0020; mysite.verizon .net/wydnorhall. Originally part of William Penn's land grant tract, this 18th-century estate has been restored and expanded. The original manor house includes 3 suites and 2 guest rooms, and there's a secluded cottage for up to 4 guests. All of the rooms are furnished with Wi-Fi, cable TV, private bath, and central air. Set just outside the city, Wydnor is quiet, clean, and a good value. Breakfast is included. $–$$.

Morningstar Inn. 72 E. Market St.; (610) 867-2300; www.morningstarinn.com. Situated in historic downtown Bethlehem, this colonial revival mansion is a convenient home base for city exploration. Common rooms include a formal parlor, sunroom, and billiards room. The 5 guest rooms, neatly decorated with a combination of antiques and modern amenities, all feature queen beds, private baths, air-conditioning, and cable TV. Breakfast is made from local ingredients and includes at least 3 choices; complimentary snacks are served throughout the day. $$.

worth more time
easton

Just northeast of Bethlehem is the third city in the Lehigh Valley trifecta. Just like its sibling cities, this smaller town is undergoing a postindustrial renaissance. Stroll through the historic area to admire the architecture and the trendy new restaurants and boutiques. Then amble south over to Center Square. Highlights here include the Crayola Experience, a kid-friendly "tour" of the crayon company's visitor center with hands-on activities, and the National Canal Museum, both of which are located in the Two Rivers Landing complex. (One ticket admits visitors to both attractions.)

day trip 04

northwest

lively villages:
phoenixville, pa; skippack, pa

One need not travel very far outside of Philadelphia for some quaint small towns—the northeast suburbs of Phoenixville and Skippack are under an hour's drive away, yet they feel like a world unto their own. Short on actual tourist sites, both Skippack and Phoenixville are simply fun to explore, each with an appealing main street to stroll and more than enough shops, spas, and restaurants to occupy a leisurely day-tripper. And because they're a relatively short distance from the city, it's easy to visit both towns in a day.

phoenixville, pa

As with so many of the region's towns, Phoenixville was built on water—in this case, the Schuylkill River and French Creek—which facilitated both the creation of goods and their transport in the industrial age. One of the main thoroughfares is, appropriately, named Bridge Street, and pretty much all of downtown is here or the intersecting Main Street. With a funky mix of shops and pubs, a regular First Friday event, a popular farmers' market, and close proximity to the Perkiomen and Schuylkill River trails, Phoenixville has become a sought-after suburb—if overlooked by most tourists to the area.

getting there

From Philadelphia take I-76 west to US 422 west, continuing on for nearly 3 miles until exit 328A. From there take PA 23 west into Phoenixville. Total travel time without heavy traffic is 42 minutes.

where to go

Colonial Theatre. 227 Bridge St.; (610) 917-0223; www.thecolonialtheatre.com. The claim to fame of this turn-of-the-20th-century theater is its appearance in the 1950s cult classic *The Blob.* Every summer during the 3-day Blobfest celebration, visitors reenact the scene where the moviegoers run screaming from the theater. It has since been restored to its earliest grandeur, and the theater shows an engaging mix of feature films, classic cinema, documentary, and cult favorites. First Fridays are devoted to horror films. Open daily.

Schuylkill River Heritage Center. 2 N. Main St.; (610) 935-2181; www.phoenixville foundry.org. Listed on the National Register of Historic Places, the foundry of Phoenix Iron Company was built in 1882. Inside, the recently completed Heritage Center tells the story of the Schuylkill River through exhibits detailing its industrial past as well as videos that run throughout the day. The center also serves as a welcome center for Chester County visitors with tourist information about area sites. Open weekends from 11 a.m. to 3 p.m. and first Fridays from 5:30 p.m. to 7:30 p.m.

Steel City Coffee House. 203 Bridge St.; (610) 933-4043; www.steelcitycoffeehouse .com. A coffeehouse in the traditional 1950s and 1960s sense of the word, Steel City is part cafe and part live music venue. For a small theater, it manages to attract a notable roster of artists, with a preference for the singer-songwriter, classic rock, and world music genres. Coffee and cakes are served at night and guests can also bring their own alcohol for a $4 corkage fee. Open daily.

blobfest

Phoenixville is typically a sleepy little town but for at least three days every year it erupts into a frenzied gathering of sci-fi, horror, and cult movie worshippers celebrating the 1958 film The Blob, *which was shot here. The weekend festival always involves a screening of the film, a reenactment of the scene when the Blob takes over the Colonial Theatre, displays of movie memorabilia, a street fair, costume contest, and live music. For a certain type of day-tripper this campy event is a great reason to visit the town.*

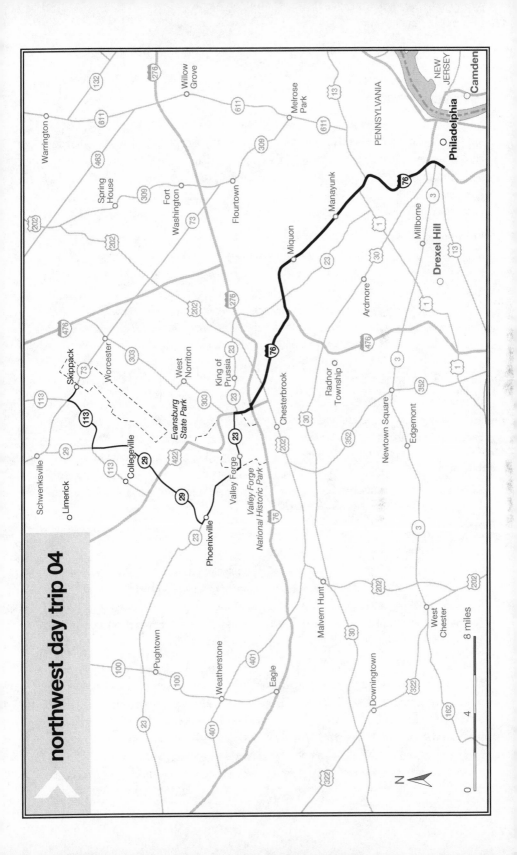

northwest day trip 04

where to shop

Best Friends. 26 S. Main St.; (610) 933-1781; www.shopatbestfriends.com. Women of all ages are drawn to this central boutique, which carries a mix of clothing, jewelry, handbags, and accessories. The emphasis is on trendy but more-than-one-season looks, with casual and dressier options from size 0 to 14. Best Friends carries brands like Bobi, Tulle, Closet Romantic, Johnny Was, and Level 99, and bags by Big Buddha and Deux Lux, plus pieces from local designers. Closed Sun and Mon.

Philadelphia Premium Outlets. 18 W. Lightcap Rd., Limerick, PA; (610) 495-9000; www .premiumoutlets.com/philadelphia. Arguably the area's best outlet mall, Philadelphia Premium Outlets is also the newest, located in nearby Limerick. The stores are laid out as an outdoor plaza with paved walkways and gathering areas. The factory stores represent the higher end of retail: Kate Spade, Brooks Brothers, DKNY, Diesel, Le Creuset, Restoration Hardware, Cole Haan, and Theory. There's also a large Last Call at Neiman Marcus outlet. Check the website for additional discounts and coupons. Open daily from 10 a.m.

where to eat

Daddy Mims'. 150–152 Bridge St.; (610) 935-1800; www.daddymims.com. Diners never leave hungry from this elegant little BYOB that specializes in tasty Creole cuisine. Chef/ owner Mims's menu takes the classics and gives them a contemporary twist. Crispy coconut shrimp is served over greens with a chili aioli drizzle. The blackened pork loin is topped with chocolate mole and served over mashed sweet potatoes. And the jambalaya is made extra special by the addition of duck confit. The colorful dining room features works by local artists. Reservations strongly recommended. Closed Mon. $$.

Majolica. 258 Bridge St.; (610) 917-0962; www.majolicarestaurant.com. A storefront restaurant with fine modern cooking, Majolica has won raves from Philadelphia critics. Diners can choose the chef's prix-fixe special in 6 or 8 courses or go a la carte for a more affordable meal. Selections might include scallop carpaccio with honey melon and prosciutto; smoked chicken over potato pave with fava beans; or fennel panna cotta with roasted strawberries and aged balsamic. Sunday brunch is served as a 4-course prix fixe. Reservations recommended. BYOB. Closed Mon and Tues. $$.

Sly Fox. 520 Kimberton Rd.; (610) 935-4540; www.slyfoxbeer.com. This hometown microbrewery in a strip mall has grown into a true contender in the beer world. The award-winning brews are fresh interpretations of classic Belgian and German styles—pils, *weisse,* saison, stout, and lager. The cuisine at this pub is designed to accompany, but not upstage them. Bavarian pretzels with sweet and hot mustard, beer-battered fish and chips, fried chicken hoagies, and flatbread pizzas are among the offerings. Visit in May for the annual goat race, in which the winner is the namesake for the season's release of Maibock beer. Open daily. $–$$.

where to stay

Morning Star B&B. 610 Valley Forge Rd.; (610) 935-7473; www.morningstarbandb.net. This small country-style inn is within walking distance of downtown Phoenixville and just 2 miles from Valley Forge National Park. The intimate, personal ambience is underscored by the small number of guest rooms (2), both decorated with a rustic aesthetic. An eco-conscious breakfast features local ingredients and the owners are happy to cater to guests with allergies. The inn has a hot tub and a billiards room, and on-site massage can be arranged. $.

skippack, pa

Skippack got its start in the 17th century when Philadelphia's founding fathers decreed that German-speaking tourists had to disperse outside of the city. In 1795 Jacob Reiff opened a general store, setting the stage for Skippack's merchant-friendly main street, eventually called Skippack Pike. Where once a furniture maker, blacksmith, and hat store lay is now a tourist-friendly shopping village with some restaurants and galleries thrown in for good measure—in short, an ideal getaway for those needing some fresh air and rural romance.

getting there

From Phoenixville, head north on PA 29/Collegeville Road and follow it for 6 miles. Turn onto PA 113 North/Bridge Road and follow for over 3 miles, then turn right onto Skippack Pike to enter Skippack. Total travel time without traffic is just over 20 minutes.

where to go

Evansburg State Park. 851 May Hall Rd., Collegeville, PA; (610) 409-1150; www.dcnr .state.pa.us. Originally part of the tract of land William Penn purchased from the Lenape tribe in 1684, this state park was established in 1979 to protect it from suburban develop-ment. Skippack Creek runs through the 3,349-acre area, offering trout fishing, while 1,000 acres of the land are open for hunting. There are also 26 miles of trails for walking, horse-back riding, cross-country skiing, and mountain biking, plus areas for picnicking, golf, and softball. The Friedt Visitor Center, occupying a 1700s farmhouse, gives a view into the life of the area's early Mennonite settlers as well as exhibits about natural history.

Grand Fromage. 3910 Skippack Pike; (610) 584-5400; www.thegrandfromage.com. Don't be fooled by Skippack's distance from Philly—this cheese shop proves you don't need to go into the city to find a cosmopolitan selection of gourmet foods. California small-batch cheddar, mushroom brie, oak-barrel aged Italian cheese, fresh mozzarella, and goat gouda are just a few of the choices here. Fromage also sells pâtés and charcuterie, plus local honey, fudge, pretzels, biscotti, and chutneys. The staff will help you put together a picnic spread or take some to go. Closed Mon.

Green Wolf's Village Barn. 4010 Skippack Pike; (610) 584-6396; www.greenwolfsvillage barn.com. The centerpiece of this mini-mall housed in an old barn is an art gallery that showcases local painters, sculptors, wood carvers, jewelers, and ceramicists. Artists are often on hand during weekends for craft demonstrations. The other stores here include the Cardinal Hallow winery, Crystal Persuasion new-age goods, Fox and Wolf cabinetry and woodworking, and Green Wolf's Elegant Junque, filled with antiques, art, gifts, and reproductions. Open daily.

where to eat

Brasserie 73. 4024 Skippack Pike; (610) 584-7880; www.skippackrestaurants.com. This restaurant and wine bar was inspired by the French Riviera, and the owners have used its dramatic atmosphere to good advantage. In winter there's a roaring fireplace to sit by, and outdoor seating and an additional bar are available in warmer months. The menu uses French cuisine as a starting point—lobster bisque; niçoise salad; quiche and crepes—but adds in some generally continental creations, such as grilled scallop and shrimp pasta in saffron cream sauce. Open daily for lunch and dinner. $$–$$$.

Italian Market. 4101 Skippack Pike; (610) 584-4050; www.skippackrestaurants.com. Step into Skippack's Italian Market for a quick-service lunch. The menu of hoagies served on fresh-baked bread is extensive and excellent (favorites include roast pork Italiano with broccoli rabe and sharp provolone; and the South Philly Special with sopressata, mozzarella, and sun-dried tomatoes), plus there are salads and kids' options to choose from. In the meantime, browse the Italian imports lining the shelves or order an espresso and one of the desserts from Milan. Open daily. $.

19 Bella. 3401 Skippack Pike; (610) 222-8119; www.19bella.com. Set just outside Skippack in the equally quaint village of Cedars, 19 Bella serves tapas inspired by the Mediterranean. The selections truly cover the entire region, with Spanish paella; Italian-style roasted eggplant stuffed with ricotta; Moroccan merguez sausage; and French beef Bourgogne. There are very few seats in the main dining room; the restaurant expands the seating options with a heated tent. BYOB. Open daily for dinner; serving lunch Tues through Sat, and brunch Sun. $$.

where to stay

Hotel Fiesole. 4046 Skippack Pike; (610) 222-8009; www.hotelfiesole.net. This modern hotel hearkens back to old-world Europe, down to the cuisine served in its 3 on-site restaurants, the detailed wood carvings, and the stained-glass ceiling in the dining room. The 16 guest rooms are each unique and decorated with heavy wood furniture and thick draperies. All have marble bathrooms, Bose clock radios, plasma TVs, and luxurious linens. Continental breakfast is included and served in the common area on each floor. $$–$$$.

appendix a:
festivals & celebrations

january

Pennsylvania Farm Show. Harrisburg, PA; www.farmshow.state.pa.us. The nation's largest indoor agricultural event. Free.

february

Midwinter Scottish and Irish Music Festival. King of Prussia, PA; www.eohebrides.com. A weekend full of performances, plus vendors and food.

Winterfest. Jim Thorpe, PA; www.jimthorpe.com. This annual event celebrates the snowy season with Civil War reenactments, ice carvings, carriage rides, and more. Presidents' Day weekend.

march

Atlantic City Beer Festival. Atlantic City, NJ; www.celebrationofthesuds.com. A weekend of tastings, with live music, food, and more, held in the Atlantic City Convention Center.

Berks Jazz Festival. Reading, PA; www.berksjazzfest.com. A weeklong music festival with over 130 events in and around Reading. March and April.

Princeton Pi Day and Einstein's Birthday. Princeton, NJ; www.pidayprinceton.com. Held on March 14, Einstein's birthday, a whimsical daylong event with lookalike contests, pie judging, and more.

april

Jim Thorpe Burlesque Festival. Jim Thorpe, PA; (507) 807-8891; www.jimthorpeburlesque.com. A weekend of burlesque performances, workshops, and other events in one of the nation's oldest vaudeville theaters.

New Jersey Folk Festival. New Brunswick, NJ; www.njfolkfest.rutgers.edu. An annual event sponsored by Rutgers, celebrating folk culture from around the world.

Springtime in the Park. Hershey, PA; (800) HERSHEY; www.hersheyinthespring.com. A month before the official opening day, Hersheypark opens for a seasonally inspired fair.

may

Cape May Music Festival. Cape May, NJ; (609) 884-5404; www.capemaymac.org. Two weeks of live performances across genres.

Chestertown Tea Party Festival. Chestertown, MD; www.chestertownteaparty.org. Remembering the lesser-known tea party that took place here during the colonial rebellion, with a reenactment, parade, street performances, and food.

Maryland Film Festival. Baltimore, MD; (410) 752-8083; www.md-filmfest.com. A 4-day event showcasing film and video from around the world.

Mayfair. Allentown, PA; (610) 437-6900; www.mayfairfestival.org. An arts and crafts, music, and food festival held annually for 5 days in May.

ShadFest. Lambertville, NJ; www.lambertville.org. An art show with live entertainment and family fun celebrating spring's shad run. Held late April/early May.

Strawberry Festival. Lahaska, PA; (215) 794-4000; www.peddlersvillage.com. A weekend-long jamboree of strawberries, with plenty of delicacies for sale.

Wilmington Flower Market. Wilmington, DE; (302) 995-5699; www.wilmingtonflower market.org. A 3-day flower and plant sale with rides, events, and other activities, benefiting children.

june

Baltimore Pride. Baltimore, MD; (410) 837-5545; www.baltimorepride.org. A weekend honoring the gay, lesbian, bisexual, and transgendered community, with parades, block parties, street fairs, and more.

Honfest. Baltimore, MD; www.honfest.com. A unique pageant in which beehived ladies compete for the Bawlmer's Best Hon title.

St. Anthony's Festival. Wilmington, DE; www.stanthonysfestival.com. A weeklong celebration of Italian culture with authentic food, winemaking competition, concerts, and more.

july

Artscape. Baltimore, MD; www.artscape.org. Billed as America's largest free art fair, Artscape features 2 days of exhibitions, performances, demonstrations, and competitions across every genre and art form.

Bastille Festival. Frenchtown, NJ; www.frenchtownnj.org. Celebrating French independence with live music, vendors, and food.

BlobFest. Phoenixville, PA; www.thecolonialtheatre.com. A celebration of the movie *The Blob* at the site where it was filmed, featuring a street fair and reenactments, and held the second weekend of July.

Kutztown Festival. Kutztown, PA; (888) 674-6136; www.kutztownfestival.com. A week-long celebration of Pennsylvania Dutch culture, with live entertainment, crafts, kids' activities, food, and folklore. Early July.

New Jersey State Barbecue Championship. Wildwood, NJ; (609) 523-6565; www.njbbq.com. A statewide grill-off, held the second full weekend of July.

august

Allentown Fair. Allentown, PA; (610) 433-7541; www.allentownfairpa.org. Dating to 1852, this fair and agricultural show runs for a week and is one of the largest in the state. Events include a carnival, talent shows, concerts, farmers' market, petting zoos, livestock judging, and more.

Boardwalk Art Show. Ocean City, NJ; www.oceancityartscenter.org. Displaying arts and crafts from local artists; held the first weekend of August.

Maryland State BBQ Bash. Bel Air, MD; (443) 823-1797; www.mdbbq.com. A barbecue-themed festival and competition held for 2 days every August.

Musikfest. Bethlehem, PA; www.musikfest.org. Ten days of music performances spanning genres, plus vendors, crafts, and food; held across the city.

september

Arts & Crafts Festival. New Hope, PA; www.visitnewhope.com. An outdoor fair with local arts and crafts, held on a September weekend.

Brandywine Festival of the Arts. Wilmington, DE. A downtown street fair with vendors, crafts, food, and music. (302) 690-5555; www.brandywinearts.com.

Doylestown Arts Festival. Doylestown, PA; (215) 340-9988; www.doylestownartsfestival.com. A street fair in the center of town with arts, crafts, furniture, and more.

Festival of the Sea. Point Pleasant, NJ; (739) 899-2424; www.pointchamber.com. A street fair with samplings of seafood from the area's restaurants, plus crafts and pony rides.

Mushroom Festival. Kennett Square, PA; (610) 925-3373; www.mushroomfestival.org. The world capital of mushrooms celebrates its main crop with a charity run, cook-off, parade, carnival, street festival, and other activities.

Polish-American Festival. Doylestown, PA; (215) 345-0600; www.polishamericanfestival.com. A celebration of Polish culture, heritage, and traditions held over 2 weekends.

RiverFest. Frenchtown, NJ; www.frenchtownnj.org. Boat races, eco-crafts, kids' activities, food, crafts, and more, held Labor Day weekend.

Whoopie Pie Festival. Ronks, PA; www.whoopiepiefestival.com. Celebrating the famous Pennsylvania Dutch treat with family events.

october

Chatsworth Cranberry Festival. Chatsworth, NJ; (609) 726-9237; www.cranfest.org. A celebration of the Pine Barren's biggest crop, held during an October weekend.

Country Living Fair. Batsto, NJ; www.batstovillage.org. Held on the third Sunday in October, this fair showcases old-time crafts, cars, and food, with antiques and other goods for sale.

Graw Days Festival. Havre de Grace, MD; www.mainstreethdg.com. An annual event recalling the horse-racing days of Havre de Grace with a street fair, speakers, demonstrations, kids' activities, and of course, horses.

Victorian Weekend. Cape May, NJ; (609) 884-5404; www.capemaymac.org. Two days of house tours, chocolate and wine tastings, theater, and more.

november

Apple Festival. Lahaska, PA; (215) 794-4000; www.peddlersvillage.com. Peddler's Village celebrates the harvest with apple delicacies, live entertainment, and kids' activities.

december

Christmas Festival. Lahaska, PA; (215) 794-4000; www.peddlersvillage.com. Peddler's Village is lit up and Santa visits via parade, with cider and other snacks.

Christmas in Cape May. Cape May, NJ; (609) 884-5404; www.capemaymac.org. Throughout December, candlelit tours, food and wine events, crafts, trolley rides, theater, and more.

Night of 100 Elvises. Baltimore, MD; (410) 494-9558; www.nightof100elvises.com. One weekend every December, Elvis impersonators and wannabes gather for 2 nights of the King's music.

Olde Time Christmas Festival. Jim Thorpe, PA; www.jimthorpeoldetimechristmas.com. Held during weekends in December, the Olde Time festival features train rides, live nativity, gingerbread houses, an arts bazaar, and much more.

appendix b: guide to regional cuisine

Birch beer: A carbonated soft drink that's a relative to root beer, birch beer was traditionally made from tree sap and is especially popular in Pennsylvania Dutch country.

Chowchow: A pickled relish usually made from green tomato, cabbage, beans, and other vegetables, frequently made and canned in Pennsylvania Dutch country.

Crab cakes: These balls of crabmeat, bread crumbs, and seasonings are traditionally associated with the Chesapeake Bay area; they're served baked, fried, or grilled.

Fasnachts: A fatty doughnut served the day before Lent, this sweet, round pastry is especially popular in the Pennsylvania Dutch territory.

Fat sandwiches: Popularized by the grease trucks of Rutgers, these decadent submarines can be stuffed with all manner of ingredients, usually some combination of french fries, chicken fingers, mozzarella sticks, and meat.

Funnel cake: Its appearance in the US is usually credited to the Pennsylvania Dutch community, and this scrawl of fried dough topped with powdered sugar is most often found at fairs and festivals.

Hoagies/submarines: Philadelphians have strict standards for the sandwiches known as hoagies—always on a long roll with Italian meats, cheeses, and a drizzle of oil and vinegar—but outside the city they are often called submarines.

Kiffle: In Allentown and Pennsylvania Dutch country, locals treasure this Slovenian holiday cookie, made from sour cream dough and stuffed with nut paste, prune butter, poppy seeds, and other fillings.

Lebanon bologna: The German settlers of Pennsylvania invented this semi-dry beef sausage that is cured, smoked, and fermented into a tangy lunchmeat.

Pork roll: Also known as Taylor ham, pork roll is a New Jersey breakfast meat in the vein of bologna or summer sausage, usually served in a sandwich with egg and cheese.

Pretzel: Germans brought the pretzel to Pennsylvania, where it has seeped into the local culinary vernacular. Pretzels can be found around the region in both hard and crispy and soft doughy forms.

Saltwater taffy: The chewy, gooey candy was given its name in Atlantic City in the 19th century—available in dozens of flavors, it's still a summertime staple.

Scrapple: Pork and cornmeal are processed together to make this Pennsylvania Dutch breakfast meat, which is formed into blocks, sliced, and fried.

Shoofly pie: The Pennsylvania Dutch have perfected this rich, coffee-cake-like pie with a fluffy molasses bottom.

Texas wiener: Despite the name, this style of hot dog topped with mustard, chili sauce, and onions was innovated in New Jersey and Pennsylvania. It can sometimes be called an "All the Way" dog.

index